MW01096389

KEEPING THE PAST
Norwood at 150

Patricia J. Fanning

American History Press
Staunton Virginia

American History Press

Staunton, Virginia

(888) 521-1789

Visit us on the Internet at:

www.Americanhistorypress.com

Cover design by Rick Bickhart/Interior design by David E. Kane

Cover Illustration: *Nahatan Street Winter Scene* by Thomas Dunlay. Courtesy of Charles and Katherine Donahue.

First Printing September 2021

Names: Fanning, Patricia J., author.
Title: Keeping the past : Norwood at 150 / Patricia J. Fanning.
Other titles: Norwood at 150
Description: Staunton, Virginia : American History Press, [2021] | Includes
  index. | Summary: "A history of Norwood, Norfolk County, Massachusetts
  as told through a series of sketches about the town. Covering the time
  period from the colonial era to the 2000s, each chapter highlights a
  certain stage of the town's history. The author is the unofficial town
  historian of Norwood, and has written this book in celebration of the
  150th anniversary of its founding"-- Provided by publisher.
Identifiers: LCCN 2021000694 | ISBN 9781939995377 (trade paperback)
Subjects: LCSH: Norwood (Mass.)--History. | South Dedham (Mass.)--History.
Classification: LCC F74.N99 F358 2021 | DDC 974.4/7--dc23
LC record available at https://lccn.loc.gov/2021000694

For T. and B.

Tell all the Truth but tell it slant –
Success in Circuit lies
Too bright for our infirm Delight
The Truth's superb surprise.

–Emily Dickinson

Contents

Preface

This is not intended to be an exhaustive account of Norwood's history. Far from it. These are subjects, happenings, and people that have intrigued me over the years. Some focus on individuals, others on place; they range from colonial to recent times and encompass war, economic depression, immigration, and injustice. There are tales of remarkable character, vision, and courage, in addition to sketches that amuse and surprise. I have attempted to place these episodes in relationship to the culture at large. No village (like South Dedham) or town (like Norwood) exists in a vacuum; significant national trends and events have always left their mark. I have tried to clarify these connections and contexts.

Too often community or popular history tends to embrace misplaced nostalgia or even downright distortion. I have sought to avoid these pitfalls. Any clear-eyed examination of the past, however, brings with it an opportunity for social criticism. There is some of that here as well.

Ultimately, my aim is to demonstrate that Norwood's past is not hoary or drab and inconsequential; it is, in fact, vivid and relevant. The great historian Barbara Tuchman once said that the secret to making history come alive is to "tell stories." Here are some of my favorites.

Chapter 1

Thomas Balch and His Parish

The Reverend Thomas Balch (1711-1774) was the founding pastor of the Church of
Christ of Dedham, Second Parish, located in South Dedham village.
(Courtesy of First Congregational Church of Norwood)

IN 1730 THERE WERE FIFTY people living in the 10.5 square
miles of what is twenty-first century Norwood, a group of resilient,
independent-minded settlers drawn by the relatively open and lightly-
wooded wilderness and the readily available water resources nearby.
The village that eventually developed in this outpost was nicknamed
"Tiot," thought to reference Native American words referring to
watering places. As they went about their daily lives, these primarily
subsistence farmers grew enough crops to sustain themselves and
their families. If they were fortunate enough to have a surplus, they
took it to market. Local historian Win Everett conjectured that for
years Tiot "was a closed community of crabbed, selfish, shrewd,

inhospitable farmers who did not like strangers."[1] Whether that bleak characterization was true or not, it is a fact that there were few residents and little or no industry in this sparsely populated region that stretched between the center of Dedham and the farthest edge of East Walpole.

The Second (or South) Parish, as it came to be called by congregants of the Church of Christ in Dedham, was set off from the Mother Church on September 2, 1728, and the separation was confirmed by the General Court in Boston in the fall of 1730. The isolated colonists, living five miles or more from the church, and rightly protesting their obligation to pay ministerial taxes and travel the considerable distance to weekly services, were finally to become a distinct parish. The inhabitants of the new precinct assembled for several months at the houses of villagers John Ellis and Nathaniel Guild until they could build a meeting house and seek a minister of their own

Upon being called to serve, Reverend Thomas Balch (1711-1774) turned this disparate assemblage of individuals, families, and farms into a community. Initially there were fifteen (male) members of the parish—not all residents of the precinct were church goers—but by the end of Balch's first year, the membership had risen to twenty-seven, including three deacons who were elected by their peers. Although the pastor was unquestionably the leader of the congregation, the deacons helped meet the additional needs of a small, but far-flung and growing parish. They might visit the sick, bring aid to the poor, or offer counsel to those facing difficulty or uncertainty. While they did not outwardly proselytize, the character deacons displayed as they went about their daily lives might bring new members into the church as well. Because of this, deacons were typically older men who were well-known and respected for their honesty and faith. Such was the case in South Dedham. Among the original three deacons was Ezra Morse, Jr. (1671-1760); the others were John Everett and John Dean. Morse, who was a child when his father came to this southern section of Dedham around 1678, eventually erected both saw and grist mills along the Neponset River near Water Street. The establishment of such mills was essential if a settlement had any chance of survival.

New England sawmills were expensive and complicated to set up.

A simple wooden mill building was easy enough to construct, but the steel-edged saw, as well as the necessary iron accessory components, had to be imported from Europe. In addition, the wooden waterwheel that kept the blade rotating required the hand of a skilled carpenter, and the retaining dam and sluice that ensured a steady flow of water was best constructed by a man with the eye of an engineer. Once in working order, a mill could be run by only one or two men, yet the business continued to be a risky endeavor: in winter, frozen streams could force a closure; in summer, a drought could hamper the uninterrupted flow of water; and a powerful spring thaw might endanger the retaining dam. Still, as one historian put it, "the sawmill built early America."[2] Pioneers who sought to build their homes and barns needed lumber and a sawmill provided it.

Gristmills faced some of the same problems, and were even more costly. The stones used to grind the grain had to be imported and, transported to the mill site—over rough and sometimes nearly impassable terrain—and set up by an expert. Much more sophisticated than simply sawing wood, successful gristmill operations required a miller who could accurately gauge the quality, age, and moisture content of a load of grain in order to set the proper speed for the rotating stones. Vital to the economic development of a nascent settlement, millers were sometimes given choice acreage for their homes and promised a percentage of every bushel of flour produced. An honest miller often made the difference between simple survival and prosperity for an individual farmer or an entire community.

Ezra Morse, Jr. had been in the milling business for more than a quarter century when approval was granted for Walpole to become its own township in 1724; his mill stood on the town's northern border. Morse served as one of that town's first selectmen and was also the town clerk for a year—during which time his penmanship was described as "closely approach[ing] the well-scratched ground of a busy hen-yard."[3] Ezra the miller had problems with Walpole, however, and in 1738 he petitioned the legislature in Boston requesting that his property and mill once again be considered part of Dedham. His wish was granted, and the boundary line between Walpole and its mother town was reconfigured, returning Morse's mill and property once again to Dedham. By that time, Morse had been a deacon of the Second Parish for two years.

More than a decade earlier, Ezra Morse had been among the south precinct colonists who met at the Ellis Tavern and voted to "procure a frame fit to set up, or raise" a meeting house.[4] Not simply a church, the colonial meeting house was the only place for rural residents to gather on a regular basis. Although men might meet at Morse's mill or at local taverns, such as those owned by Paul Ellis or Reuben White, entire families traveled to Sunday services. The meeting house became the place for socializing and gossip-sharing, and provided many residents with their first sense of community. Due to its importance, there was always much discussion about the building's location and size. After several meetings, it was agreed to erect a forty by thirty-six-foot structure at the center of the precinct (near today's Morrill Memorial Library), and, as was the custom, everyone contributed what they could to the effort, be it land, materials, labor, or money.

A house for their new minister was raised nearby. Unlike the simple clapboard-covered "salt-box" farmhouses featuring a steeply pitched roof and central chimney that most parishioners had built for themselves, the parsonage was a large, two-story home with a generous gambrel roof, extended rear ell, and well-proportioned central entrance. Reverend Thomas Balch, who had been selected from among three candidates to become the minister of the new church, arrived in 1736.

Born on October 17, 1711 and baptized in Charlestown, where his father, Benjamin, was a blacksmith, Thomas Balch had attended Cambridge Latin School and graduated from Harvard College in 1735. A rather reticent adolescent but ambitious scholar, Balch was a hard-working student but one without pretension or prejudice. Upon his call to the South Dedham parish, he was offered an annual salary of 120 pounds and sixteen cords of wood. He accepted the calling—his first and only ministerial position—and was ordained as pastor of the Church of Christ in Dedham, Second Parish, on June 20, 1736 at the age of twenty-five. In October of the following year, Balch married the former Mary Sumner of Roxbury, and together they raised a large family.

Although Balch was "never prominent among the clergy of the province,"[5] as one source noted, he was a gentleman of good character and, despite his youth, displayed sound judgment in both ecclesiastical and social matters. Balch was regarded as a serious, if somewhat conservative, preacher; more important, it was said that he was always prudent and respectful in his communications. Looking back in later years, he was pleased "never to have had the least misunderstanding"[6] with any of his congregation, a remarkable accomplishment for the times. During his first decade as pastor, for example, the revivalism of the Great Awakening—a call for people to seek a more emotional connectedness to their God—spread across the colonies. Thomas Balch was a "New Light," one of those who acknowledged the calling of the revivalists and the veracity of their conversion experiences. However, Balch seemingly wore his personal beliefs lightly and avoided any discord among the "Old Lights," those who were not as quick to embrace such spiritual attachments. Avoiding confrontation and discord was among his gifts. And yet, as his Harvard College biographical sketch asserted, "Parson Balch was far from being a pacifist."[7] In March of 1745 the minister himself became a willing participant in the historic Siege of Louisbourg. It was undoubtedly the most famous encounter during King George's War (1740-1748), one of a series of military episodes (historically referred to as the Colonial Wars) faced by English colonists in defense of the Crown.

Both the French and the English believed that control of Nova Scotia and Cape Breton Island was vital to the possession and eventual settlement of the northern interior of the continent. Provincial frontiersmen also felt they would continue to suffer the threat of Native American attack until the French, known to be allies of several tribes, were defeated. Thus, even though New England merchants were conducting lucrative trade with the French fortress located at the mouth of the St. Lawrence, the English king demanded its capture.

Built by the French beginning in 1720, the walls of Louisbourg enclosed approximately 100 acres. Three bastions protruded from its fortified wall on the landward side, two more on the seaward; two parapets overlooked the narrow harbor entrance. For all these barricades and ramparts, however, the fortress was vulnerable to a land assault and was defended by a force of around 500 inexperienced French soldiers.

The colonial recruits, aged sixteen to seventy, were equally untested. Most were farmers, fishermen, millers, tavern keepers, even drifters, whose only military experience was at the gathering of local militias where soldierly drills and maneuvers were supplemented by picnics, ale, and familial entertainments. Led by similarly unseasoned officers, the assembled volunteers, most of whom turned out in their everyday clothes, were expected to supply their own weapons—likely a bulky (over five feet long), heavy (between ten and fifteen pounds) and inaccurate flintlock, which took several time-consuming steps to reload. Recruited by a cadre of propagandists promising the opportunity to seize great sums of money and valuables from soon-to-be-defeated Louisbourg merchants, over 3,000 Massachusetts men agreed to serve, including eight from South Dedham.

Michael Bright, Hugh DeLap, Eleazer Fisher, Ebenezer Sumner, John Thorp, Samuel Thorp, Samuel Wetherbee, and William Wetherbee, each left their families and homesteads behind and, in March of 1745, began the journey to Cape Breton. Rev. Balch, who joined these eight villagers, was eager to participate in what he considered a holy crusade against the Roman Catholic French forces. For Protestant clergymen like Balch, the expedition was a proving ground; the capture of Louisburg would confirm God's satisfaction with the tenets of their Church in Massachusetts. One pastor even brought along an ax—the instrument of God's wrath—to destroy the Anti-Christ altars within the fort.

Arriving at Louisbourg, the ragged band of colonial troops, some barefoot and dressed in tatters, dragged artillery and provisions up steep hills and through bogs, sinking to their knees in mud, until finally planting their equipment in a commanding position. On April 28, 1745, they laid siege to the fortress while British ships blockaded the port. After a few skirmishes, some lost, some won, two months later, on June 28, the beleaguered French officially surrendered. With the take-over of Louisbourg, New England colonists were the victors in the only significant engagement of King George's War. Both the New Lights and the Old Lights of the Great Awakening felt the victory was due to God's intervention on their behalf. The successful expedition also strengthened the New England settlers' belief that the American "citizen-soldier" was superior to the European regulars, and they were angered when the British contended that their naval presence was actually responsible for the victory.

British leaders celebrated the fact that only 53 French troops and 101 New Englanders were killed in the encounter, yet the expedition took a heavy toll among South Dedham's small contingent. Samuel Thorp, 33, and Hugh De Lap, 27, a skillful gunner, were killed at Cape Breton during the siege. Even more deadly was the accompanying onset of disease. Severe illnesses plagued the colonial camps because of the lack of proper clothing, the inadequate food supply, and the insufficient sanitary facilities. Dysentery, a disease contracted by the ingestion of contaminated food or water, ravaged the troops. Smallpox and rampant fever sickened or killed many more. Such diseases lingered, adding to the mortality figures even after the soldiers had returned home.

John Thorp, 30, and Eleazer Fisher, 46, died in October and November, respectively, after their return. Both deaths were carefully recorded by Rev. Balch, who had arrived home safely in July, as being related to their Cape Breton experience. In November, 1745, Balch entered the death of "Lieut. Ebenezer Sumner, my dear brother-in-law, aged about 23, soon after his return from Cape Breton." The young man, Balch wrote, was "a promising, hopeful young gentleman."[8] In all, the South Precinct had lost five of the eight volunteer-soldiers who participated in the Siege of Louisbourg, a staggeringly high percentage. In 1903 during Norwood's second Old Home Day celebration, a commemorative stone dedicated to the memory of all nine participants, including Thomas Balch, was unveiled in Guild Square.

Convinced that he had God's approval after the Louisbourg victory, Rev. Thomas Balch resumed his ministerial duties. Within a decade, however, many of his parishioners were again called to military service. In April 1755, Captain Eliphalet Fales (1717-1781) enlisted to fight in the French and Indian War. Among his company of recruits were seven from the South Dedham area: Ebenezer Everett,

David Fairbanks, Moses Fisher, John Hawes, Benjamin Holden, John Scott, and William Woodcock. Together they made their way to the shores of Lake George in New York. There they engaged in a fierce battle on September 8, and by nightfall Moses Fisher and John Scott had been slain. While the provincials defeated the French and their Native American allies in that encounter, the colonial troops took note of the fact that not one British soldier or officer was present during the fighting.

A year later, in May 1756, Captain William Bacon (1716-1761) mustered a company of men from Dedham, Walpole, and Roxbury as part of Col. Richard Gridley's regiment in the Crown Point Expedition. (Gridley subsequently became George Washington's Chief Engineer and one of the most distinguished military men in New England.) Bacon, one of the original fifteen members of the Second Parish, was a successful farmer and was widely-respected among his peers. According to early historian Fred Day, Bacon had originally owned land that covered acres between today's Walpole and Nichols Streets. Eventually he sold that property to the Guild family and moved to a larger parcel that stretched from Clapboardtree Street eastward to the meadows, including all of what became known as the Ellis neighborhood. The Crown Point Expedition brought the militia company through Western Massachusetts and across rugged, unsettled New York territory. According to Bacon's diary,[9] by October, the provincials gathered near Fort William Henry [named after the king's son]. The fort was built in an irregular quadrangle about 130 yards at its widest point with four bastions anchoring its corners. The shores of Lake George were in the northeast, and Fort Edward stood a short distance to the southeast.

Over the next three months combat with the French and their Native American supporters, combined with a variety of illnesses, inflicted casualties among the company. By their December return, six had fallen in battle, two had been taken prisoner, and twenty-three were sick. Once again, a trail of death followed the South Dedham volunteers home. Solomon Bullard, Jr. died in Leicester, New York; Timothy Lewis at Lake George; John Woodcock at Fort Edward; Joseph Lyon at Still Water; and, at Albany, William Lewis and Joseph

Whittemore. Captain Bacon entered each death in his diary. Both Lewis and Whittemore were parishioners of the Second Parish. In addition, Rev. Balch's son and namesake, Thomas, died at Albany while on his way back from Crown Point. As one historian wrote, "To his father's great sorrow he never lived to get home."[10] William Bacon noted that on November 22, 1756, he sent a sergeant into Albany to retrieve young Balch's belongings; his gun was recovered but his pack and money could not be found. Heartbroken, the reverend recorded the loss in the parish records despite the fact that his son's body remained far away: "My dear son Thomas, being 18 years and 18 days old, died at Albany. He was upon his return from Lake George, being of Captain Bacon's company in an expedition to Crown Point. He died of camp disorder."[11] The disease was probably dysentery.

It was most likely a sorrowful and much diminished Captain William Bacon who made his way back to the South Precinct to report to his neighbors and friends the loss of so many men. When he died nearly five years later, on May 21, 1761, at 45 years of age, it was said that his death was due to lingering effects of the war. Writing in the 1930s, nearly 200 years later, local historian Win Everett felt that Bacon's face as depicted on his gravestone in the Old Parish Cemetery was "the finest and most human in the [grave] yard." Although it is doubtful that stone carver George Allen, Jr. was actually attempting an accurate portrait of Bacon, Everett continued to muse, "You will have no trouble seeing the Captain's long, lean intelligent face which is framed in a full wig with three curls on each side. The eyes are large and commanding. The lips are straight and firm. It is a real soldier's face."[1]

Throughout the 1750s and 1760s, South Dedham, according to Win Everett, continued to be dominated by small farmers "of straight, pig-headed British descent, isolated way out in the woods, miles from the scanty civilization of Dedham village. They were uneducated, as we understand it today, some of them could not write their names..."[13] It was a hard life, particularly during the long, harsh New England winters. Tilling the rock-filled soil was no easy task but farms sprang up throughout the precinct, owned by the Kingsbury, Fisher, Fales, Dean, and Sumner families. To supplement a diversified harvest, many residents kept the usual array of farm animals. When not called away for military service for Great Britain—the conclusion of the Anglo-French conflicts came with the Treaty of Paris in 1763—men worked from daylight until dark clearing the land, chopping wood, plowing fields, cultivating crops, and caring for animals. Each homestead was virtually a self-contained economic unit.

Life for women was perhaps even more strenuous. Cooking was done over a fireplace or wood stove, either of which required continual monitoring and feeding with cords of wood. Heavy buckets of water had to be toted from a good distance for meal preparation and bathing. Meals were a time-consuming chore. Kneading dough and baking bread; picking, cleaning and cutting up vegetables; plucking chickens, cleaning fish, or preparing meat, and cooking over an open fire were all arduous tasks. When crops were ripe, women harvested vegetables and then set to work pickling and preserving to ensure there would be food until the next planting.

One of the most physically-challenging responsibilities for women was washing clothes. This chore required carrying enough water to fill the wash tub and then building a big enough fire to heat it. Once hot enough, women spent hours bent or kneeling over a rough washboard to scrub out the dirt and grime; all the while the soap, made by hand from lye and animal fat, was so abrasive that it burned their skin. Each article of clothing was then wrung out by hand and hung on a clothesline to dry. Hours later, ironing was a terribly hot and even dangerous job as heavy, heated flatirons were carried back and forth from the fire to press the fabric. All of these chores, plus keeping a home relatively clean and free from soot and debris, were exhausting, and were repeated daily in an endless cycle of labor.

In addition to this perpetual toil, women often had to endure extreme loneliness. In most cases, their homes stood a quarter- or half-mile away from one another in the still relatively uncultivated wilderness. There were no paved roads, only narrow cart paths carved out by repeated use. After sundown, there was no visible light; when the clouds covered the moon, the pitch-dark night was populated only by scurrying rodents, nocturnal animals thrashing through the underbrush, and night birds soaring through the sky in search of prey.

Occasionally a solitary colonist or Native American traveler might pass. It is little wonder that the weekly visit to the meeting house for services and socialization took on such significance. In a few of the households in South Dedham, however, a family's burdens were lightened by the labor of slaves.

Northern slaveholding was different from that practiced in the South, where dozens, sometimes hundreds, of slaves, worked on a single plantation. In New England, those who claimed human property held only one or two in a household and treated them much like indentured servants. Sleeping in attics, cellars, and back rooms, the enslaved—euphemistically referred to as "servants"—most often worked alongside their masters in the home, on farms, in shops, or as craftsmen. Women slaves were particularly valued for their ability to perform domestic work, the arduous cleaning, sewing, and cooking chores that required working in hot kitchens and freezing outer buildings. There were fewer slaves in Massachusetts than any other colony, but in 1721 their number was approximately 2,000. Three decades later, in 1754, the number of Black slaves in the town of Dedham was around twenty.

According to historian Elise Lemire, in her carefully researched work, *Black Walden*, only those with the most wealth, education, or prestige were slaveholders; it was a sign of economic or social position. Virtually all the owners of slaves in the Concord area held the honorific title of reverend, doctor, colonel, captain, or deacon, a clear indication of a profession, military office, religious or social standing. The same held true in the southern district of Dedham. There are few surviving records of human bondage in the parish, but in every instance, the owners were at the top of the existing social hierarchy. Reverend Thomas Balch unquestionably held the most prestigious position in the precinct, along with his wife, Mary, who was referred to as "Madam" Balch. Used as a formal form of address to identify a woman of high social standing, the title even appears on her gravestone. And the couple owned slaves.

Rev. Balch carefully registered all baptisms, marriages, and deaths that occurred during his tenure. On March 24, 1745, he recorded that "Flora, our negro woman [was] delivered of a still born child." A few months later, there was an even more poignant entry. On August 13, Balch noted the death of "our negro child, Peter, about 7 months old." The following day, August 14, he wrote of the passing of "Flora, our negro woman, aged about 18 years." It is possible, perhaps even likely, that Flora had given birth to twins sometime in March, one stillborn, one named Peter. Rev. Balch was away on the Louisbourg expedition from early March until July, and may well have recorded the date inaccurately. Then, some months later, both the child Peter and his mother, Flora, died. That Thomas Balch felt this woman and her children were his property is indicated by the lack of a last name, and his use of the possessive: "our negro child" and "our negro woman."[14]

For Balch to hold slaves was not at all unlawful. Slavery was first legalized in Massachusetts in 1641, nearly a century before Balch arrived in the district, and it was not until 1783 that the state essentially abolished the practice. Nor was it outside the mainstream of his religion. Cotton Mather, whose beliefs and legacy still reverberated in Massachusetts Bay at the time, believed that the Bible sanctioned slavery. He felt that Christianity provided a proper framework for servitude, one that upheld the humanity of slaves but required obedience to their masters. In return, Christian slave-owners had a responsibility to care for the material well-being of their human property.

Balch was not the only slaveholder in the small village of South Dedham. On October 5, 1765, the minister "Baptised a Negro child of Captain Fales named Cesar."[15] As was the case with the parson, Captain Eliphalet Fales (c. 1717-1781), veteran of the French and Indian War, gave his slave only a first name, an effective way to distinguish his human property from society in general, and the family in particular. The name Cesar (or Caesar) conformed to the customary slave names used in New England. According to Lemire, most were given "place names, biblical names, classical names, or a diminutive form of these or common English names." As it happened, the name Caesar was "one of the most popular slave names in colonial New England. A man who owned a Caesar said to the world he believed in a republican government."[16]

It was also common to baptize a child born into bondage. Cotton Mather and other church leaders encouraged slave baptisms, believing it would ensure the proper treatment of a slave. And English colonists were assured that baptism did not infringe upon ownership but might act as a further restraint: Christian slaves may expect the spiritual rewards of Heaven only by accepting their place and obeying their masters. Thus, children born into slavery were often baptized before being given away or sold.

A third slave-owning family in South Dedham was that of Deacon Nathaniel Sumner (1720-1802), once again a well-educated and well-respected member of the community. Born in Roxbury, Sumner was a graduate of Harvard, where he studied theology. Around 1740 the General Court allowed Dedham to annex a considerable portion of his estate, which had stood within the borders of Sharon. With this annexation Sumner was allowed "to do duty and enjoy privileges" within the Second Precinct.[17] Chosen to be a deacon of the parish in 1752, after the death of John Everett, Sumner was also a representative to the General Court in Boston and served as a Dedham selectman for nineteen years. Owning a slave or two would enable Sumner to fulfill his religious and political duties while still maintaining his farm and considerable assets. There is no record of the number of slaves Sumner may have owned, but in 1774, "a baptized Negro belonging to Nathaniel Sumner" died. Her name was Eunice.[18]

Well before that time, the surviving children of Thomas Balch had reached adulthood. Madam Balch gave birth to eight children; she was 21 at the time of her first pregnancy, 44 at her last. The youngest and eldest of the children were both named Thomas. In 1766, nearly five years after the death of their first-born child, Rev. Balch recorded the birth and baptism of another son by the same name, to, as he put it, "bear up the name of my deceased son, Thomas."[19] Balch's third son, Benjamin, born in 1743, followed in his father's footsteps. He graduated from Harvard College in 1763, continued his theological studies with his father and, by 1764, became a minister in Machias, Maine, and later in Mendon, Massachusetts. He served as a lieutenant in a colonial company that participated in the Battle of Lexington on April 19, 1775, and subsequently was a chaplain for provincials on both land and at sea, earning the nickname "The Fighting Parson." Following the Revolution, he settled as the minister for a Barrington,

New Hampshire, congregation for thirty years until shortly before his death in 1815.

Three of Rev. Balch's daughters married clergymen. Lucy was the wife of Rev. Moses Everett of Dorchester; in 1777, Hannah married the Rev. Jabez Chickering, who had succeeded her father as minister to the parish; and Mary Balch, the Reverend and Madam Balch's eldest daughter, married Manasseh Cutler, a Yale graduate. Cutler had arrived in the village to become the precinct's school master in 1765. Within a year he had wed the pastor's daughter and moved to Martha's Vineyard. Three years later, Cutler, a man of boundless curiosity and intellect, who qualified for legal, medical, and divinity degrees, decided to enter the ministry. He studied with his father-in-law for almost two years before being called to a parish in Ipswich Hamlet. Cutler served in the Continental Army as chaplain during the Revolution and, later, as chronicled by famed historian David McCullough in his book *The Pioneers*, worked tirelessly to open the Northwest Territory to settlers. Finally, Balch's remaining daughter, Elizabeth, taught in the village school during the summer of 1763. Three years later, she married Jonathan Dean and they raised their family of boys—one named Balch in honor of her father—in South Dedham.

Meanwhile, Tiot village grew and diversified. By 1765 there were some 431 residents and, in 1766, Manasseh Cutler reported teaching close to 100 student-scholars in the South Precinct's schoolhouse on Pleasant Street. Balch's congregation expanded as well, and outgrew its original meeting house, which was deemed inadequate and in disrepair. Plans were drawn up in 1768 and on June 26, 1769 the "new and second meeting house [at] the head of Penniman's Lane" (near today's Lenox Street) was constructed.[20] Parishioners again contributed to the purchase of materials, including clapboards, and supplied dinner and "sufficient drink" for the men who provided the labor. Directly beside the new church, a building called the "Noon House" was erected for use by parishioners between Sunday's two services, especially those who traveled a considerable distance. Rev. Balch was no doubt gratified by the increase in his congregation, from 15 upon his arrival to approximately 200 when he delivered his final sermon on October 7, 1770. During his time as the South Church

The Balch parsonage stood on the site of today's 17 Walpole Street,
near the first meeting house of the South Parish.
(Courtesy of First Congregational Church of Norwood)

of Dedham's first pastor, he had also baptized 637 worshippers and
performed 148 marriages.

On January 8, 1774, after a brief illness, Rev. Thomas Balch
died in the parsonage that had become his home. He had married,
raised a family, and led his parishioners from this house. Manasseh
Cutler wrote about the death in his journal: "This day my honored
father, the Rev. Mr. Balch, departed this life, at 8 o'clock in the
morning, in the 63rd year of his age, and the 38th of his ministry...
An irreparable loss to his family and friends, and much lamented by
his people. He left a sorrowful widow and 7 children to lament his
exit." Although he had traveled from Ipswich, Cutler did not attend
the funeral. "I was unable (from a severe attack of pneumonia) to
go out," he wrote, "but ventured down to see the corpse, before it
was carried out of the house." And, he added, "The parish buried
him in a very honorable manner."[21]

With eight ministers in attendance as pall-bearers and four
underbearers, Balch was carried ceremoniously from the parsonage

to the meeting house for prayers and hymns. For nearly four decades, the Reverend Thomas Balch had been the ecclesiastical, social, and cultural center of Dedham's South Precinct. He had seen his congregation through hardship and victory, war and peace. After the customary final viewing by parishioners, the procession led by the Church Sexton and including family, friends, congregants, and even strangers, made its way to the Parish Cemetery, where the beloved minister was interred. His gravestone stands there still, at the pinnacle of the graveyard, surrounded—as he would have wished—by those who knew him best.

Sources, and Notes

The records of the South (or Second) Church may be found in *The Record of Baptism, Marriages, and Deaths, and Admissions to the Church and Dismissals Therefrom, Transcribed from the Church Records in the Town of Dedham, Massachusetts, 1638-1845*, Don Gleeson Hall (ed.), (Dedham, Mass: Office of the Dedham Transcript, 1888). Most of the biographical information on Thomas Balch came from Clifford K. Shipton, "Thomas Balch," *Biographical Sketches of Those Who Attended Harvard College in the Classes 1731-1735*, (Boston: Massachusetts Historical Society, 1956), pp. 273-277. David Freeman Hawke's *Everyday Life in Early America* (NY: Harper & Row, 1988) was most helpful in his descriptions of mills, meeting houses, and colonial village life. Information on the Colonial Wars can be found in Robert Leckie, *"A Few Acres of Snow": The Saga of the French and Indian Wars* (NY: J. Wiley & Sons, 1999) and *Yankees at Louisbourg* by George A. Rawlyk (Nova Scotia: Breton Books, 1999). Walter R. Borneman also discussed the Crown Point Expedition in his *The French and Indian War* (NY: Harper Collins, 2006). Slavery in colonial Massachusetts is discussed in *Black Walden: Slavery and its Aftermath in Concord, Massachusetts* by Elise Lemire (Phila: University of Pennsylvania Press, 2009), and in Tony Williams, *The Pox and the Covenant* (Napierville, IL: Source Books, 2010). Local history books that were especially helpful are Williard De Luce, *The Story of Walpole, 1724-1924* (Norwood, Mass: Ambrose Press, 1925) and Isaac Newton Lewis, *A History of Walpole, Massachusetts* (Walpole, Mass: First Historical Society of Walpole, Mass., 1905). Finally, an essay titled "History of Norwood, Massachusetts" by Francis Tinker published in *History and Directory of Norwood, Mass for 1890* (Boston: Press of Brown Bros, 1890), pp. 9-58 focused on South Dedham and Norwood in particular.

1. W. W. Everett, "Four Periods of Growth," *Norwood Messenger* (hereafter *NM*), 10 March 1933, p. 1.
2. Hawke, p. 145.
3. Lewis, p. 205.
4. Tinker, p. 12.
5. Shipton, p. 276.
6. Shipton, p. 277.
7. Shipton, p. 274.
8. Dedham Records, p. 162.
    Note: Francis Tinker wrote in 1890 that there was a tenth volunteer from South Dedham who participated in the Louisbourg Expedition—Nathaniel Corry, 40, who died at Cape Breton alongside Samuel Thorp. Corry's name is not listed on the commemorative stone.
    It appears that the South Parish lost at least one additional congregant to the island fortress, however. Mary Dehaughty, a woman in her 40s, died at Cape Breton in 1745, too. During the Colonial Wars, British regulations allowed women to serve as nurses and laundresses among the troops; many were the wives of soldiers, and they drew a soldier's ration. According to South Parish records, Rev. Balch had performed the marriage of Mary Thomas and John Dehaughty, both Dedham residents, in May of 1742. Mary had been received into the South Church in full Communion (an indication that she had had a conversion experience) the following year. It is likely that John Dehaughty was part of an earlier expedition to the Louisbourg vicinity and Mary had accompanied his regiment (six women were allowed

per regiment). While there is no subsequent record relating to
John Dehaughty, Balch recorded that Mary Dehaughty died at
Cape Breton in January 1745. (Dedham Records, p. 161, 145,
168)

9. "Extracts from the Diary and Note Book of Captain William
Bacon - 1756," in *The Dedication of A Monument to the Memory
of the Men of Walpole and Vicinity who Served in the French
and Indian War* (2 November 1901). Walpole Historical Society
Collection.

10. Lewis, p. 106.

11. Dedham Records, p. 164.

12. W. W. Everett, "Portrait of Gravestones of Tiot," *NM*, 23 October
1934, p. 1.

13. W. W. Everett, "Birth and Babyhood of Tiot," *NM*, 2 October
1934, p. 3.

14. Dedham Records, p. 162.

15. Dedham Records, p. 159.

16. Lemire, p. 27.

17. Tinker, p. 23.

18. Dedham Records, p. 167.

19. Dedham Records, p. 158. According to Francis Tinker, this
second Thomas, named in memory of his brother, was taken
prisoner while serving on a war vessel during the Revolution,
taken to Halifax, and died there. (p. 19).

20. Tinker, p. 24.

21. William Parker Cutler and Julia Perkins Cutler, *Life, Journals and
Correspondence of Rev. Manasseh Cutler*, Volume 1, (Cincinnati:
Robert Clarke & Company, 1888), pp. 44-45.

Chapter 2

The Annals of Aaron Guild:
A Tale Most Fabulous and Forged

ON A LOVELY JULY DAY in 1902 the townspeople of Norwood gathered on the lawn of the Congregational Church on Walpole Street to witness the unveiling of a unique monument. At 4:00 p.m. sharp, Milton H. Howard, a well-known builder and chairman of the historical committee of the town's first ever "Old Home Day," opened the festivities. Surrounded by a multitude of men, women, and children, with several residents seated in their horse-drawn carriages for a better view, Howard uncovered a granite boulder with gold-lettering carved into its level-seamed face. The inscription read:

> NEAR THIS SPOT
> CAPT AARON GUILD
> ON APRIL 19, 1775
> LEFT PLOW IN FURROW, OXEN STANDING
> AND DEPARTING FOR LEXINGTON,
> ARRIVED IN TIME TO FIRE UPON
> THE RETREATING BRITISH

Attorney Harold E. Fales delivered the main historical address, noting that the tribute paid to Aaron Guild "should not be understood merely as an honor to an individual. We honor Aaron Guild, but we honor him more as a type of many who showed their heroic devotion, for the heroes that day were numbered by thousands."[1] Officials were, of course, linking their own brief history—it had been barely thirty years since the town was incorporated—to the Revolutionary War and the nation's founding a century earlier. With this day and with this memorial, as Fales indicated, they sought to bind their community to the "heroic traditions" of the brave "undisciplined

The dedication of the Aaron Guild commemorative stone took place during
Norwood's 1902 Old Home Day celebration.
(Courtesy of the Morrill Memorial Library)

farmers" of Massachusetts who took on the formidable British forces.
They were not alone in this quest.

Old-time New England was fading from memory by the turn of
the twentieth century. Once a collection of small towns dominated by
like-minded Yankee farmers, the region was becoming unrecognizable
due to the throes of industrialization, urbanization, and immigration.
Over three-quarters of Massachusetts residents now lived in cities. The
population of Boston had more than doubled between 1870, when it
was home to about 250,000, and 1905, when it reached nearly 600,000.
Even more significant, the recently developed railroad and streetcar
lines had fostered an urban sprawl; Brookline and Cambridge, for
example, had tripled in size during the previous three decades.

Only thirteen miles from the city, Norwood was part of the modern transportation network. It was already industrialized, with tanneries, an ink mill, and large-scale printing establishments attracting an influx of new residents. In 1870, two years before its incorporation, the town had been home to 1,560; in 1900, the number had risen to 5,480, and by 1905, it was well past 6,500. This rapid growth had resulted in the same unease and resentment toward immigrants felt in Boston, Massachusetts at large, and America as a whole.

Dignitaries like Woodrow Wilson, then president of Princeton University, bemoaned the fact that, in contrast to the "sturdy stocks of the north of Europe" who had built this nation, now the country was being overrun by "multitudes of men of the lowest class from the south of Italy and men of the meaner sort out of Hungary and Poland." These immigrants, Wilson continued, possessed "neither skill nor energy nor any initiative of quick intelligence." It was, he wrote, "as if the countries of the south of Europe were disburdening themselves of the more sordid and hapless elements of their populations." In Massachusetts, Wilson's sentiments were enthusiastically echoed by Senator Henry Cabot Lodge, who forcefully declared the need to close America's gates to "races" he found "most alien"—those from southern and eastern Europe. As early as 1891, Lodge had demanded immigration restriction in order to "guard our civilization against an infusion which seems to threaten deterioration."[2] The memory of the pastoral New England village was in jeopardy.

In truth, that memory was itself a myth. Although many small villages like South Dedham had been relatively homogeneous, overall colonial New England had been inhabited by a variety of English and other European settlers, as well as Native Americans and Africans. But the reality of this diverse population had been forgotten, and the arrival of new "alien races" caused a wave of nostalgia for an imagined past. Late nineteenth century writers, artists, and cultural entrepreneurs reinvented the region's history, casting as sole founders the white, Protestant farmers with lives purportedly centered on freedom, faith, and family. This included men like Aaron Guild.

To sustain that fiction, ancestral-based organizations, like the Sons of the Revolution, the Daughters of the American Revolution, and the Colonial Dames of America, were formed to bestow status on those who had occupied the land for generations, to celebrate their ancestors' past glories, and, in no small measure, to set themselves apart from recent arrivals. Another manifestation of this revisionism was an attempt to instill proper Yankee values into a newly-arrived diverse population. For the first time in 1902, Massachusetts set aside the last week in July as "Old-Home Week;" and legislation was passed to encourage towns to commemorate their history, promote good citizenship, and "stimulate our people to higher ideals." Sons and daughters who had moved away—who had, according to the local newspaper, "gone forth to all portions of this broad land, building up new communities, making them stronger, better and purer for their presence"—were invited to return to their home towns to renew old acquaintances, make new friends, and be feted by a grateful community.[3]

In a more modest observance of civic pride, Norwood held an Old Home Day. Former residents returned to Village Hall to view an historical exhibit and to eat a luncheon of "cake, crackers, lemonade and dainties." Following the Guild Memorial ceremony, there was a supper at the Universalist Church, a band concert, and closing exercises presided over by businessman Frank Fales, who suggested that some wealthy Old Home Day visitor might show his loyalty to Norwood by donating the cost of a new town hall.

The *Norwood Advertiser and Review* estimated that between 150 and 200 former residents returned to Norwood on Old Home Day, most from neighboring towns (Walpole, Medfield, Canton, and Attleboro), or other Massachusetts communities (Brockton, Lynn, Melrose, and Springfield). A few, though, traveled across state lines from New Hampshire, Rhode Island, New York, and Connecticut. The newspaper assured its readers that during the Village Hall gathering, where stories were told and memories recalled, "all lines of caste, clique, nationality, creed, and faction were broken down."[4] Even more, all were in agreement with Harold Fales that Aaron Guild was the perfect representational figure for the townspeople to celebrate.

But who was this Aaron Guild? And why was he selected as the town's representational patriot? After all, Francis Tinker's "History of the Town," the first published account of Norwood's history which appeared in the *History and Directory of Norwood, Mass., for 1890,* only mentions Guild in passing, and, in fact, omits him entirely from the list of responders to the April 19, 1775 alarm. As with so many symbolic historical figures, the details are a bit murky, complicated, and more than a little comic.

Born in 1728, Aaron Guild had spent his entire life in the village of South Dedham. His farm encompassed the land on which both the Morrill Memorial Library and the Congregational Church stood, a fitting spot for his commemorative stone to be placed almost two centuries later. Guild's house had been just across the Wrentham Road (today's Walpole Street), the route of the first regular stage coach between Boston and Providence, which had opened in 1767. Guild was well-known in the village, was a member of the Church of Christ in Dedham's Second Parish (by 1902, the First Congregational Church), was married three times, and had raised a large family. In addition, he was a veteran of two conflicts—the Colonial Wars and the American Revolution—and died in 1818, at the age of 90, having witnessed, but not participated in, yet another war. And now, almost a century after his death, he was being designated a hero.

It was not until the 1930s that local newspaperman Win Everett questioned Aaron Guild's prominent position in community folklore—in addition to the commemorative stone, in 1906, a depiction of Guild, his oxen, and plow had been adopted as Norwood's town seal. Among the many historical sketches Everett published in the *Norwood Messenger*, an April 1936 article introduced his reservations. "With all due respect to the judgment of those who picked out Aaron Guild to be our traditional Norwood Revolutionary hero," Everett wrote, "it has seemed to me that Nathaniel Sumner's name and record were somehow lost in the shuffle. He appears to the writer to be a much bigger ace than Aaron." Everett obviously had some literary fun describing Sumner on his horse flying past the walking Aaron Guild on his way to the infamous 1775 muster, but he seemed quite sincere as he made his case in Sumner's favor. The newspaperman allowed that Guild was a farmer who owned considerable acreage, served in the war, and married multiple times, but as he bluntly pointed out, "that seems to cover it."[5] Sumner, on the other hand, had a truly distinguished career.

Born in 1720, Nathaniel Sumner was a 1739 graduate of Harvard College, where he studied theology. Although he never served as a minister, he became a deacon of the Second Parish in 1752 while Rev. Thomas Balch was the pastor. On the secular side, Sumner was a representative to the General Court for several years between 1756 and 1770, was a Dedham selectman for nineteen years, and a delegate to the colonial convention held in Faneuil Hall in 1768. On April 19, 1775, like Aaron Guild, he responded to the alarm. Both men were considered aged (Sumner was 55, Guild was 47), but were ready to defend their homes in the face of British hostilities.[6]

Only a month earlier, in March of 1775, as tensions rose between the Crown and the colonies, a Dedham town meeting had voted to raise a company of 60 Minutemen, each bound into nine months service. This contingent had barely begun to train when the events of April 19 unfolded. Surprisingly, although Dedham was only a few miles from Boston, the town did not hear of the near-dawn military engagement at Lexington until an express rider, traveling a circuitous route through Needham and Dover, arrived at around 9 o'clock in the morning. The word was spread by church bells, signal guns, and, to reach outer villages like Tiot, additional riders. Minutemen, militia companies, and volunteers hurried to their agreed upon meeting places. The men of South Dedham all hastened to gather in Dedham center; they did not set off for Lexington as Norwood's Guild monument states.

According to the annals   of Dedham, well over three hundred men responded to the Lexington alarm. Unlike some communities, which mustered their full contingent before heading toward the conflict, Dedham sent their militiamen out in small groups as soon as they had gathered. Under the command of Capt. William Bullard, 59 men assembled from the Second Parish and were sent to Menotomy (Arlington) where they soon skirmished with the British regulars. But neither Aaron Guild nor Nathaniel Sumner was among them. According to multiple sources, elder men, many of them veterans of earlier conflicts, were not dispatched until much later in the day when they were "led by Hezekiah Fuller and Nathaniel Sumner, two of the oldest and most respected of the citizens." And with that, Win Everett closed his defense of Deacon

Nathanial Sumner as Norwood's most prominent Revolutionary War figure, one deserving of a memorial.[7]

Regardless of the actual events of that April day, Aaron Guild, who had received his promotion to captain in the militia in 1771, did participate, albeit briefly, in the war that followed. He spent a few days at Dorchester Heights in March of 1776 and later that year served a total of four months with his company, guarding Hull Harbor. For the most part, however, military activity by-passed Dedham.

Nearly twenty years earlier, in 1758, Aaron Guild, at the time a thirty-year-old father of small children and an ensign in His Majesty's service, had marched to Lake George in upstate New York during the Seven Years War (1756-1763). As in the preceding King George's War (1740-1748), this episode of what is referred to as the French and Indian War was characterized not by constant combat but lengthy periods of inaction punctuated by occasional violence. From the end of May until the first week of July, while part of the company of Capt. Eliphalet Fales in the regiment of Colonel Nichols, Guild kept a diary.[8] In this account, he carefully recorded distances covered and meals eaten. For example, his May 29, 1758 entry read: "Marched to Mr. Dwight's (3 m) and refreshed then marched to Mr. Graus's (3 ½ m) and breakfasted, then marched to Mr. Warner's in Hadley (2 m) and dined, supped, and lodged."

It was a long and sometimes miserable journey for these rather ill-prepared recruits. Following two days of "A Great Rain," on Sunday, June 4, they "marched on through mire and hills and brooks, through valleys and swamps in a hideous and untrod way (10 m) and camped." Later that evening, the inadequately-trained sentry was startled by the cry of an owl. Thinking it was the shrieking of the enemy, he abandoned his post in fear, flung away his gun, and ran into the camp shouting in alarm, whereupon, Guild records, he "fell over a stump, log, or rock and broke out one of his teeth." Otherwise uninjured, the militia continued their march the next day, only to have a tree accidentally fall on one of the men, breaking his arm. The disheveled and mishap-prone contingent eventually arrived at Fort Miller near Saratoga, New York, on June 18. There they received news that the French had raised a flag of truce. On the evening of June 20, however, their bad luck continued when "a gun accidentally went off," wounding one of the men. Exhausted from these trials, the company rested for the next three days.

On June 25, they heard heavy gunfire coming from the direction of nearby Fort Edward, a fort held by colonial forces. A scouting party, which included Aaron Guild, was sent to see if hostilities had resumed. Instead of encountering the enemy, however, they found militia men firing off their weapons just "to clean their guns." Relieved that it was yet another false alarm, Guild and the others returned to camp. For the next week or more, Capt. Fales' company remained on site, reinforcing the fort while the rest of the regiment was ordered elsewhere. Once his service was completed, Guild was dismissed, and he began the long trek home from Lake George. Guild's diary stops at July 7, 1758, but his troubles did not.

Aaron Guild summarized his travails in a petition sent on January 15, 1760 to Thomas Pownal, the Captain General and Commander-in-Chief of His Majesty's colonial force in Massachusetts.[9] Shortly after he started for South Dedham, Guild's health became "much impaired through fatigue and hardship" and he was forced "to purchase a passage to New Marlboro in a wagon." Once there, he lay "sick of fever" for six days in the home of John Thompson, incurring the cost of lodging and a doctor's care. Guild subsequently hired a horse and driver to get home, a journey that took six days because of his "extreme weakness." Even after he reached South Dedham, Guild convalesced for another month and "was not able to do anything of any value for some time after." It was certainly an ignominious end to his participation in the military campaign.

With his petition, Aaron Guild was seeking reimbursement from Pownal for both the expenses he had incurred and for his lost time. But that was not all. In addition, he sought compensation for another loss, writing: "Also your humble petitioner had a servant named Isaac Little who enlisted into and served in the same company and was taken by the enemy at the fight near Half-way Brook by which means he has not only lost his service, but also a valuable gun worth 2 pounds, 8 shillings which was taken with him by the enemy." Thus, Guild was asking for compensation not only for his out-of-pocket expenses and time lost to illness, but the loss of his servant and his gun as well.

Aaron Guild was not the only one looking for recompense, however. Apparently, word of Isaac Little's capture had reached South Dedham soon after it had occurred. On September 7, 1758—more than a year before Aaron Guild's petition—his wife had submitted her own plea to Pownal. "This is to inform your Honor," Anna Guild wrote, "that my servant Isaac Little of Dedham was, or I am well afeared, taken captive at the Half-way Brook in a skirmish with part of Col. Nichols' regiment and should be redeemed...."[10] It seems from these petitions that Isaac Little was not simply a hired hand working on the Guild farm but an indentured servant, a man whose labor had been contracted through an arrangement that had already cost the Guilds a considerable sum. His status as such is confirmed by the Muster Roll of Captain Eliphalet Fales' company which identifies Aaron Guild as Isaac Little's "Master."[11]

Indentured servitude for household work or farm labor was quite common in colonial New England. Immigrants from Great Britain became indentured in America in return for free passage and, often, the promise of a plot of land. Some estimate that between 1620 and 1775, these voluntary servants accounted for two out of every three arrivals from the British Isles. The town of Dedham was known to have condoned such arrangements for immigrants as well as for native-born young adults, and children, with selectmen deciding how long householders could keep a servant (usually between one and four years) before they must "clear the town of him or her" to ensure the servant would not become a public charge. After 1710, Dedham residents brought in servants not only for household work or farm labor but also to serve as tenant farmers on their excess acreage. The circumstances of Isaac Little's entry into servitude is unknown, as is his exact status—he may have been a tenant farmer on part of Guild's expansive property—but the couple's reaction to his capture makes it clear that they had an investment in Little and expected to be compensated by the colonial government for his loss.[12]

Neither Aaron nor Anna Guild seemed to know what had happened to Little after he was carried off by the enemy. Amazingly, however, Isaac Little was able to tell his own story. On February 16, 1760, a mere month after Aaron Guild's petition, Isaac Little stood before Justice of the Peace Nathaniel Sumner—the need for Little to swear to the truth of his account to Sumner is a further indication of his lowly status—and described his ordeal.[13]

On July 20, 1758, Little and nine others had been ordered to guard a courier from Half-way Brook to Lake George. During their return, they were confronted by an army of about seven hundred. Four of the party were killed; Little and the others were captured. After a month in the hands of Native Americans, Little recounts, he "stole away from them & ran to the French," who, in turn, brought him to Quebec where he was confined for about three months "enduring very great hardships, being almost starved for want of provisions."

Following his detention in Canada, Isaac was put on board a British vessel which carried him across the Atlantic to Dartmouth, England. From there, Little continues, he "was obliged to travel to London (230 miles)…without any money & hardly any clothing." He was then sent to Portsmouth and "from thence to New York" where he arrived in May 1759, "after a tedious passage of three months at sea." Once back in the colonies, instead of being released to return to his home, Isaac was given a choice: "go into the 55th Regiment or on board a man-of-war." He chose the former, although complaining that he "thought it very hard to be detained and obliged to go in service again." Little remained with the troops until January of 1760 when the regiment went into winter quarters and he obtained a furlough. It was a remarkable tale, one with which His Majesty's representatives apparently sympathized. Isaac Little was awarded 8 pounds; Aaron Guild received 40 shillings, considerably less.

After his 1936 review of these accounts in an article titled, "The Dolesome Adventure of Aaron and Isaac," Win Everett agreed with the colonial authorities. "Of all the characters in this little drama," Everett concluded, "the writer's heart warms to the gritty and patient Isaac." In the end, Everett made a rather droll suggestion: "Why not substitute Isaac for Aaron on the town seal?"[14]

In addition to sponsoring Old Home Day in 1902, the Norwood Business Association and Board of Trade held a contest to design a town seal. More than eighty designs were submitted by pupils of the Norwood Public Schools. The judges generously noted that the selection process was "rendered more difficult because of the general excellence, skill, taste and ideas" shown in the submissions. Designs incorporated assorted flags, eagles, and crests and ranged from depictions of King Philip to factories, colonial homesteads, and printing presses. Grace Weaver, who sketched smoking factory chimneys to represent industry and fruit to indicate prosperity, was given special recognition as was George Boyden who drew a likeness of "Capt. Aaron Guild leaving his oxen and plow to go to the Concord fight." The winning entry—by high school student Ethel Hubbard— was a representation of the Hook, a familiar landmark to those who knew their history. The *Advertiser and Review* described the design in detail: "Set within a wreath is the stable yard and corner of the old Sumner tavern, showing the edges of the three buildings, with a horse tied to a large hook which projects from the exterior of one of the buildings. Beneath the picture and wreath is a well-executed iron hook, and around this design are the words, 'The Hook.'"[15]

Ethel Hubbard received a check for her original drawing but, in case there were any misunderstandings, the Board of Trade included a careful caveat: "The committee does not wish it to be understood that in making these awards it has finally determined upon the design for a seal which it will recommend." Instead, they clarified, the committee "made its selections for the purposes of this contest in accordance with its terms," terms that apparently did not guarantee that officials would adopt the first-place design as their new town seal. And there the matter rested until February 1905, when a Norwood town meeting voted to appoint a committee of three —Milton H. Howard, John R. Parker, and Elmer Barker—to "make recommendation as to the adoption of a new seal and report at a future town meeting." After a year of deliberations, the committee presented their report and town meeting voted to adopt their suggestion. Aaron Guild, along with his plow and oxen, made their inaugural appearance on the cover of the *35ᵗʰ Annual Report of the Town of Norwood* for the year ending January 31, 1907.[16] What brought Aaron Guild to the attention of the committee—other than George Boyden's contest submission—was not explained. There were, however, several descendants of Guild still living in the area around 1900 to advocate on his behalf.

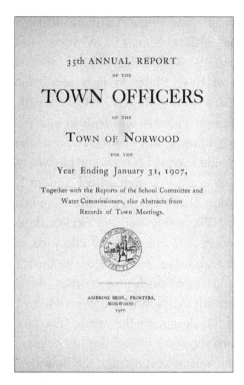

35th ANNUAL REPORT
OF THE

TOWN OFFICERS

OF THE

TOWN OF NORWOOD

FOR THE

Year Ending January 31, 1907,

Together with the Reports of the School Committee and
Water Commissioners, also Abstracts from
Records of Town Meetings.

AMBROSE BROS., PRINTERS,
NORWOOD.
1907.

Norwood's new town seal featuring Aaron Guild first appeared in the
35th Annual Report of 1907. (*Courtesy of the Morrill Memorial Library*)

The National Society of Daughters of the American Revolution (DAR) accepted a Norwood chapter into their organization in 1975. The local group took as its namesake, Aaron Guild. Founded in 1890, the DAR was one of the associations created to memorialize the country's colonial era history. The DAR and other self-described "patriotic" groups drew withering criticism from historian Howard Mumford Jones in a 1938 *Atlantic Monthly* article titled, "Patriotism —But How?" Calling for a "patriotic renaissance" in the face of the Great Depression, Jones warned that "selfish interests have adopted the star-spangled manner." Declaring that organizations from both the right and the left had agendas that included the desire "to call somebody else un-American," he continued, "Patriotism may not always be the last refuge of a scoundrel, but it is too often a convenient disguise for a one-hundred-per-center who wants somebody else to go back home."[17] As if to prove Jones' point, in 1939 the DAR refused permission to renowned opera singer Marian Anderson to perform before an integrated audience in Constitution Hall, their national headquarters in Washington, D.C., because of her race. In response, with the assistance of First Lady Eleanor Roosevelt, she gave her concert on the steps of the Lincoln Memorial to a crowd of 75,000.

Earlier in the decade, artist Grant Wood had taken up his brush to parody some of America's fables. His aim, in many instances, was to use satire to mock those individuals and groups "who perpetuated deceptive elaborations of historical truth," such as the myth of George Washington chopping down a cherry tree. One of his works was titled *Daughters of Revolution* (1932), a portrait of three elderly women standing before a lithograph reproduction of Emanuel Leutze's 1851 painting *Washington Crossing the Delaware*. The carefully rendered, unsmiling trio in their sensible matronly dresses, one with a collar of hand-tatted lace, stand in for a generation of women who revered their ancestors. The central figure grasps a blue and white Willow Ware tea cup with its faux Chinese landscape in her slender elongated fingers. The sturdy star-studded frame, which echoes that of the lithograph in the background, was part of Wood's portrait as well. The title, etched into this painted border, *Daughters of Revolution*, is an unmistakable reference to the Daughters of the American Revolution, an organization Wood had clashed with previously.[18]

Four years earlier, the DAR had publicly objected to Wood's having a stained-glass window—part of the Cedar Rapids, Iowa, Veterans Memorial Building—manufactured in Germany less than a decade after the end of the Great War. *Daughters of Revolution* was thought to be the artist's revenge. Wood's lampoon intentionally called into question the women's brand of patriotism; he felt the group's admission requirements "betrayed the American principle of egalitarianism" and highlighted their hypocrisy. While the DAR criticized Wood's German-produced stained glass, they had embraced the German-born Leutze's iconic painting with gusto.[19]

Learning from such controversies, the DAR re-examined its aims, added more local chapters—like the Contentment Chapter in Dedham (1947) and the Aaron Guild Chapter in Norwood (1975)—and focused its activities on preservation, education and community service. In 1983, the Aaron Guild Chapter of the DAR placed a plaque on Aaron Guild's grave in the Old Parish Cemetery.

In the spring of 1903, Norwood debated whether to hold a second Old Home Day. Despite the fact that Massachusetts had scheduled its Old Home Week celebration for July, a few residents recommended postponing the event until later in the year. Some proposed promoting the day as a kind of civic holiday to demonstrate citizenship, since the object of Old Home Week across the state was to inspire residents to do good works. A third group believed the day should be designated as a time for "social reunions," a kind of family reunion for the community. James Folan, business owner and Board of Trade member, contended that everyone was trying to "throw cold water on the whole thing." He objected to the fact that some members of the Old Home Day Committee "appeared to insinuate that no people ever went away from Norwood, or if they did go away, they never wanted to come back," making the whole idea pointless. After that meeting, there was some question whether the celebration would take place at all.[20]

In spite of these questions and concerns, beginning on July 23, 1903, Norwood's second Old Home Day actually was spread across two days. Most of the festivities took place in a tent erected especially for the occasion, large enough to hold 1,200 people. Dedham town clerk and historian Don Gleason Hill made a presentation on Wednesday, followed by a dedicatory address on Thursday by the Hon. Frederick Stimson, also of Dedham. There was, of course, a concert by the Norwood Brass Band as well. The highlight of the events was the unveiling of a second historical monument. This time the committee had reached even farther back in history to the Siege of Louisbourg in 1745. With Milton H. Howard once again serving as master of ceremonies, its drapery was lifted and the lettering etched into the stone paid tribute to the nine men from South Dedham who had participated in that military action during the Colonial Wars: Rev. Thomas Balch, John Thorp, Capt. Eleazer Fisher, Samuel Thorp, Lieut. Ebenezer Sumner, Michael Bright, William Wetherbee, Hugh DeLap, and Samuel Wetherbee.[21]

The monument stood in a small park near the Everett School. The site was historically linked to the Guild family. Not to Aaron, however, but his brother, Captain Moses Guild (1725-1789), who had also answered the call on April 19, 1775. Guild's son and namesake, Moses Guild (1755-1829), founded a freight hauling business along the Norfolk and Bristol Turnpike (Washington Street) around 1806. The company housed wagons in a barn built near the spot where the Louisbourg stone was ultimately placed. The business made the family one of the wealthiest in the village. The Guild house, standing across from the barn at the juncture of today's Washington and Walpole Streets, was a well-recognized landmark. There was even a legend that the Marquis de Lafayette had spent the night in the house in 1825 on his way to the dedication of the Bunker Hill Monument.

In 1843, with the freight business waning, the barn became a grist mill, and later a store. For a time, Col. O. W. Fiske rented the structure, installed steam-power, and manufactured playing cards there. Ever after referred to as the "old steam mill," it was converted into a tenement house for Irish immigrants and even later became a carpenter's shop. At the turn of the twentieth century it was torn down and a public band stand was erected in its place. The house was moved to the corner of Broadway and Park in 1911 to make way for the construction of the Talbot Block, said to be Norwood's first modern, multi-story apartment building. Having owned the property on both sides of what is now Guild Street, it seems likely that it was Moses Guild, not Aaron, for whom Guild Street was named, although in 1947 Win Everett indicated the street name was a tribute to Major Aaron Guild.[22]

The Everett School was replaced by a new federal Post Office in 1933 and Central Street was extended to form a more sizable space surrounding the band stand which was torn down in 1955. During Norwood's centennial celebration in 1972, the park, which had been known as "Guild Square Park," was beautified by the Women's Community Committee, and dedicated as the Aaron Guild Memorial Park, essentially erasing the history of the site and the legacy of the Moses Guild family.

In 2006 Norwood's Veterans Services Director, Ted Mulvehill, came before the Board of Selectmen proposing to alter the town seal. It seemed that Aaron Guild, who had graced official flags, documents, and memorabilia since 1907, was wearing a red coat, a color only British

regulars would have worn on that April day in 1775. A few members of
the Board of Selectmen felt the coat should not be changed because
"it has been red since 1972 [Norwood's centennial year], and it's
important to keep its historical heritage alive." Others offered that the
scarlet jacket had been added by the Centennial Committee "to make
it attractive."[23] In fact, although the original design had been in pen
and ink, a colorful seal was introduced on a stained-glass window in the
new Municipal Building's Memorial Hall in 1928, but somehow went
unnoticed until the 1972 celebration, when it appeared on various
souvenirs and bumper stickers. Some renderings even had Guild
depicted in a double-breasted, fully-buttoned-up British uniform!

As discussion continued around town, residents were split on the
question. Most, like the selectmen, thought the color of Guild's coat
was insignificant, a rather comical gaffe. But Mulvehill persisted in
his sartorial argument, and a year later returned to the selectmen to
unveil a new town flag with Aaron Guild wearing a brown coat. He has
worn one ever since. Despite Win Everett's preferences, at least when
people look at Norwood's town seal today, they know Aaron Guild was
a colonial militia man, not a Redcoat.[24]

Aaron Guild may not have been the most skilled (or healthy)
colonial recruit or the most generous of "Masters," and he may not
have actually headed to Lexington in 1775 as his monument claims; he
may have even, through no fault of his own, been granted his brother's
rightful place in history at the corner of Washington and Guild. But he
was a life-long resident of Tiot, a church goer, and an affluent farmer,
and, most important, unlike Nathaniel Sumner whose farm stood on
the outskirts of the village, Aaron Guild lived in the right place—near
the center of town.

Sources and Notes

1. "Old Home Day," *Norwood Advertiser and Review*, 1 August
   1902, p. 1.
2. Woodrow Wilson quoted in Adam Hochschild, "American

Chronicles, Obstruction of Justice," *The New Yorker*, 11 November 2019, p. 30; Henry Cabot Lodge quote: Daniel Okrent, *The Guarded Gate* (NY: Scribner, 2019), p. 38. Also see, James M. Lindgren, *Preserving Historic New England* (NY: Oxford University Press, 1995).

3. "Old Home Week," *Norwood Advertiser and Review*, 9 May 1903, p. 1.

4. "Old Home Day," *Norwood Advertiser and Review*, 1 August 1902, p. 1.

5. Win Everett, "Silhouette of Old Tyot, Number 4," *Norwood Messenger* (hereafter *NM*) 21 April 1936, p. 1.

6. Sumner's biography in: Francis Tinker, "History of the Town," *History and Directory of Norwood, Mass., for 1890* (Boston: Brown Bros., 1890) p. 52.

7. Herman Mann, *Historical Annals of the Town of Dedham from its Settlement in 1635 to 1847* (Dedham, 1847), quoted in Everett, "Silhouette of Old Tyot, Number 4." For events of April 19, 1775, see also: Robert B. Hanson, *Dedham, Massachusetts, 1635-1890* (Dedham, MA: Dedham Historical Society, 1976) and David Hackett Fischer, *Paul Revere's Ride* (NY: Oxford University Press, 1994).

8. Quotes taken from: "The Diary of Ensign Aaron Guild," printed in the pamphlet *The Dedication of a Monument to the Memory of the Men of Walpole and Vicinity who Served in the French and Indian War*, 2 November 1901. Walpole Historical Society Collection.

9. Quotes taken from: "The Petition of Aaron Guild of Dedham" dated 15 January 1760, Massachusetts State Archives Collection,1629-1799, Digital Records, Volume 78, Military, 1758-1760; Film #2363837, DGS 007703423, Image 1404 (p.761).

10. Quotes taken from: "The Petition of Anna Guild" dated 7 September 1758, Massachusetts State Archives Collection, 1629-1799, Digital Records, Volume 78, Military, 1758-1760; Film #2363653, DGS 007703422, Image 731 (p. 694).

11. Muster Roll dated 3 February 1759 in His Majesty's service under

Captain Eliphalet Fales in Col. Ebenezer Nichols Regiment (date entered service 7 May 1758,),Massachusetts State Archives Collection, 1629-1799, Digital Records, Volume 97A, Muster Rolls, 1757-1759; Film #1783687, DGS 007705825, Images 660 & 662.

12. Indentured servants in general: Don Jordan and Michael Walsh, *White Cargo: The Forgotten History of Britain's White Slaves in America* (NY: New York University Press, 2008) and Dedham in particular: Barry Levy, "Girls and Boys: Poor Children and the Labor Market in Colonial Massachusetts," *Pennsylvania History* 64 Summer, 1997) pp. 287-307.

13. Quotes taken from: "The Petition of Isaac Little, servant to Aaron Guild of Dedham" dated 16 February 1760, Massachusetts State Archives Collection,1629-1799, Digital Records, Volume 78, Military, 1758-1760; Film #2363837, DGS 007703423, Image 1286 (p. 697).

14. Win Everett, "The Dolesome Adventure of Aaron and Isaac," *NM* 1 September 1936, p. 1.

15. "They Stick to 'The Hook'" and "Award in Town Seal Contest," undated newspaper clippings, Norwood Historical Society Collection.

16. "Award in Town Seal Contest," undated newspaper clipping, Norwood Historical Society Collection; *34th Annual Report of the Town of Norwood*, year ending January 31, 1906, p. 21; *35th Annual Report of the Town of Norwood*, year ending January 31, 1907, p. 21.

17. Howard Mumford Jones, "Patriotism—But How?" *The Atlantic Monthly* 162 (5) (November 1938) p. 590.

18. Emily Braun, "Cryptic Corn: Magic Realism and the Art of Grant Wood," in *Grant Wood: American Gothic and Other Fables*, edited by Barbara Haskell (New Haven, CT: Yale University Press, 2018) p. 73; Glenn Adamson, "Willow Weep for Me," in *Grant Wood: American Gothic and Other Fables*, edited by Barbara Haskell (New Haven, CT: Yale University Press, 2018) pp. 39-48.

19. R. Tripp Evans, *Grant Wood, A Life* (NY: Alfred A. Knopf, 2010)

p. 156-157.

20. "Old Home Week," *Norwood Advertiser and Review*, 9 May 1903, p. 1.

21. "Norwood Old Home Week," *Norwood Advertiser and Review*, 7 August 1903, p. 3.

22. Bryant Tolles, Jr., *Norwood: The Centennial History of A Massachusetts Town* (Norwood: Town of Norwood, 1973) (The Everett School was named for Israel Everett, a South Dedham veteran of the Revolutionary War who was wounded on April 19, 1775.); Marcia M. Winslow, "Recollections of Old South Dedham," 1902, 43-page typescript, Norwood Historical Society; Win Everett, "La Fayette Stayed at Old Norwood Home," *NM*, 4 May 1934, p.1; "Names of Streets Recall Noted Citizens," *Official Commemoration and Chronicle Issued in Honor of the 75ᵗʰ Anniversary of the Town of Norwood* (Norwood, MA: Norwood Daily Messenger, 1947) p. 71.

23. Brian Falla, "Red is seen as dead wrong in town seal," *Daily Transcript*, 29 August 2006, pp. A1, A8; Luke Drummey, "Considering a turncoat…, *Norwood Bulletin*, 28 September 2006, pp. A1, A9; Brian Falla, "Board recolors historic image," *Daily News/Transcript*, 19 September 2007, pp. A1, A10.

24. Peter Schworm, "He was a patriot, not a redcoat," *Boston Sunday Globe South*, 1 October 2006, pp. 1, 11.

Chapter 3

For the Union Dead

"There is always the deepest eloquence of sermon or poem
in any of these ancient graveyards..."

-Walt Whitman (*Specimen Days*)

ENCIRCLED BY COMMERCIAL BUILDINGS and parking lots,
the Old Parish Cemetery has stood silent vigil in the center of town for
well over 250 years. Unless you happen to glance out an office window
or catch a glimpse from a passing train or car, you may not even realize
it is even there. One of the earliest indications that a disparate group
of people were forming a community, the burial ground of the Second
(or South) Parish of Dedham was founded in 1741, a physical symbol
that these few families had set down roots in this place and sought to

keep their dead close by. It is a hilly two-acre piece of land with sandy soil. Part of it was donated in 1740, and by 1827 the congregation had raised enough funds by subscription to double its size. A portion of it was lost, washed away by a great storm around 1850. As one historian wrote, "There is no record of the many graves so destroyed, but it is certain that no small number disappeared at that time."[1] Still, the citizens persevered and continued to make the solemn journey along Cemetery Street (now Central) into the graveyard to bury their dead.

In 1880, after the village had become the town of Norwood, residents had the foresight to establish a second burial place, one that provided room for expansion. As that cemetery was developed, the Parish Cemetery saw fewer and fewer interments. They ceased altogether in the mid-twentieth century, leaving the rough terrain with its quaint colonial markers to languish, virtually forgotten. Among the slate and stone and sepulcher, however, there are sixteen who shared a common cause, men who, in the words of early town historian Francis Tinker, "took their lives in their hands and went forth and stood as a wall of fire, and hurled back the mad surges of the legions of slavery."[2] Four of them perished in the endeavor; the rest returned home to pick up their lives and remember.

Historian Tinker was quick to point out that those who left South Dedham to fight in the Civil War "were humble men and filled no high stations."[3] They were farmers and carpenters, teamsters and tannery workers. They were young, with an average age of twenty-six; four were teenagers. Several did not start off life in this village, but family and circumstances brought them to this sacred ground upon their deaths. They mustered into various regiments, mostly in Massachusetts, although two signed up in Rhode Island, one each in Maine and Michigan, and one joined the US Navy, and their terms of service varied. The majority enlisted for three-year stints while others were "nine months men."

Support for the abolitionists' fierce principles was strong in South Dedham, due in no small part to the proselytizing of Reverend Edwin Thompson, a Universalist minister. He lectured for the cause throughout Massachusetts, often in the company of well-known advocates William Lloyd Garrison and Wendell Phillips. Thompson had even addressed a meeting of the Norfolk County Anti-Slavery Society alongside Frederick Douglass in 1844, while serving as a leader of South Dedham's Universalists.

Founded in 1793 in Oxford, Massachusetts, Universalism embraced the doctrine of universal salvation for all human beings, in sharp contrast to the more conservative doctrine still adhered to by the South Church of Dedham. In addition, its followers strongly advocated for temperance, women's rights, prison reform, and the abolition of slavery. In 1827, several Tiot families, mostly young and of a liberal outlook, broke from the South Church and formed the First Universalist Society of South Dedham. The rift between the two denominations was deep, and it took many years for the rupture to heal. Still, despite this schism, Universalists buried their dead in the graveyard that had, to that point, been exclusive to the congregants of the South Parish. The society's first pastor is interred in this place, as is Rev. Edwin Thompson, close by the men who had shared his beliefs.

Sumner Ellis, a nineteen-year-old laborer from a South Dedham family, was the first to sign up for a three-year enlistment into the Union forces. On July 3, 1861, he joined Company F of the 18th Massachusetts Volunteers, which began forming in April of that year. Company F was called the "First Dedham Company" because the majority of its requisite 101 soldiers were from Norfolk County and Dedham. In August of 1861, the 18th arrived in Washington, D. C. to fight as part of the Army of the Potomac. It saw its first real combat near Fort Corcoran, Virginia, and took part in most of the major battles of the Peninsula Campaign. Considered a "good soldier" with "an army record to be proud of," Ellis was wounded at the Second Battle of Bull Run on August 30, 1862. The culmination of General Robert E. Lee's campaign in Northern Virginia, this battle (also called the Second Manassas) was fought on a much larger scale than the First Battle of Bull Run had been a year earlier. Although not a total defeat, only the precipitous retreat by Union forces avoided a calamity. Ellis was struck on the final day of combat and, according to later accounts, "his life was saved only in an almost miraculous manner." He received a discharge for his gunshot wound but, following his recovery, reenlisted in Company F of the 56th Massachusetts Regiment and served to the end of the war.[4]

Ellis attended reunions for the survivors of the 18th Massachusetts Volunteer Militia and was a member of the local chapter of the Grand Army of the Republic (GAR). When Sumner Ellis died of heart disease on January 11, 1897 at the age of fifty-four, eight of his fellow GAR members served as pallbearers, and their chaplain praised him for being "brave, generous, and kind." Townspeople, too, recalled Ellis as a "man of pleasant disposition and kindly heart." He was part of a large old time Norwood family with various branches spread throughout the area.[5]

Two other veteran sons of the Ellis clan are buried in Old Parish, as well. Albert Ellis and Alfred Ellis were not siblings, but each came from the neighborhood of South Dedham colloquially referred to as the "Ellis section." In August 1862, one month after Lincoln's pleas for more volunteers to support the Union, both Albert and Alfred enlisted in Company I of the 35th Massachusetts Regiment. Dubbed the "Second Dedham Company" because 65 of its officers and men were from the area, Company I was fully enrolled by mid-August and, with little time for training, was ordered to report to the front.

Dressed in their pristine uniforms with shiny brass buttons and carrying their newly-issued weapons, the freshly-minted soldiers headed south on a train to Virginia. During the trip, one Dedham volunteer wrote in his diary that he "could not help feeling a sort of pride to be steaming along thinking of the great work we were going to do," although admitting he "could not keep the tears from my eyes as I thought of home, left perhaps forever."[6] Most of these young men had never been very far from Dedham village, and must have borne a striking resemblance to Henry Fleming, the main character in Stephen Crane's Civil War novel, *The Red Badge of Courage*. Like Fleming, who naively enlisted in an effort to seek glory, danger, and a glimpse of the wider world, Albert and Alfred were farmers. Perhaps similarly bored with the daily monotony of the farm and the tedium of small town life, they signed on for three years.

By September 14, 1862, the 35th was in action at the Battle of South Mountain. It is not too difficult to imagine that one or both of them felt like Crane's Fleming: "He wished, without reserve, that he was at home again making the endless rounds from the house to the barn, from the barn to the fields, from the fields to the barn, from the barn to the house. He remembered he had often cursed the brindle cow and her mates, and sometimes flung milking stools. But, from his present point of view, there was a halo of happiness about each of their heads, and he would have sacrificed all the brass buttons on the continent to have been enabled to return to them."[7]

Three days later they were at Antietam in Maryland, one of the deadliest and most gruesome battles of the Civil War. As historian James McPherson wrote, "the number of casualties suffered at Antietam was four times greater than the number of American casualties at the beaches of Normandy." Thousands were either killed outright, or later died of their injuries; another fifteen thousand were wounded, many severely. That day, September 17, 1862, was simply "the bloodiest single day in American history" and its horrors haunted many of its survivors for the rest of their lives.[8] The battle ended the Confederate invasion of Maryland and clearly marked the end of the innocent patriotic bravado that had driven many like Albert Ellis and Alfred Ellis to enlist.

Alfred Ellis was wounded at Antietam, but he remained with the 35th as Company I regrouped and engaged in the Battle of Fredericksburg on December 13, where the Union met one of its worst defeats. After a winter encampment at Newport News, Virginia, the regiment moved south and west to participate in the sieges of Vicksburg and Jackson, Mississippi. Through the summer of 1863 they shifted to Kentucky and down through the Cumberland Gap to take part in the siege of Knoxville and other maneuvers in Tennessee, well into the spring of 1864.

Back in Virginia, Alfred Ellis was wounded once again during the Battle of Peeble's Farm (also called Poplar Spring Church) on September 30, 1864, but continued on active duty. He was promoted to corporal and then sergeant on January 1, 1865, during the Siege of Petersburg, the ten-month strategy that eventually led to Lee's surrender in April of that year. Alfred Ellis was finally mustered out, along with Albert Ellis and the rest of Company I, on June 9, 1865. Twenty-four of their comrades had died (20 of battle wounds, 4 of disease) and a few dozen had been discharged early because of disability; thus, only 45 of the original 101 enlistees mustered out together that June. They had served under the command of eight generals, including McClellan, Sherman, Meade and Grant, traversed a good portion of the eastern United States, and had played a part in several of the war's most significant battles. At last, their three arduous years of service had come to a close.

Although Albert and Alfred Ellis were not siblings, there were three brothers from Dedham who did serve in the war whose grave markers stand in the old cemetery: Charles, Benjamin, and Eugene Phipps. Their father was a cabinetmaker, likely employed at the Everett Furniture Factory located in the center of South Dedham village. Benjamin and Charles enlisted as privates within a week of each other in September 1861, in the 24th Massachusetts Regiment. Benjamin, nineteen, who listed his occupation as a varnisher and probably worked at the Everett factory with his father, mustered into Company C on September 12. A week later, twenty-four-year-old Charles, a teamster, joined Company A of the same regiment.

Although the 24th was splintered and assigned to different brigades for much of the war, on May 1, 1864 the regiment was reunited in Virginia. There they engaged in the battle at Drury's Bluff, where 11 men were killed and 54 wounded on May 16. Moving north, the regiment encamped on the banks of the James River for two months. Then, from August 14 through August 16, they fought in the battle of Deep Bottom (also called Deep Run), Virginia. Among the soldiers killed in action at Deep Run on August 16, 1864, was Charles W. Phipps, eldest of the Phipps children. Less than a month later, Benjamin, still only twenty-two, was mustered out, although the 24th itself continued to maneuver throughout the Richmond area. Following Lee's surrender on April 19, 1865, the regiment was sent to Richmond itself, where they stood guard duty until January 10, 1866. Four days later, the remainder of the regiment arrived in Boston Harbor, where they were discharged.

Despite his young age—born in 1851, he would have been 14 in 1865—Eugene (his given name was actually Amos Eugene) Phipps enlisted in Company E of the 1st Rhode Island Regiment and was mustered into the Rhode Island Light Artillery (RILA) unit on

March 16, 1865. Just three months later, with the end of the conflict, Company E was apparently disbanded, and on June 14 Eugene was discharged. He eventually became a house painter and lived the majority of his life in Boston. In 1887, when a swing staging gave way, Phipps was thrown some forty feet to the ground, badly bruising, but not breaking, both legs. Twenty years later, however, in 1907, he died at the age of fifty-six as the result of a similar accidental fall. Near the center of the graveyard at the edge of the slight rise of a grassy slope, the three brothers were reunited, brother Benjamin having predeceased Eugene in 1866. Each brother has his own small marble regimental marker.[9]

Three official Union army regimental stones mark the graves of the three Phipps brothers–Amos Eugene, Benjamin, and Charles. Charles was killed in action. (*Courtesy of John M. Grove*)

Historically, garrison commanders were charged with burying their dead, but with the start of the Civil War and its massive loss of life, the War Department created the first organized system of marking interments, erecting uniform wooden headboards with rounded tops at each soldier's grave. Shortly after the war ended, a Cemetery Branch was established within the Office of the Quartermaster General and given the charge of maintaining national military cemeteries. As burials reached into the hundreds of thousands, however, it was recognized that wooden headboards were inadequate and impractical as permanent memorials. Following several years of discussion and debate over size and material (marble or galvanized iron), in 1873 the first official design for headstones was adopted. The War Department chose a slab design of marble (or some other durable stone) cut four inches thick and ten inches wide, with a slightly curved top, to be set with twelve inches of the stone extending above the ground. Referred to as the "Civil War" type, the stone had a sunken shield on its face in which the name of the soldier, his company and regiment, were carved in bas relief. In 1879, Congress authorized this same stone design to be placed at the graves of veterans in "private village or city cemeteries" as well.[10] Thus, the standard-issue stones of the three brothers—one a casualty of war, the other two surviving veterans of the conflict—stand shoulder-to-shoulder, with no further adornment, a tribute to one family's willing participation in the effort to save the Union.

A short distance away, two young soldiers are memorialized in the family plot of Reverend H. G. Park. Harrison Greenough Park was born in Providence, Rhode Island in 1806, and graduated from Brown University in 1824. Following his graduation, Park studied both law and theology and was called to be the pastor of the South Church of Dedham in December 1829. A year later, he married Julia Bird, whose father George Bird owned a papermill on the Neponset River in East Walpole. The couple lived in South Dedham village and had four children before Julia Park died in May 1835. A few months later, the minister resigned his pastorate and moved his young family to Danvers and subsequently, Burlington, Bernardston, and later Westminster, Vermont. In 1837, Park married Elizabeth Bird, a sister of his first wife, once again bringing him into the Bird family orbit. For a brief time, Park even became a partner in the Bird & Son paper company along with his father-in-law, George Bird, and his two brothers-in-law, Josiah and Francis William. The Rev. Park and his wife, Elizabeth, had nine children.

One of their sons, Henry Martin Park mustered into Company H of the 40th Massachusetts Regiment in August of 1862, at the age of nineteen, for a three-year enlistment. The regiment was attached to the Second Brigade and was stationed primarily near Washington, D.C. In August of 1863, the troops sailed to Folly Island, South Carolina, where they participated in siege operations against Forts

Wagner, Gregg, and Sumter. In February of 1864, the 40th was part of an expedition to Florida. There it fought in the Battle of Olustee, the only major battle of the Civil War fought in Florida, which ended in a Union retreat to Jacksonville.

By May the regiment was back in the Richmond area, where it entered a series of battles near Bermuda Hundred, Virginia. On May 20, 1864, Henry Park was wounded, after which, according to a later account by his captain, he stood his ground, loaded and fired his carbine. A second wound below the knee forced him to leave the field of battle but, before he could reach shelter, he was hit a third time. Gravely wounded, Park was taken to the hospital at Fort Monroe, Virginia, where he died on June 6, 1864, just four days shy of his twenty-second birthday . The chaplain of the regiment tried to console the youth's grieving parents with words that alluded to Henry's state of mind and faith: "His last hours were cheered by a trust in his Saviour. The prayers and fidelity of his parents, and God's merciful dealings with him on the battle-field for the defense of his country, were the means to prepare his soul, and purify it through Christ's blood, for a life of eternal blessedness."[11]

The chaplain's letter is a moving example of the kind of condolence letter families received during the war, correspondence meant to reassure those left behind that their loved one had experienced a "Good Death." Historian Drew Gilpin Faust describes these heartfelt and well-intentioned communications, composed by writers who "understood the elements of the Good Death so explicitly that they could anticipate the information the bereaved would have sought had they been present at the hour of death." Relatives were comforted by eyewitness accounts attesting that their son, or husband, or brother, "had been conscious of his fate, had demonstrated a willingness to accept it, and shown signs of belief in God and his own salvation...."[12] No doubt the regiment's chaplain realized how meaningful a testimony to such sentiments would have been to Harrison Park, a clergyman himself.

When news of Henry's death arrived, the Park family was already in mourning, however. In 1863, Julia Bird Park, the eldest daughter of H. G. Park and his second wife, Elizabeth, had married John Henry Hale, a young carpenter from Bernardston, Massachusetts. On August

21, 1863, John Hale enlisted and mustered into Company I of the 9th Massachusetts Regiment, determined, like his brother-in-law Henry, to defend his country.

The 9th Regiment had originally been formed in June of 1861, recruiting primarily Irish-Americans to its ranks since its initial funding came from Patrick Donahoe, publisher of the *Boston Pilot*. In July 1862, the 9th was part of the Peninsula Campaign waged in and around Richmond. During that action the unit suffered heavy losses and its commander, Colonel Thomas Cass was mortally wounded.[13] Following Cass's death, Colonel Patrick Robert Guiney, an Irish immigrant from County Tipperary and Boston lawyer, took command. The 9th fought in the Second Battle of Bull Run, Antietam, and the Battles of Fredericksburg and Chancellorsville, and was subsequently assigned to hold a strategically important position during the Battle of Gettysburg in July 1863. Thus, by the time John Hale and other freshly-mustered recruits joined the regiment, it was an experienced, and somewhat war-weary unit.

On April 30, 1864, the regiment, with Colonel Guiney at its head, received orders to join the command of Lieutenant General Ulysses S. Grant. On May 5, they engaged in the Battle of the Wilderness, the first battle of Grant's Virginia Overland Campaign. The 9th suffered severe losses, including the wounding of Colonel Guiney, who was shot in the eye. On that date and in that battle, Private John Henry Hale, the husband of Julia Bird Park, was killed. Married less than a year, Julia brought her husband back to South Dedham where he was interred in her family's lot. A month later, she witnessed her own brother being buried there as well.[14]

One more young man with South Dedham roots was slain during the war, and brought home to this ancient graveyard. Willard F. Rhoades, the son of Deacon Lewis S. Rhoades, enlisted for three years in Company B of the 1st Michigan Cavalry in August of 1861 at the age of twenty-three. Organized in Detroit, this regiment was part of the famed Michigan Brigade, a unit that fought in every major campaign of the Army of the Potomac, beginning with Gettysburg in July 1863. It was at Gettysburg that the brigade's brash youthful commander, George Armstrong Custer, rallied his troops with the cry, "Come on, you Wolverines!," that gave the brigade its nickname. Willard Rhoades had been promoted to the rank of Quartermaster Sergeant on June 30, just prior to the battle. After Gettysburg, the Michigan Brigade was assigned to scouting and patrol duty throughout the Centreville, Virginia, area for the remainder of 1863. Centreville, and all of Fairfax County, was a location sought after by both sides of the conflict because of its elevated topography. There, on November 6, 1863, Willard Rhoades was killed by a Confederate sniper who had penetrated the Northern encampment.

While there is good documentation that these four men were interred in the South Dedham cemetery along with their forefathers and loved ones, other soldiers were not so fortunate. The nation was ill-prepared for the scale of death the Civil War inflicted and, as hundreds, sometimes thousands, of bodies fell on the battlefield, their removal and respectful burial became a logistical nightmare of gargantuan proportions. At Antietam, for example, General Robert E. Lee ordered his army into a retreat. This action left the dead of both sides—thousands of men and an inestimable number of horses and mules—to be attended to by the Union Army, a ghastly and demoralizing task. At times, the combatants issued a truce to allow each side to bury their comrades, but, more often, the mortally wounded and dead were left where they fell for hours or even days. Additionally, no arrangements had been made to keep formal records of the identification and burial of soldiers, records which would have enabled later retrieval and reburial.

Instead, a haphazard, unofficial network of agents, embalmers, and undertakers followed, and one might say preyed upon, the armies. They made a good profit for their services—the location, retrieval and return of the dead to their grieving families. Alternatively, the New England Soldiers Relief Association, and similar groups, were organized to help arrange payment for the disinterment of bodies, as well as for the services of embalmers, the purchase of metallic coffins, and the shipment home of the deceased to an honored grave. Still, family members traveled to military hospitals, encampments, and even the battlefield seeking to retrieve their kin, a harrowing and truly horrifying ordeal.[15]

It is easy to understand how Henry M. Park, who died in the Fort Monroe Hospital, was likely to have had his death recorded, his remains identified properly, and his body returned to Massachusetts. Similarly, the family of Willard Rhoades, who lost his life in a non-battle encounter, may well have been able to make proper arrangements without much difficulty. But Charles Phipps and John Hale were killed in action, and may easily have been hurriedly interred in a battlefield burial; particularly Hale, who was slain in the Battle of the Wilderness, where some 1,700 Union deaths occurred. And yet, by some miracle, they all returned home.[16]

Two of South Dedham's "nine months men" who are buried in Old Parish Cemetery survived the war as well. William H. Gay and Charles J. Guild, cabinetmakers, enlisted in Company D of the 43rd Massachusetts Regiment together on August 25, 1862. The regiment trained in Readville, Massachusetts, a town just outside of Dedham. They left Boston on October 24, and for much of their tour they were stationed near New Bern, North Carolina, where their most significant encounter was the Goldsborough Expedition in December of 1862. Ordered to destroy the strategically significant Wilmington & Weldon Railroad Bridge across the Neuse River, a vital link in the Confederate supply chain, the Union troops faced three engagements—at Kinston, White Hall, and Goldsborough—on their way. They set the bridge on fire and destroyed three miles of tracks to hamper its reconstruction. During their return, skirmishes with Confederates slowed their progress. At one point, the Confederates ripped apart a dam on a millpond, forcing the Union soldiers to cross a rapidly-rushing neck-high stream on foot. They arrived back in New Bern just before Christmas. Gay and Guild were mustered out on July 30, 1863, a two-month delay Gay thought worth noting. "We received our pay and discharge papers," he wrote, wryly noting that "We were paid for eleven months service and I came to the conclusion that to enlist for nine months means eleven."[17]

Upon his return from the war, Charles Guild left South Dedham. He died in Worcester in 1874 but his body was returned to his hometown. William Gay went on to become an active member of the George K. Bird Post No. 169 of the Grand Army of the Republic

(GAR) headquartered in Norwood. Founded in 1884, this fraternal organization's membership consisted of army, navy, and marine veterans of the Union forces during the Civil War. In addition to the camaraderie of associating with others who had shared similar experiences, Post 169 aimed to collect and preserve historic artifacts relating to the war, to assist sick or disabled Union veterans and their families, to teach lessons of patriotism to the younger generations, and to hold exercises and decorate the graves of their comrades on Memorial Day. The post had a peak membership of 170 at about the time it received its charter from the national GAR organization in 1899.[18] William H. Gay became an officer of the Bird Post in 1900. One of the longest-lived of Norwood's Civil War veterans, Gay died at his home on Howard Street in Norwood on June 7, 1919.

None of the five remaining Civil War veterans who are interred in the Old Parish Cemetery were born in South Dedham, but each became associated with the town of Norwood later in life, associations which led them to be buried in the hallowed ground of the town's old cemetery.

John Benjamin (J. B.) Fuller was born in Walpole, and had been a currier in the leather business in Providence prior to his enlistment in the 11th Rhode Island Regiment. Following the war, he lived in Norwood and worked at the tannery. He was the oldest recruit from this group of sixteen, and when he died of heart disease in 1895, he was seventy-four years of age.

Andrew Keene was born in and grew up in Pembroke, Massachusetts. He served in both the 1st and the 4th Massachusetts Cavalry regiments during the war. He was a bootmaker by trade and spent most of his life in Sharon and Stoughton, but was a member of Norwood's newly-founded GAR Post when he died in 1884. Keene's immediate family is buried in Old Parish as well.

Leonard Lowell was a Maine native who was drafted into Company E of the 9th Maine Infantry. A few years after the war, he married Frances (Fannie) Gay, a South Dedham native, the daughter of well-known and respected veterinarian Jarvis Gay. Lowell was a conductor for the New York & New England Railroad and, later, for the street railway in Woonsocket, Rhode Island. A member of South

Portland's G. A. R. chapter, Lowell was buried in the old cemetery as were his wife, son, and in-laws.

Lewis G. Stone was a machinist who was drawn to Norwood when the New York & New England Railroad car shops relocated to the town from Readville in 1876. Born in Maine, he had resided in Newton, Massachusetts prior to his enlistment in the 32nd Massachusetts Regiment in August of 1862. A few months later, Stone was discharged with a disability. In later years he lived in Roslindale and joined the Abraham Lincoln Post No. 11, GAR chapter of Charlestown. He was employed at the Registry of Deeds when he died in 1907.

Finally, James Erastus Hawes was the only Old Parish veteran who was a sailor. Born in Wrentham, Massachusetts, he was thirty-eight years old and married when he enlisted in the United States Navy in 1862 at New London, Connecticut. During his one-year term of service, he spent time on the USS *Sabine*, one of the first sailing frigates to see action in the Civil War. Actively deployed along the Atlantic coast in search of Confederate raiders, the *Sabine* was employed in the hunt for the infamous CSS *Alabama* in October of 1862. Hawes also served on the USS *Stars and Stripes*, which, following repairs, was recommissioned and assigned to the waters off the Gulf Coast of Florida. Following the war, Hawes lived on Guild Street in South Dedham, then Norwood, until he sold his home in 1890. In 1895 he died a widower at the age of seventy-one in Attleboro. His body was brought back to Norwood by his surviving children to be interred with his deceased wife, Esther, and their infant son.

The Civil War changed the way Americans viewed death and, as Drew Gilpin Faust declares, "acknowledged a new public importance for the dead."[19] Traditionally, families took responsibility for their losses, which were individual and private. But, after the war, the memory of the participants became a public charge. Coordinated by the federal government, a chain of national cemeteries was created and a massive effort to identify, retrieve, and re-inter hundreds of thousands of remains took place. On a more local level, monuments to the dead were erected on town commons, public parks, and in village cemeteries to ensure that communities would not forget the sacrifices made in the name of the nation. In Norwood, the Grand Army of the

Republic aided in this effort. A Civil War cannon, dedicated to the memory of South Dedham residents who lost their lives in the conflict, stands in Highland Cemetery; beside it is a memorial to the Unknown Dead of the war. It was placed there in 1905 by the Women's Relief Corps of the GAR.[20]

A cluster of veterans died between 1895 and 1897 (J. B. Fuller, James E. Hawes, Leonard Lowell, Sumner Ellis) when the Old Parish Cemetery was still an active burial ground. Ten years later, in 1907, when Eugene Phipps and Lewis G. Stone were laid to rest, a significant change had occurred. Highland Cemetery on Winter Street had become the primary burial ground for the town. In fact, several prominent families had even disinterred their dead from the colonial graveyard and moved their remains and stones into expansive lots on the purposefully designed grounds of Highland.

By 1919, when the Old Parish Cemetery received its last two Civil War veterans, it had become a sleepy, half-forgotten artifact of the distant past. In June 1919, a solemn ceremony for William H. Gay, seventy-nine, was held in the quiet graveyard, with a scattering of gnarled old trees providing shade. Gay's large granite stone, with its GAR decal embedded in its base, stands near the equally impressive monuments of Rev. Edwin Thompson and Rev. Harrison G. Park, where veterans Henry Park and John Hale were laid to rest.

The final veteran of the Civil War to be buried at the Old Parish Cemetery was Alfred Ellis. In July of 1919, only a month after William Gay's funeral, eighty-six-year-old Alfred Ellis died. His obituary in the *Norwood Messenger* ran under the headline: "Death of Aged Civil War Veteran." The article included a recapitulation of his descent from two of the families (Ellis and Dean) who had helped to found South Dedham village, and a review of his wartime service. Ellis had been a charter member of the George K. Bird GAR chapter and had held all the offices in the post, except that of commander, "which he declined, not caring to accept the responsibilities of the position."

The obituary saved the longest paragraph for a description of Ellis's devotion to his family and community. "Mr. Ellis was a family man, fond of his home, where his chief interest centered," the writer explains, going on to name his sons, his grandchildren, and great-grandchildren. He had returned to South Dedham after his military service and, except for a brief stint as a cabinet maker, "was a farmer most all his life till he retired from active work." It was noted that Ellis "was a good citizen. [He] always took a great interest in town meeting, which he attended regularly. He made a holiday of the annual town meeting day, and before the community became a separate town he drove to Dedham when town meeting was held there." Perhaps most significant, Ellis "made it a point to vote at every election."[21]

Mustered in a private, promoted to corporal and then sergeant, and wounded twice, Alfred Ellis was the epitome of the Civil War volunteer. He was a modest family man who was drawn into battle to save the nation he believed in, who returned to his beloved hometown to live out his quiet life in peace. And when it was over, his family and friends and community laid him in the family plot in Old Parish Cemetery, less than a mile from the house in which he was born, lived, and died.

It has been over a century since the last veteran was interred at Old Parish Cemetery; in fact, there have been no new burials here for more than sixty years. The elaborate wrought iron fencing and gates that had once encircled the plots of prominent citizens have all been removed. Much of the finely etched lettering on marble obelisks has weathered to near illegibility. So, too, the bas relief names and regiment designations on the porous Civil War markers. The once ominous colonial-era epigraphs have softened with age.

Enclosed as it is, this land is protected from the twenty-first century cacophony outside its boundaries. Its silence and permanence make this a profoundly contemplative place and a material testament to the past. But the intimacy of this space is its strength. If passersby should enter and walk among the ancient stones, they would find not an impenetrable barrier but a window through which the hopes and fears of earlier generations could be seen. An open cultural text, an outdoor museum, the Old Parish Cemetery is a vivid reminder of human fragility and mortality. Each individual buried here has a lesson to impart. The tale of these sixteen men, whose love of country, as Francis Tinker noted, was "pure and deep," is just a sampling.

The Old Parish Cemetery remains a contemplative outdoor museum nearly 300 years after its founding in 1741. *(Courtesy of John M. Grove)*

Civil War Veterans Buried in Old Parish Cemetery, Norwood

Albert Ellis (1835-1903)

Alfred Ellis (1833-1919)

Sumner A. Ellis (1843-1897)

J. B. (John Benjamin) Fuller (c.1821-1895)

William H. Gay (1840-1919)

Charles J. Guild (1825-1874)

John Henry Hale (1837-1864)

James H. Hawes (1824-1895)

Andrew J. Keene (1829-1884)

Leonard Lowell (1836-1896)

Henry Martin Park (1842-1864)

Amos Eugene Phipps (1851-1907)

Benjamin F. Phipps (1842-1866)

Charles W. Phipps (c. 1836-1864)

Willard F. Rhoades (1838-1863)

Lewis G. Stone (1835-1907)

৩৯৩৯৩৯

Sources and Notes

Norwood's history can be found in Bryant Tolles, *Norwood: The Centennial History of a Massachusetts Town* (Norwood, MA: Norwood Printing Company, 1973) and Patricia J. Fanning, *Norwood: A History* (Charleston, SC: Arcadia Publishing, 2002). An early historical essay titled "History of Norwood, Massachusetts" by Francis Tinker published in *History and Directory of Norwood, Mass for 1890* (Boston: Press of Brown Bros, 1890), pp. 9-58 contains general history and material about Civil War volunteers. Information about individuals and families were researched on Familysearch.org and Ancestry.com. Civil War Records, regimental histories and battle histories were located online.

1. F. Holland Day archive, Norwood Historical Society, notes on Old Parish Cemetery.
2. Tinker, p. 37. There are many more Civil War veterans interred at Highland Cemetery.
3. Tinker, p. 37.
4. Sumner Ellis, obituary. *Norwood Advertiser & Review*, 15 January 1897, p. 4. Ellis was discharged on June 17, 1865, with a disability.
5. Ibid. There are more than 75 members of the extensive Ellis family buried in Old Parish Cemetery. Two of Sumner Ellis's brothers, Warren and Henry, also enlisted in the Union army. They are not buried in Old Parish.
6. Diary of Henry W. Tisdale, quoted in Charles Fanning, *Mapping Norwood* (Boston: University of Massachusetts Press, 2010), p. 87.
7. Stephen Crane, "The Red Badge of Courage," in *The Portable Stephen Crane* (NY: Viking Press, 1969), p. 206.
8. James M. McPherson, *Crossroads of Freedom: Antietam* (NY: Oxford University Press, 2002), pp. 3-6.
9. The names of Charles, Benjamin, and Amos Eugene Phipps were somehow left off of the Civil War Veterans' Roll of Honor placed in the Municipal Building in 1928. On November 11, 2020, that error was rectified.

10. This gravestone design was for the Union Army veterans only. Stone manufacturers in several states were contracted to supply headstones. In 1906, Congress authorized the Cemetery Branch to furnish stones for the graves of Confederate soldiers who died and were buried in federal cemeteries. These stones were to be the same size and material with slight variations—a pointed rather than curved top and no shield. In 1930, regulations authorizing Confederate headstones to be inscribed with the Confederate Cross of Honor were implemented.

11. Quotes from both Park's captain and the Chaplain's letter were published in Henry Martin Park's obituary, dated 18 June 1864. Typescript in Norwood Historical Society archives.

12. Drew Gilpin Faust, *This Republic of Suffering: Death and the American Civil War* (NY: Alfred A. Knopf, 2008) p. 17.

13. Thomas Cass was buried with full military honors at Mount Auburn Cemetery, and a statue of him was erected in Boston Common.

14. A monument dedicated to John Henry Hale and his brother, James, is in Bernardston, Massachusetts, to commemorate their sacrifice.

15. Faust, *This Republic of Suffering*, p. 87.

16. George K. Bird Post No. 169, Grand Army of the Republic, archives at Norwood Historical Society, and Town of Norwood cemetery plot plans, indicate the final resting place of these veterans.

17. Diary of William H. Gay, typescript, Norwood Historical Society.

18. Upon the death of its last member in 1934, the post automatically disbanded. (Tolles, p. 174). Interestingly, the namesake of the George K. Bird Post, George Kurtz Bird, was born in Boston and had no affiliation with the town until after his marriage to Hattie Ellis of West Dedham. The couple then settled in Norwood. Bird was a Civil War veteran and was especially devoted to the welfare of Norwood's veterans. He worked in Boston. Bird died in 1877 in Dorchester. His good works were remembered when the post was formed in 1884.

19. Faust, *This Republic of Suffering*, p. 101.

20. It is somewhat ironic that this monument, dedicated "to those who lost their lives in the conflict," is at Highland Cemetery. All of the South Dedham comrades who lost their lives in the Civil War are buried at Old Parish Cemetery. Highland did not exist until 1880.
21. "Alfred Ellis Passes Away, Death of Aged Civil War Veteran," *Norwood Messenger*, 26 July 1919, p. 7.

Chapter 4

The Greening of Norwood

HISTORIES OF THE IRISH in and around Boston have frequently overlooked the arrival of immigrants directly from the Emerald Isle to more rural locations. The story of the Irish in Norwood brings to light a unique migratory trend, experience, and advancement.

Norwood began life as South Dedham (also known as Tiot), a part of the town of Dedham, which was founded in 1636. More than 200 years after its first settlers arrived, Tiot was primarily an Anglo-Saxon Protestant, Congregationalist, community of less than 1,000 individuals.[1] Then things began to change. As fate would have it, the Norfolk County Railroad was expanding through the center of the village, and two large tanneries, a furniture factory, and an ink mill were seeking workers. At the exact same time, the Irish were being driven from their home country by a disastrous multi-year potato blight and subsequent famine.

One of Norwood's first Irish settlers was Thomas Ford, who recounted how he had left Ireland in the 1840s: "After a long voyage of seven weeks and three days, I landed Good Friday morning with many of my brother Irishmen in Boston. I stayed there a few weeks, but as Boston could not afford employment for all of us, some had to go elsewhere to earn a living. I started from there one morning, I knew not whither, and I cared less provided I had the prospect of finding work. I walked onward until I reached Dedham. There I learned that a railroad was being constructed in this district known as South Dedham [and] I received employment from the men in charge of the railroad construction." As Ford recalled, "there were but few Irishmen in South Dedham at this time," and they found little in the way of housing until Moses Guild converted an old wagon barn into a tenement.[2]

Built by Moses Guild to store cargo and freight wagons, this structure
was converted into housing for early Irish immigrants.
(Courtesy of the Morrill Memorial Library)

The Moses Guild family, who owned a large farm, had become
prosperous by running a fleet of freight wagons between Boston and
Providence. They had stored their wagons and equipment in the
center of Tiot. After the frieight business waned, the Guilds rented
the building to a man named O.W. Fiske, who converted it into a
steam-powered factory that produced playing cards, much to the
chagrin of local churchgoers. From then on it was referred to locally
as the "old steam mill." When Fiske vacated it, the building was
turned into a tenement for Irish immigrants. Both floors of the gray-
shingled wooden structure, which was approximately 40 x 70 feet in
size, were divided into 12 by 12-foot rooms. Lighting was provided by
whale oil lamps and lanterns, a bucket-well provided water, and the
sanitary facilities consisted of a single outhouse. As more Irish arrived,
several families crowded into the haphazardly renovated building.
And, as one of the steam-mill's former residents, Patrick Pendergast,
recalled,"Kings, Queens, Jacks, and Aces covered the boards."[3]

This early group of Irish pioneers came primarily from counties
Cork, Galway, and Mayo in the west of Ireland. "In general, the first
Irish were rough, tough hewers of wood and tillers of bog," local
historian Win Everett summarized nearly a century later. "They also
knew horses and how to handle them. These talents secured them

heavy-duty jobs" on the railroad, and later on in factories and on farms.[4] At the outset, these immigrants were desperately poor and, as Everett indicated, willing to take on almost any work just to survive. A man with farming skills could secure a place on one of several farms in the area. Besides the railroad, others found employment at industrial sites such as Willard Everett's furniture factory, Fisher Talbot's carpet shop, George Morrill's ink mill, and the Winslow and Smith tanneries. The latter were particularly popular places of employment.

Founded at the end of the eighteenth century, Abner Guild's small tannery on Hawes Brook, built to process the rawhides of local farmers, had met with immediate success. In 1791, Guild took on an apprentice, John Smith, a seven-year-old boy from a poor family. Smith learned the trade, and eventually succeeded Guild in the arduous enterprise. John Smith continued to run the tannery until 1831 when he turned it over to his son, Lyman Smith, and his son-in-law, George Winslow. By the time the Irish began arriving in South Dedham, Smith and Winslow had dissolved their partnership and each had established a distinct family business. Winslow and his sons continued at the original tannery location on Endicott Street under the name George Winslow and Sons, and after the elder Winslow retired it became Winslow Brothers. There, by the end of the century, many Irishmen, including Pat Tobin, Pat Gahagan, Billy Mahoney, Pat Mahoney, and Mike Cooney, were able to find work. Meanwhile, Lyman Smith and his sons, Charles and John, built a tannery beside the railroad tracks at the northern end of town.[5]

After a few years of steady employment and frugality, most tenants of the steam mill apartments moved into neighborhoods near the Lyman Smith and Sons tannery and the E. D. Draper and Son foundry on Railroad Avenue. They settled into two enclaves: one came to be called "Dublin," located along Railroad Avenue west of Washington Street; the other, "Cork City," stretched out to the east of Washington Street. In both neighborhoods, the Irish created a flourishing community of their own.

Most significant to this growing ethnic community was the establishment of the Catholic Church. Michael Fagan, one of the town's earliest Irish immigrants, later recalled the events that led to the formation of St. Catherine of Siena parish. Arriving in Boston in September 1847, Fagan wandered "from one place to another in search of work and home." He came upon South Dedham and within a short period of time found employment on a farm, acquired a room in the steam mill, and learned there was an "Irish Church" in Canton (and another in Roxbury). Fagan called the news "a great relief" since the Catholic faith was "the only inheritance of the average Irish voyager." He promptly joined the nearly one hundred laborers who walked the "hard, lonesome road to Canton" to hear Mass "in a small stone house" near a viaduct. This was the practice until November 1848, when a missionary priest passing through South Dedham offered to say Mass in the home of Peter Kelly, an Irishman who had recently moved out of the tenement. As Fagan recalled, "The news of his coming spread like wildfire and the house could not hold all that came to be present at the first [M]ass."[6]

For the next decade, the South Dedham Irish continued to walk to church services in Canton and Roxbury, with an occasional visit by Father Patrick O'Beirne of St. Joseph's Church in Roxbury. On significant holy days Mass was celebrated in the dining room of the residence of Patrick Fahy at 407 Nahatan Street, a house that is still standing today. By 1860, as the number of Catholics continued to climb, a succession of priests began to hold Mass on a semi-monthly basis in the community, often in Village Hall, which was rented for that purpose by Irish immigrants Richard and Abbie Oldham. This practice continued until 1862 when the Universalist Society of South Dedham erected a new church on the corner of Washington and Nahatan Streets and offered to sell their former building to the Catholics. As Win Everett tells the story, George B. Talbot, of the Universalist Society, came up with the idea and brought it to Richard Oldham; Michael Fagan recalled that Joseph Day and Lyman Smith had approached him with the suggestion. Either way, the property was purchased for $3,300 and the building was dedicated to St. Catherine of Siena on August 3, 1863. Thereafter, Mass was celebrated every Sunday in, as Michael Fagan put it, in "our own building, out of which no one could drive us."[7]

In 1890, almost twenty years after Norwood was officially

incorporated, the first resident pastor arrived at St. Catherine's. Father James Troy was beloved by all, and he oversaw a rapid expansion of the parish during his seventeen years of service. The bond he formed with the Norwood community continued even after he was transferred to St. Vincent's in South Boston in 1907. At Troy's untimely death in 1915, his body was returned to Norwood. Following a lengthy procession through the center of town—all stores were closed in deference to the priest—Father Troy was interred at Highland Cemetery where a large Celtic cross was placed on his grave.[8]

Under the stewardship of St. Catherine's second pastor, Reverend Thomas McCormack, a new church building, still one of Norwood's landmarks, was erected and dedicated in 1910. Designed by the firm of Maginnis and Walsh, architects noted for their innovative ecclesiastical designs, it is an English Perpendicular Gothic-style building of gray Roman brick with Indiana limestone trim. The 1,200 seat structure was further distinguished by two Connick stained glass windows. Residents living in the Dublin and Cork City neighborhoods were no doubt proud to note that Joseph Conley, John Horgan, and Christopher O'Neil were the first baptisms held in the new church on December 25, 1910, and the first marriage was that joining Ellen Donovan and Cornelius Cleary on April 17, 1911. The original church building was renamed Columbia Hall, and served as a meeting room until its demolition in 1927 to make way for a rectory.[9]

In addition to the founding of St. Catherine's parish, the Norwood Irish started their own neighborhood stores with Peter Flaherty's grocery in Dublin and Thomas Casey's in Cork City leading the way. T. J. Casey, born in County Cork in 1826, emigrated to America in 1850 and settled immediately in Moses Guild's tenement. He worked at the tannery, the South Dedham Tavern, and was a partner in the Bell & Casey foundry prior to opening his grocery business.

In 1882, Casey erected a community building behind his store. This became the center of neighborhood social activities including public concerts and dances, as well as weddings, and private parties. Casey Hall, as it was known, was also the home of the Norwood chapter of the Ancient Order of Hibernians (AOH). Founded in 1880 by Patrick Spillane, Patrick Walsh, Edward Fay, and Thomas Casey himself, the

AOH became one of the town's most popular fraternal organizations. Its stated purposes, "to promote the friendship and unity of Irish Americans, to give aid to widows and orphans, to provide for the sick, to befriend the stranger, and to support the cause of an independent Ireland," were maintained well into the twentieth century. The AOH also purchased a substantial plot at Highland Cemetery for the burial of fellow Irishmen who died too poor to afford their own.[10]

In 1912, the Norwood Gaelic Club, an organization whose purpose was to promote a United Ireland, pay sick benefits, and perform other beneficial activities for the community, was founded by Patrick Kelly, Daniel Collins, Michael Lydon, and Peter Flaherty. Like the AOH, the Gaelic Club chiefly promoted the unity of local Irish-Americans. They also sponsored dances, parties, festivals, and concerts, as well as a popular and successful Gaelic football club. In 1927 the Norwood Gaelic Mutual Benefit Association held the formal opening of its headquarters in the Conger Block, a commercial building erected a few decades earlier by James W. Conger, a real estate developer who lived at 239 Railroad Avenue, in the heart of Dublin. Conger was also a town selectman between 1909 and 1914. Located at the corner of Railroad Avenue and Washington Street, at the crossroads between the two Irish enclaves, the block which had retail space on the ground floor and the hall above, became a landmark. The Benefit Association and Gaelic Club met in that hall, designated Gaelic Hall, until the mid-1950s.[11]

Because of the solid social supports of this community, family and acquaintances from Ireland began to emigrate not simply to America, but to Norwood in particular. One family whose migration was well documented was the Oldham family of County Cork. Richard Oldham, one of the earliest of the Irish to arrive in South Dedham in 1852, quickly found employment at the Talbot farm and a room in the steam mill tenement. Richard's brother, John, arrived in 1853 and, as was often the case at the time, John and Richard sent money to Ireland to pay for the passage of two more siblings, Robert and Nancy. Richard Oldham and his wife, Abbie, whom he met at Catholic services in Canton, became leaders of the church in South Dedham, working tirelessly to raise enough money to purchase and establish the first church in the village.[12]

John J. Gillooly (left) and Richard E. Oldham. Sons of Irish immigrants, each went on to serve on Norwood's Board of Selectmen.
(Courtesy of Gillooly Funeral Home)

Like many Irish immigrant women, Abbie Linnehan had formerly been a domestic servant. She had lived and worked in the home of Mr. and Mrs. Ebenezer Dean until her marriage to Richard Oldham. The couple's son, Richard E. Oldham, born in 1855 in South Dedham, attended village schools and became a station agent for the New York & New England Railroad. In 1899, he quit the railroad to become an insurance agent. He served as selectman for the town of Norwood from 1901 to 1911. Another son, John P. Oldham, was born in 1859. He too worked for the railroad as a fireman, then worked as a custodian for the Norwood School Department in 1900. He became the supervisor of custodians, buildings, and grounds for the public schools, retiring in 1938. The John P. Oldham Elementary School was named for him in 1963.[13]

Another son of immigrants who found local politics and business to his liking was John J. Gillooly. The son of mason William Gillooly, John was born in the Cork City neighborhood and lived in Norwood all his life. Like his father, he started out as a mason and builder but, before too long, he became a well-regarded undertaker with an office in the center of town and a home at 126 Walpole Street—still the site of Gillooly's

Funeral Home. Gillooly was involved in many civic projects, was one of the first trustees of the Municipal Light Department, and was the first Irish-American to be elected to the Board of Selectmen in 1891.[14]

Although more difficult to trace, there is some documentation concerning the migration of Irish women to South Dedham as well. According to Patrick Pendergast, only two women lived in the steam mill apartments: "Mrs. Smidy and Mrs. Nugent," both widows. Michael Fagan could recall only six Irish women in South Dedham when he arrived: "Ellen Lynch, Mary Graham, Margaret Gaynor, Abbie Linnehan (later Mrs. Richard Oldham), Mrs. John Sullivan," and one other whose name he could not recall. Abbie Linnehan had arrived in Boston alone in 1848, not an uncommon circumstance among Irish immigrant women. She had traveled to South Dedham to meet a married friend, Peg Sullivan, most likely the Mrs. John Sullivan whom Fagan remembered. Like Linnehan, two other female pioneers were also live-in domestics: Mary Casey in the house of John Morse, and Catherine Hepan [sic] in the home of the Talbot family. Day-only domestic servants included Catherine Cuff and Catherine Devine, both of whom lived with their own families although employed as domestic help.[15]

As the neighborhoods expanded, the vast majority of the Irish remained in the working class. Many sons of Irish immigrants joined the town's public works, police, and fire departments. New arrivals continued to find employment at the tannery, the railroad car shops, the American Brake Shoe & Foundry, the George H. Morrill Company, and often at the Plimpton Press, which stood within a few blocks of both Dublin and Cork City.

The Plimpton Press was founded by local residents Herbert and Howard Plimpton. Born in Walpole, Herbert had trained as a compositor, pressman, and binder at a time when bookmaking was largely a process completed by hand labor. In 1882, he initially opened his press in Boston, where he was among the first in the industry to advocate for the use of labor- and time-saving machinery. According to several sources, the first folding, sewing, rounding, and backing machines were used in Plimpton's Boston plant. Plimpton also used the first cover-making machine and invented the first gathering machine.

In 1897, attracted by concessions offered by the Norwood Business Association, Plimpton moved his press work and binding operations to property east of the railroad tracks on land bounded by Lenox and Nahatan Streets. In 1904, he brought the remainder of his business to Norwood and, by the following year, the firm employed about 600. In 1913, the business was incorporated as the Plimpton Press, and during the 1920s it employed upwards of 1,000 workers. Publishing primarily textbooks, at its peak the Plimpton Press could roll 50,000 volumes off its presses daily.

By this time, Norwood had become a very stratified community. The owners of the large manufacturing firms were at the top, with the primarily immigrant, working class at the bottom. At the outset, these wealthy industrialists controlled the town and, not unexpectedly, resisted attempts to unionize. As noted in a later newspaper account, "Because of prejudice against the organization of working men…it was difficult for them to secure a meeting place 'up town.'" But the doors of T. J. Casey's hall were always open, and "became the first rallying place for members of local trade unions. There they met unhindered and laid the foundation for organized labor in the community."[16]

Like much of America, Norwood had entered a time of rapid growth. The town's population was approximately 5,500 in 1900; 8,000 in 1910; and nearly 12,000 in 1920. Within this environment, the second and third generations of Irish Americans were gaining respect, not only among their immigrant peers but also the community-at-large. In 1890 Edward Pendergast and Daniel Callahan, both born in South Dedham to Irish immigrants, succeeded Thomas Casey and prospered in their store on Railroad Avenue. A few years later, Daniel Callahan joined his brother, John, in the furniture business. Callahan's Norwood Furniture Company occupied a large building in Norwood's main commercial district for decades. According to a publication of the Norwood Business Association, Callahan's offered "practically everything in house-furnishings which could meet the taste or needs of any class of patrons in this town."[17]

A third brother, Cornelius Callahan, educated at Williams College and Harvard Law School, straddled the divide between immigrant Norwood and the more established community in his own unique way.

A member of the Ancient Order of Hibernians, the Norwood Gaelic Club, and the Holy Name Society, Callahan was active in the Total Abstinence Society and the Norwood Board of Trade. He practiced law in Norwood and was elected to the School Committee in 1904. He remained on that board until 1920, serving as chairman during his last four years in office. He died suddenly in 1925, after which Norwood's Callahan Elementary School was named after him.[18]

Another successful Irish-American was James Folan who, in 1887, opened a small shoe store at the corner of Washington Street and Railroad Avenue. He increasingly became involved in the town's business community and helped organize the Norwood Business Association. Most significantly, however, Folan constructed commercial buildings. One of them, the Folan Block, still stands at the corner of East Cottage and Washington Street in Norwood center. He also put up multi-family dwellings in South Norwood, a neighborhood that grew dramatically with the arrival of immigrants from southern and eastern Europe in the early part of the twentieth century.[19]

James E. Pendergast was the grandson and namesake of steam mill resident James Pendergast, who had fled Ireland around 1850. The younger James, born in 1877, began working in his uncle's grocery store, Pendergast and Callahan, as a teenager. Almost twenty years later he was appointed to the position of town accountant; in January 1915, when the municipal government was restructured, he became the town clerk and accountant. A highly respected official, it was said of Pendergast that he was always "busy in the public interest. No case is too small, or too insignificant, to have his personal attention. No case is too large or too involved to have his fullest comprehension." Pendergast continued in office until his retirement in 1939.[20]

Just behind the Folan Block on Washington Street stood a small wooden building with a sign reading "T. B. Mulvehill's." It was the home away from home of Thomas B. Mulvehill, the son of Irish immigrants who arrived in Norwood from nearby Westwood around 1907. Having given up his job as a streetcar conductor, "Tom Mul" as he was known, opened a livery stable and auto rental business, with a backroom fit for the exchange of gossip about current events and local politics. A member of the Ancient Order of Hibernians and the Democratic Party, Mulvehill became a significant political figure. He was the first Democrat elected to the state legislature from Norwood in 1915, and climbed the local political ladder to become the Chairman of the Board of Selectmen. Although not the first man of Irish descent to be so honored, Mulvehill served from 1919 until 1931. During his time in office, significant public projects, including a re-designed town center and common, a new municipal building, and state armory, came to fruition.[21]

Finally, the career of Agnes Curtin demonstrates that Irish American women, too, embraced career and civic opportunities. Curtin had grown up in Norwood's Dublin neighborhood. Her father, Timothy Curtin, was born in County Clare in the midst of the famine years and had come to America in the 1870s to work on the railroad. After losing his leg in a railroad accident, he became the crossing gate tender at Railroad Avenue until his death in 1898, when Agnes was sixteen. Agnes finished high school, graduated from Bridgewater Normal School, and, in 1904, began teaching at the Balch Elementary School in South Norwood. There she taught first grade to a diverse classroom of Irish, Polish, Lithuanian, Italian, and Syrian children. Curtin was also an active member of St. Catherine's parish, a Girl Scout leader, and an advocate for women's suffrage. As evidence of her personal reputation and the increased influence of the Irish in Norwood, Agnes Curtin was elected to the town library's Board of Trustees in 1912.[22]

Despite the success and acceptance of the second and third generations, the Irish had initially encountered discrimination and disdain. Michael Fagan recalled that the Guilds hired him and others, "although inclined to be suspicious because we were Irishmen." Fagan also recounted the story of a woman he met on the road from Dedham one morning in April of 1861. "Hearing my footsteps, she turned around, and seeing my real Irish clothes, she made a dash over the stone wall and paddled through water to make her escape." Years later, having made her acquaintance, he asked about the incident. "The reason for my acting so, Mr. Fagan," the woman explained, "was because I heard of the Irishmen that were in South Dedham, and learned to look upon them as savages." Even after John Gillooly was elected to the Board of Selectmen, total acceptance remained elusive. In January of 1892, for example, Rev. Achilles Loder of the First Congregational Church warned of the "foreign element" then coming to America, assuring his parishioners that "Seventy-four per cent of the Irish who come here are criminals."[23]

Two decades later, when municipal reform was promoted by progressive businessmen in Norwood, ethnic and class animosities resurfaced. The Irish were the most vocal of the ethnic groups, and at an open hearing on proposed town charter changes, Daniel J. Collins, one of the founders of the Gaelic Club, stood to refute the statement that "the working class were incapable of serving on a committee." Insulted by the characterization, he protested that, in fact, "There are men in the factories capable of filling any position." As the debate heated up, reformers appealed to Irish residents with a poorly written parody of a Finley Peter Dunne "Mr. Dooley" column entitled "Mr. Hooley on the Town Charter." In the Norwood version, Mr. Hooley, a shopkeeper —not a saloonkeeper as in Dunne's original—tries to persuade his friend Mr. Hennessey of the merits of political reform. Finally, as late as the 1920s, a store owner, H. E. Rice, reportedly offended his Irish customers. There are different versions of the story. Either Rice put a "No Irish Need Apply" sign in his store window in the Conger Block, or he displayed a bright green pig on St. Patrick's Day. In any event, legend has it that St. Catherine's pastor called for a boycott of the store, a move which was embraced by his parishioners and ultimately forced the store's closing.[24]

By that time, there was no denying the success of the Irish within the as yet relatively small community. In 1918, statistics showed that "the Irish and their descendants comprised over forty per cent of the town's total population" of about 12,000. And there was no doubt they had swiftly moved into government and politics, with John Gillooly leading the way as selectman in 1891. John Callahan was elected to the Board of Water Commissioners in 1893, Richard Oldham became a selectman in 1901, Cornelius Callahan joined the School Committee in 1904, Agnes Curtin took her seat on the library board in 1912, and by 1915, James Pendergast was the town clerk and accountant. Thomas

Mulvehill led the town through much of the 1920s and into the 1930s, when a new group of Irish-Americans took their place in the political arena. By mid-century, the next generation, which included Eugene Murphy, Daniel Collins, Charles Donahue, Thomas Foley, Clement Riley, and Walter J. Dempsey, dominated the Board of Selectmen as well as other elected positions.[25]

The stability and relative affluence of the Norwood Irish continued to foster a rather remarkable chain migration throughout the first half of the twentieth century, an influx that made Norwood one of the most Irish communities in southeastern Massachusetts. Even after the Depression of the 1930s and the World War of the 1940s, the migration to Norwood continued unabated. An analysis of the 1950 United States Census statistics, compiled by Frank Sweetser of Boston University's Department of Sociology, demonstrated that, with the exception of the anticipated cluster of Irish-born residents in portions of Boston, the Dublin and Cork City neighborhoods of Norwood held the highest concentration of Foreign-born Irish in the entire Metropolitan Boston area.[26]

In fact, from 1946 into the 1960s, another large migration from "the old country" occurred, consisting chiefly of single young adults forced out by a stagnant Irish economy and a lack of confidence in Ireland's ability to recover from the post-war doldrums. In Norwood, this wave of arrivals was chiefly a continuation of the migration that had begun a century earlier. An immigrant did not just wander into this suburb, as one might into cities like Boston or New York. These immigrants knew Norwood; they had family here and many had visited before.

This migratory pattern was confirmed anecdotally by Gaelic scholar Maureen Murphy. She recounted that, in the mid-1960s, when she was learning the Irish language among the insulated communities along the Gaelic-speaking south Connemara coast, she would ask people if they had ever been across the width of Ireland to Dublin. Many of her respondents replied (in Gaelic), "I haven't been that far, but I've been to Norwood." In fact, Gaelic was often heard around the streets of Norwood. "When they wanted to keep secrets, they would speak in Irish," reported one younger resident years later.

Located on Central Street, this small building, known as the Irish
Heaven, was a popular spot for Irish-speakers. Even in 2012, it remained
nondescript, without signage. *(Author's collection)*

It was, according to many, the language of the neighborhoods.
Gaelic was also common in local spots such as the "Irish Heaven,"
a barroom located in a small, two-story clapboard-covered house
on Central Street which was tucked between a commercial
building and the original location of Norwood's Municipal Light
Department. There was no sign over the door; the Irish just knew
it was there. Máirtín Ó'Cadhain, the most accomplished twentieth
century writer of fiction in the Irish language, spent many hours
among Gaelic-speakers at the Irish Heaven. Norwood even figures
in Ó'Cadhain's 1949 masterpiece work *Cré na Cille*, translated
as *Graveyard Clay*. One of the main events in the novel is a key
character's immigration to "Big Brian's family in Norwood," a place
referred to as "that bitter bee-hive."[27]

What had it been like living in Dublin and Cork City in the days
when these neighborhoods of "neat, cottage type homes on large
lots," were a tiny piece of Ireland in America? Longtime residents
remembered chickens kept for fresh poultry and eggs. Some families
even kept a few cows. Large vegetable gardens and an assortment of
fruit trees grew in backyards, and the bounty was universally shared

when the harvest came in. Odd jobs like plumbing, carpentry, and electrical work were handled by homeowners, while more extensive projects such as roofs, additions, or house painting were tackled by friends and neighbors. Later, people recalled milk deliveries, meat and fish wagons, and traveling salesmen who brought dry goods and clothing. Even during the Depression, one old-timer recollected, "With everyone in the same modest circumstances, there were few extras and no reason for anyone to feel deprived." Of course, for a time, there was "a great rivalry" between the younger generations in the neighborhoods. "In the old days," one Dubliner recalled, "they used to throw stones at us when we crossed the tracks" into Cork City. Competition in sports was especially keen. But, by the 1950s and 1960s that rivalry had dissipated into good-natured boasting.[28]

Migration out of Ireland slowed during the 1960s and 1970s— and there was some return migration back to Ireland as well— due both to increasing prosperity at home and the passage of the 1965 Immigration Act in the United States, which placed certain restrictions on the immigration of traditional European nationalities like the Irish. Confident in their place in the town and having now spread far beyond the boundaries of Dublin and Cork City, by the 1970s and 1980s both neighborhoods were holding "reunions" for former residents. Not unlike the "Old Home Day" celebrations promoted by Yankee Norwood during the first decade of the century, current and former neighbors and friends gathered to recall the close-knit communities of their childhoods. As one attendee put it, they were there to reminisce about "the Dublin that exists only in the archives of our hearts and our memories."[29] Those who spent their youth in Cork City no doubt felt the same way.

Despite Ireland's modest prosperity in the 1960s and 1970s, the international recession of 1979 and 1980 hit the country hard, and both inflation and unemployment soared. A new generation of Irish immigrants, whose ambitions could not be satisfied at home, made their way to America—and Norwood. Unlike previous generations, however, these Irish men and women were "undocumented" or "illegal aliens." Compliance with Immigration Laws required a prospective migrant to be sponsored by a close family member, such as a parent or sibling, in order to secure entry. Connected primarily to aged aunts and uncles, this new wave arrived on tourist visas. When their visas expired, however, the young adults remained in the United States, living without proper documentation, working "under the table," and socializing primarily among themselves.[30]

In Norwood, a good number of these recent residents lived with elderly relatives or were welcomed into unlicensed "boardinghouses," homes with extra bedrooms owned by families or friends known to kin back in Ireland. They most often worked for roofing, plastering, masonry, and landscaping contractors. It was hard, entry-level, often seasonal labor, not unlike the type of work their ancestors had found upon arrival in South Dedham more than a century earlier. Eventually, some returned home to Ireland, while others obtained a "green card," giving them the right to live and work in the United States. Many simply remained in the hidden economy. After a 1986 revision to the Immigration Act loosened restrictions on Irish immigration, even a fair percentage of these came out of the shadows to make their status legal.

By the 2000 United States Census, 37.4 percent of Norwood's population identified as Irish or of Irish ancestry; most of these, if asked, still traced their heritage back to the counties of Cork and Galway, and the wild land on the west coast of Ireland where most Norwood Irish pioneers like Thomas Ford, Thomas Casey, and Richard Oldham had begun their journey.[31]

The increase of the Irish and Irish American population in suburban Boston has been attributed primarily to migratory patterns after World War II, when the Boston Irish who served in the war took advantage of the G. I. Bill and moved to locations on the south shore. Then, common wisdom says, the white flight of the 1970s further increased their numbers. But the history of the Irish in Norwood goes against these assumptions. Begun with the nineteenth century famine Irish and bolstered by a chain migration that continued well past the mid-twentieth century mark, Norwood's Irish population has a distinctive story to tell.

๛๛๛๛๛๛

Sources and Notes

An earlier version of this piece was published as "The Greening of Norwood: Irish Migration and Life in a Massachusetts Town," in The Dublin Seminar for New England Folklife, Annual Proceedings, 2012, *The Irish in New England*, (Deerfield, MA: Dublin Seminar for New England Folklife, 2016) pp. 105-117. I thank the Dublin Seminar for permission to use this essay in this collection. I especially want to thank Seán Ó Coistealbha for his insights into the Irish immigration to Norwood of the 1970s and 1980s.

1. For history of Norwood, see Bryant F. Tolles, Jr., *Norwood: The Centennial History of a Massachusetts Town* (Norwood, MA: Town of Norwood, 1972) and Patricia J. Fanning, *Norwood: A History* (Charleston, SC: Arcadia Publishing Co., 2002).
2. "Thomas Ford," *Check List of Foreign-Born Folks (Irish and German) Settling in So. Dedham between 1845 and 1865*, compiled by Willard W. Everett, no pagination, Norwood Historical Society; "Thomas Ford," (obituary) *Norwood Advertiser*, 17 June 1904, p.1.
3. Win Everett, "Old Manuscript Recently Uncovered Here Lists Tyot's First Irish Families," *Norwood Messenger* (hereafter *NM*) 21 February 1947, p. 1,2.
4. Tolles, *Norwood: The Centennial History*, p. 77; Joseph F. Gould, "Racial Survey of Norwood, III. The Irish," *NM*, 19 July 1913, p.1; Win Everett, "Blue-Book of Tyot's 'Mayflower' Irish and German Settlers Divulged," *NM*, 7 March 1947, no pagination, clipping folder, Morrill Memorial Library Collection.
5. Photograph of Winslow Brothers' tannery workers, names written on reverse, Norwood Historical Society Collection.
6. Michael Fagan, "History of the Catholic Church in South Dedham Now Norwood," *NM*, 23 November 1895, p. 5, reprinted in *NM*, 24 June 1932, p.1. The "small stone house" was located on the property of the Revere Copper Mill in Canton.
7. Fagan, "History of the Catholic Church in South Dedham Now Norwood;" Tolles, *Norwood: The Centennial History*, p. 157;

Saint Catherine of Siena, 75th Anniversary, (Norwood, MA: Saint Catherine of Siena, 1965), pp. 2-3. "Richard Oldham," *Check List of Foreign-Born Folks.*

8. *Saint Catherine of Siena, 75th Anniversary*, p. 5.
9. *Saint Catherine of Siena, 75th Anniversary*, p. 6; Tolles, *Norwood: The Centennial History*, p. 158.
10. "Thomas Casey," *Check List of Foreign-Born Folks*; "Ancient Order of Hibernians," *Official Commemoration and Chronicle Issues in Honor of the 75th Anniversary of the Town of Norwood*, (Norwood, MA: 1947), p. 24.
11. "Norwood Gaelic Club," *Ibid.*, p. 22.
12. The Oldham family history is detailed in a series of letters from Nancy Oldham, County Cork, Ireland, to her son Richard Oldham in South Dedham, 1849-1863, photocopies of typescript, Norwood Historical Society. Also see, "Richard Oldham," *Check List of Foreign-Born Folks*. Most of the Oldham family remained in Norwood, where today the Oldham Elementary School can be seen in the former Dublin neighborhood.
13. "The Board of Selectmen," *Norwood, One of the Newest and Most Progressive Towns in Massachusetts* (Norwood, Mass.: Ambrose Bros., Printers, c.1910) pp.78-79. One of John P. Oldham's grandchildren, Dr. Philip Oldham Coakley, became Superintendent of Schools in Norwood and the Philip O. Coakley Middle School was named in his honor.
14. "William Gillooly," *Check List of Foreign-Born Folks*. William Gillooly was the first Catholic interred in Highland Cemetery in 1888.
15. Win Everett, "Old Manuscript Recently Uncovered," *NM*, 21 February 1947, p. 2; Fagan, "History of the Catholic Church in South Dedham Now Norwood; "Richard Oldham," *Check List of Foreign-Born Folks*; U.S. Bureau of the Census, Census of Dedham, Massachusetts, South Precinct, 1860.
16. "New Town Charter Debated," *NM*, 7 February 1914, p. 1.
17. Tolles, *Norwood: The Centennial History*, p. 219; "Pendergast & Callahan," *Norwood: One of the Newest and Most Progressive Towns in Massachusetts*, p. 105; "John F. Callahan," *Norwood: One of the Newest and Most Progressive Towns in Massachusetts*, p. 106.

18. Cornelius Callahan file, Norwood Historical Society.

19. "James M. Folan," *Norwood: One of the Newest and Most Progressive Towns in Massachusetts*, p. 97.

20. Win Everett, "An Irishman Looks at Liberty," *NM*, 14 August 1934, p. 1, 5; "The Story of a Local Official," *NM*, 12 May 1923, p. 10. Pendergast died a year later.

21. Thomas B. Mulvehill file, Norwood Historical Society; Edmund W. Mulvehill, Jr. (Mulvehill's grandson), interview with author, 2020.

22. Agnes Curtin file, Norwood Historical Society; Patricia Scanlon (Curtin's daughter), interview with author, 2007.

23. Fagan, "History of the Catholic Church in South Dedham Now Norwood;" "Correspondence,"*NM*, 2 January 1892, p. 5.

24. "Debate Over Town Charter," *NM*, 7 February 1914, p. 2; "Mr. Hooley on the Town Charter," *NM*, 7 February 1914, p. 4; Tom Bowman, "Dublin: More akin to County Galway than it is to County Norfolk," *The Daily Transcript*, 22 June 1982, p.8. The story of H. E. Rice, although it may be apocryphal, persists among elder Irish Americans in the community today.

25. "The Pioneers of Norwood," *The Civic Herald*, vol. 5, no. 1, (January 1918), p. 12.

26. Frank L. Sweetser, *The Social Ecology of Metropolitan Boston: 1950*, (Boston, MA: Division of Mental Hygiene, Massachusetts Department of Mental Health, 1961), Figure 5-D.

27. Charles Fanning, *Mapping Norwood: An Irish American Memoir*, (Amherst, MA: University of Massachusetts Press, 2010), p. 11; Bowman, "Dublin: More akin to County Galway than it is to County Norfolk," p. 8.

28. "Dublin Reunion," 18 September 1977, pamphlet. Norwood Historical Society; Bowman, "Dublin: More akin to County Galway than it is to County Norfolk," p. 8.

29. "Dublin Reunion."

30. On this migration, see: Linda Dowling Almeida, *Irish Immigrants in New York City, 1945-1995* (Indianapolis: Indiana University Press, 2001).

31. United States Bureau of the Census, Census of Norwood, 2000.

Chapter 5

Swedeville, A World Apart

FROM ITS INCEPTION it was a self-contained village apart, an enclave bounded by Chapel Street on one side and railroad tracks on the other. Between the two, there was the semi-circular loop of Cedar Street and Savin Avenue, with side streets Quincy and Melville Avenue and Johnson Court branching off for good measure. "I lived there all my life," Augie Mattson, who was born to Swedish immigrants in 1899, recalled in a 1982 interview. "It really was all Swedes; the Finns came later."[1] And, although the neighborhood was eventually dominated by those Finnish immigrants, the nickname affixed by townspeople in the early years—Swedeville—survived.

Only a handful of people of Swedish birth resided in Norwood until the 1890s when a still small but significant influx occurred. By 1895, over one hundred immigrants called Swedeville home; ten years later some five hundred of Swedish birth or parentage occupied the sturdy, one- and two-family homes built by the carpenters and masons who were among the newly-arrived Scandinavians.

Religion was important to the Swedish immigrants, and Swedish Congregationalists became members of Norwood's First Congregational Parish as early as 1889. With the arrival of additional émigrés, they worshiped together with Swedish Baptists and Swedish Lutherans in a house at the corner of Chapel and Cedar Streets. Originally the home of George S. Winslow, the structure was moved to that site in 1894, with plans to install a dry goods and grocery store on the first floor and "a club house" upstairs. The large, open second floor space was ideal for the combined services.[2]

A few years later, however, each denomination formed their own distinct parish, but not before receiving criticism from Rev. Achilles

Loder of the First Congregational parish. He was quoted in the *Norwood Messenger* as saying, "There are many Swedes in Norwood who are without religious instruction from week's end to week's end.... So they drift along with no quickening along the lines of temperance, morality, and the higher life." An indignant reply came from a Mr. Olson, who put the question to Loder: "On whose authority do you publish that the Swedes in Norwood are without religious instruction?" While assuring *Messenger* readers that the Swedish community held frequent religious meetings, Olson suggested, "Would it not be best for each one to attend to his own affairs?"[3]

In 1898 local Swedish Baptists incorporated as part of the larger Swedish Baptist Church of Boston, and began to hold services in a small chapel on Cedar Street. Four years later, with their membership bolstered by a Sunday School, Young People's Society, and Missionary Circle, the congregation moved to a newly built church on Chapel Street, opposite Savin Avenue. The Reverend Anders Kallgren was the pastor of the church during this crucial period of growth, when the congregation increased from twelve members to over fifty. Kallgren left Norwood for a time but returned to the community and built a substantial retail and residential structure on Chapel Street next to the church. There he ran a dry goods and shoe store and lived with his family in the apartment on the floor above. The Swedish Baptist Church remained on Chapel Street until the mid-twentieth century when the sanctuary was moved to the corner of Walpole and Berwick Streets and was enlarged. It continues in use today as the Trinity Community Church.

Similarly, in 1898 the Swedish Lutheran community organized their own parish with Carl Johnson, August Peterson, and Axel Carlson among the first officers and trustees. One year later, their first clergyman, along with his congregation, dedicated their own church building on Cedar Street. The Swedish Lutheran community continued to worship there for some forty years until the current Emmanuel Lutheran Church, designed by local architect Harry J. Korslund, was completed in 1939. A handsome building set at the corner of Berwick and Gardner Streets, the church stands only a short distance from its original Swedeville location.

The dry goods and shoe store at 39 Chapel Street was built by Rev. Anders Kallgren. He lived with his family above the store.
(Courtesy of Connie Wold)

Meanwhile, in June of 1902, Swedish Congregationalists began to hold services in the homes of their members. On March 21, 1904, the Norwood Swedish Congregationalist Church had built and occupied a new building on Savin Avenue. A Sunday School, Ladies Sewing Circle, and a Young People's Society were rapidly formed as the group gained more members. They erected and moved into a second meeting house on Chapel Street in 1909, where the congregation remained until they disbanded around 1939. Both this building and the Swedish Lutheran Church building on Cedar Street were eventually converted into private residences.

Many of these pioneer Swedish immigrants, some of whom originated from Åland, an archipelago of islands that dots the waters between Sweden and Finland, had been poor farmers, fishermen, and tradesmen. Coming to America had been the last resort of a conservative, risk-averse people who saw no opportunity in their homeland. Once here, they settled together to help maintain what they could of their customs and ethnic heritage. They quickly formed a local chapter of the Order of Runeberg, a fraternal and benefit association organized to maintain Swedish traditions. Frequent gatherings held at the former Turnhall in the German neighborhood on Wilson Street helped preserve family histories, folk dances, and customs. Elaborate smorgasbords featured familiar foods like Swedish coffee bread with cardamom, Swedish meatballs, pickled herring, rice pudding, and a crisp rye bread called kanckebrod. Another fraternal organization, the Siljan Lodge of the Order of Vasa, was formed in 1906. During the peak of Swedish habitation of Swedeville, there were also two temperance societies, a male singing society, a literary society, and a third benefit society called Einghet ("Unity").

Many Swedish men, like the Finnish males who followed them, found work at local industries such as the tanneries, Bird & Son, and the ink mill. Others found at least seasonal employment at the Norwood Ice Company. This unique enterprise was established in 1868 at Ellis Pond off Walpole Street and became one of the largest of its kind in the area. Paul Ellis had first harvested ice from the pond in the winter of 1860 and soon began selling the ice to local residents, farms, and dairies. Within a few years, he had a near monopoly on the ice business in the Norwood, Dedham, and Walpole region. Harvesting the ice crop was a familiar routine for men from Scandinavian countries, and became the first job of several Swedish and Finnish immigrants, including Otto Granroth, Algot Johnson, Viktor Suomi, and John Wuori. In Norwood, watching the harvest was entertainment; families lined the perimeter of Ellis Pond to watch the men at work.

Once the ice reached a depth of at least a foot, it was time to harvest. First, any snow that had accumulated on top of the ice was removed using horse-drawn scrapers and plows. The entire ice field was then marked off and scored. A channel was created from the center of the pond to the icehouse in order to float the cut ice to shore. Using special saws and instruments, the scored ice blocks were separated, then moved along the channel with float hooks and placed on either a horse-powered hoist or, later, a conveyor belt. Once carried up into the icehouse, the heavy blocks were positioned and piled within a few feet of the roof. Sawdust or straw was placed between layers of ice and as building insulation to keep the heat out during the warm weather. It was arduous, sometimes dangerous, labor, and it was temporary, except for the few men who worked in the icehouse or delivered to customers.

Norwood Ice Company was a thriving business for decades. In 1909, shortly after it was taken over by the Winslow Brothers & Smith tannery, its holdings included five huge icehouses able to store some 10,000 tons of ice. Ten years later, the first refrigerators appeared. By the 1920s, with household refrigeration common, the need for natural ice production abated and the men who worked there were forced to seek other employment.

By that time, Finnish immigrants in Norwood outnumbered those from Sweden. According to one local historian, "Finns could be found in almost every house of the streets of Swedeville." Arriving almost a decade after Swedish immigrants, the Finnish population grew rapidly. On December 16, 1903, the first Finnish-American child, Toivo Manula, was born in Norwood; the first marriage within the community occurred on September 3, 1904 between John Heiskanen and Maria Widerholm. That year, there were twenty-five Finnish immigrants in town; within ten years, there were 500. Together they created and maintained a nearly self-sufficient community of their own. Homes featured well-kept yards, carefully-tended flower and vegetable gardens, and flourishing berry bushes, pear and apple trees. There were barber shops, ice cream and candy stores, restaurants, saunas, a pool room, and a cooperative store. In addition, the call of traveling vendors added to the sights, sounds, and activity of the small neighborhood. Nearby, Finnish Hall hosted all manner of social, athletic, and cultural events. Unsurprisingly, as one resident put it, "While homogeneous as a village, every household had its own history, secrets, dreams, ambitions, joys and sadness."[4]

Finnish emigration was prompted by both financial and political factors. As in many European countries, an increase in population and the modernization of farming and fishing methods led to a surplus of workers and lower wages, causing young people to look for opportunities elsewhere. There were also distinctive political aspects to the Finnish diaspora. Located in northernmost Europe, bordered by Sweden to the west, part of Norway to the north, and Russia to the east, Finland was conquered by Russia in that country's 1809 war with Sweden. Once annexed by Russia, the country became the autonomous Grand Duchy of Finland within the tsar's empire.

After a severe famine between 1866 and 1868, which killed 15% of the Finnish population, and the subsequent easing of Russian regulations, a Finnish nationalist movement began to strengthen. Under the reign of Nicholas II, however, many of Finland's existing self-governing rights were rescinded. In 1899, Emperor Nicholas abolished Finland's constitution and began an aggressive campaign for the country's "Russification." By 1901, the tsar ordered that Finnish males be conscripted into the Russian military; many chose to migrate to America instead.

Although there were concentrated Finnish settlements in the upper Midwest, including in Michigan, Minnesota, and Wisconsin, several smaller enclaves appeared in Massachusetts: Fitchburg, Worcester, and Boston among them. Even though it was a small town, Norwood's industrial base made it a prime destination for skilled and general laborers alike. And once the first contingent of Finns found employment, a chain migration brought family and friends to the community.

Unlike the Swedish immigrants before them, most of Norwood's Finns did not attend church. Many felt resentful that the Lutheran Church in their homeland had required tithes, even from the poorest farmers. Some were reportedly forced to give up their only cow, or precious farm equipment to meet the demands of local clergy. Once in the United States, they believed the Lutheran hierarchy here did not adequately support workers struggling for higher wages or better working conditions. Because of this, Finnish immigrants often embraced socialism, whose promises of fairness and equality for all seemed just. They joined the Socialist Party of America in greater numbers than any other ethnic group and were consistently at the forefront of demands for workers' rights and unionization.

Even within the American Finnish community, however, the Norwood enclave drew criticism because they had no organized church or temperance society. According to one Finnish-American historian, "The evangelists and pastors working in Norwood considered it a 'Sodom' as far as the Finns were concerned; they were not receptive to the Word of God." Still, in Norwood, the Finns were praised for their literacy, gender egalitarianism, and reliability. In one study, Norwood's

Board of Trade concluded that "the Finnish people ranked ahead of the other foreigners in intelligence." In addition, their work ethic was considered exceptional. The Finns, it was said, "could be depended on to be on hand Monday mornings."[5]

While some men found employment at the Norwood Ice Company, others became valued workers at the tannery, the railroad car shops, and at the Bird & Son paper, roofing, and linoleum plants. They also took on the heavy labor of road construction and the massive project of carving Willett Pond out of southeast Norwood's landscape. On the other hand, Finnish women, both single and married, sought domestic service jobs in the homes of the wealthy, whose large estates were always in need of not only maids to do the cleaning and serving, but also cooks and laundresses. The women who took these positions worked long hours— on average two hours longer per day than industrial workers—with little time to relax or even eat. Experienced cooks, who were expected to prepare all manner of meals, breads and desserts, were most often married women. Many lived in Swedeville and walked to and from their jobs; some even traveled miles to mansions in Dedham and Walpole.

Young, unmarried women became maids or part of the serving staff. A few had live-in quarters, residing most commonly in tiny third floor rooms, but these positions often came with strict rules regarding time off. Most Finnish domestics rented rooms from acquaintances in Swedeville, often in the homes of fellow employees. A few—mostly new arrivals—rented rooms in what became known locally as "the Suitcase House" or "the Bachelor House." Owned and operated by the Siivonen family and located in the heart of Swedeville, the house contained a warren of clean, well-kept rooms that were convenient and affordable, even if there was a long line at the bathroom door each morning. More males than females lived at the house but even a few married couples found it a pleasant introduction to the neighborhood. Soon enough, as they became familiar with their new environs, these young people moved on to more spacious rooms, a nearby apartment, or even a small home of their own.

Shortly after the number of Finnish immigrants began to increase, three familiar institutions—a social hall, a cooperative store, and a sauna—became the mainstays of the vibrant Swedeville neighborhood.

The earliest gathering of immigrants interested in organizing a labor society met in 1903, when there were fewer than 100 Finns in Norwood. By February 1904, the group was meeting weekly. On March 20, 1904, eighteen residents were inducted into a society called Imatra 29; less than a month later, a new name, INTO ("zeal"), was chosen for this Finnish Workingmen's Association and the group joined both the American Socialist Party and the Finnish Socialist Federation.

At first, the association rented a local hall for their meetings but, in 1905 INTO bought a piece of land across Chapel Street. Unable to obtain a construction loan from a local bank due to their association with socialists, undeterred members raised the money for materials and built what became the first Finnish Hall with volunteer labor. The dedication took place on January 6, 1906, and from the outset the 30-by 60-foot building was filled with the kind of entertainment, food, and camaraderie for which it became well-known. A women's sewing club, groups for children and young adults, a choir, band, drama, and sports clubs were established before long, and Finn Hall became the focal point of social life in Swedeville.

Calisthenics, a hugely popular form of gymnastic exercise in Finland, was one of the first sports to be organized. It consisted of movements completed in unison by groups of men and women, and was an essential feature at regional competitions at Finnish club picnics across Massachusetts. Intended to increase fitness and flexibility, teams were judged on the graceful choreography of positions assumed and held in a deliberate synchronized fashion. Eventually interest in the practice waned, and more competitive track and field events became popular. Within a decade or so, young people were participating in gymnastics, pyramid building, table tennis, basketball, and volleyball at Finn Hall, while the more serious athletes entered relay racing and distance running events at contests as far away as the Midwestern United States and Canada.

One sport that drew nearly fanatic supporters in the Finnish community was Greco-Roman wrestling, a style of wrestling which forbids holds below the waist, a restriction that results in an emphasis on throws, because participants cannot "trip" an opponent to the ground. Greco-Roman wrestling has been included in summer

The Finnish Workingmen's Association of Norwood (called INTO) erected this
meeting hall off Chapel Court in the early twentieth century.
(Courtesy of Aira Koski Johnson)

Olympics since 1904, about the time INTO began sponsoring a team.
Local matches, which could take hours to complete, were held at Finn
Hall, Lithuanian Hall, and the Civic, and several Swedeville natives
went on to earn regional and even national titles.

The most famous Norwood wrestler was John Maki, who won
the world lightweight championship in 1914. Born in 1883 in Lapua,
Finland, where his father was the village blacksmith, Maki arrived
in Norwood in 1902. Having learned the trade from his father, Maki
was almost immediately employed as a blacksmith for the town of
Norwood, and later was hired as an auxiliary police officer. He married
and had five children. An avid Greco-Roman wrestler, Maki first
entered local matches and then moved on to regional and national
bouts. He traveled to Nebraska in 1914 where he defeated, in straight
falls, the reigning world lightweight champion, Owen Daily. In January
1915, the *Norwood Messenger* proudly carried a detailed account of
the match which took place before "one of the largest crowds" ever
gathered in Daily's home state.[6] Two other Swedeville athletes, Anton
Koivisto Birch and Viktor Kuusela, followed in Maki's footsteps. Birch
won the gold medal of the New England Amateur Athletic Union in
1916 and Kuusela, who lived on Savin Avenue, won one gold and two

silver medals in regional competitions between 1920 and 1923.

Another popular entertainment in Swedeville was live theater. Several men and women within the community had received dramatic training in their homeland, and quickly formed an Actor's Club under the auspices of INTO. The group became part of a surge in membership and interest. As the Finnish Workingmen's Association grew and the number of its activities increased, members realized they had outgrown the original Finn Hall. In 1912, with the local bank once again refusing to issue a loan to this perceived band of immigrant radicals, INTO volunteers nearly doubled the size of Finn Hall. During the renovation, the Actor's Club insisted that the building be fitted with a professional, fully-equipped stage, a switchboard to control batten, foot, spot, and house lights, and dressing and make-up rooms. Painted backgrounds and most stage settings, which sometimes required rather elaborate construction, were also handled by volunteers, while the furniture and props necessary for each production were borrowed from Swedeville neighbors. Sylvia Wiik often provided piano accompaniment for any musical numbers, and several women took on the task of prompter, secreted into a recess specially built into the stage floor. Under the direction of paid professionals, many well-known Finnish dramas and original works were performed at the hall to enthusiastic audiences for several years.

If elaborate music was required for any of the club's theatricals, INTO was well-prepared. In addition to piano and choral music, the association sponsored the Sävel Band. John Waihela, an extraordinarily talented musician (it was said he could play every brass instrument in the band) became the director when it was formed in 1906. An all-male band, the Sävel played as the calisthenics team marched into competition, at Finn Hall dances, for outdoor festivals and picnics, and even for funerals, when they sometimes followed the hearse to the cemetery. Busy most weekends at Finn Hall, area social clubs, and various venues around eastern Massachusetts, Waihela led the band for over twenty years. During much of that time he was employed at the Readville car shops and lived with his family in Swedeville.

INTO was not solely a recreational and social institution,

however. Education was important to these new immigrants as well. Lectures, political speakers, and other programming was offered throughout the year, and there was a well-stocked library that held thousands of volumes, most in the Finnish language, for patron's reference and enjoyment. On Sundays classes were held to acquaint the younger generation with the traditions, history, and language of Finland. While the elders did not want their children to be unaware of their ethnic heritage, they were proud of their new homeland as well. Organized groups discussed current events in both Finland and the United States, keeping interested members well-informed, and newcomers enrolled in U.S. citizenship classes whenever they were offered at the hall.

Of course, as in any neighborhood, there were "unofficial" institutions too. There was the "Us Girls," women who thought of themselves as "the original support group, lending ear and heart to one another during the good times and the bad" and the "Night Hawks," working women who gathered in the evening—sometimes sporting costumes—to share conversation and laughter. Finally, a particularly ingenious group of a dozen or so teenaged boys scavenged lumber, built a clubhouse ("No Girls Allowed"), and innocently ran a baseball lottery until they learned it was illegal. They made enough profit, however, to buy themselves matching club jackets which they wore proudly for years.[7]

As the Finnish Workingmen's Association began to thrive, the group sought a suitable place to hold outdoor picnics, recreation, and sporting events. They found a fitting location in Walpole on land that contained both a grove of pines and an open field. Later known as Finn Farm, the six-acre-plus site held several rustic structures: a kitchen and food preparation building, a cinder running track, and well-designed athletic fields. Weekend days at the farm included morning programs of speakers, music, poetry reading, and even theater skits. In the afternoon there might be athletic contests, and evenings were devoted to food, relaxation, good company and conversation. Picnic days in Walpole became a much appreciated and well-earned "summer retreat" from the everyday labor and worries of the whole neighborhood.[8]

In 1909, the Finnish community of Norwood opened a
cooperative store. It was incorporated as The United
Cooperative Society of Norwood in 1921.
(Courtesy of Aira Koski Johnson)

In 1909, INTO members opened a retail cooperative food store
in conjunction with the TURVA ("security") Cooperative Store in
Quincy, Massachusetts. Cooperative stores were chiefly a derivative
of the socialist movement in Finland and other European countries.
By 1900, Finnish immigrants in the United States had embraced
the concept, which enabled a proportionate share of store profits
to be returned to investors who were often also customers. These
cooperatives were fairly successful in the United States and served a
real need within Finnish communities. Located at 47 Savin Avenue
in the building which had been the first home of the Swedish
Congregational Church, the Cooperative Store, as one Swedeville
resident recalled, was where people "could buy groceries that were
part of the Finnish diet: cardamom seeds for the sweetbread, hardtack
bread, rye bread, lingonberries, herring, smoked salmon, and dried
codfish." In addition, a customer could hear and speak his own native
language there. "It was at the coop where he felt comfortable—where
he was among his own kind."[9]

At various times the second floor of the building housed a shoe store, a dry goods store, a restaurant, and an apartment for the store manager. Around 1917, the Coop expanded to include a dairy and milk bottling enterprise in Walpole, which delivered to homes in Norwood, Walpole, Westwood, and Canton. Eventually, the store severed its relationship with Quincy and, in 1921, its name was changed to United Cooperative Society of Norwood. Staffed by local residents, it was a mainstay of the community through two world wars. By the 1950s, however, competition from the new "supermarket" concept had taken its toll, and second generation Finnish-Americans began drifting away. The dairy was eventually sold to Garelick's Milk Company, and the Cooperative Store closed in 1953. After reimbursing its shareholders, the Cooperative Store's remaining funds were contributed to the March of Dimes, the Norwood branch of the American Red Cross, and the Norwood Hospital.

Throughout the early twentieth century, however, the Cooperative Store provided an anchor to Swedeville's many small, family-run retail establishments. There were two variety stores on Chapel Street and one on Savin Avenue. There were barbershops, shoe repair shops, and small grocery stands, including those owned by Olavi "Whitey" Huttunen, Guido Stuntzner, Kusta Anttila, and Wilho Maenpaa. George Peterson opened an express company on Chapel, a family ran a stamping mill business (manufacturing metal washers for Bird & Son roofing) in their backyard on Savin Avenue, and Karl Roth had an auto repair shop on Johnson Court. When the second-floor restaurant in the Coop building closed in the 1920s, Aina Ahlfors opened her own restaurant at her Savin Avenue home. Equipped with a coal-fired black stove, oversized soapstone sink, and a broad table for food preparation, Ahlfors served simple but hearty meals and desserts family-style to boarders from around the neighborhood. She also provided breakfasts, complete with homemade muffins and breads, and even offered boxed lunches for the men to take to their jobs at the tannery or the press or the ink mill. Aina Ahlfors sold her house and business to Lüisa and Karl Sandberg in 1933 and they kept it running until 1940.

One of the most enterprising entrepreneurs in Swedeville was Willehard Karki. After purchasing the business and building at the corner of Savin and Melville Avenues from Kustaa Anttila, Karki turned the flat-roofed, concrete and clapboard-sided two-story structure into a neighborhood institution, known simply as "Karki's." No signage was required. Three large windows—two facing Savin Avenue and one facing Melville—provided ample room not only to display store products but also posters advertising local social and athletic events. Decades later, Aira Johnson could still describe the store's interior from memory: "[There was] a large mirror on the back wall to visually enlarge the room, as well as two long counters over large cabinets. The back counter was used for coffee cups, plates and napkins, a coffee pot, and baked goods. The counters were built to face one another, leaving comfortable walking space between them. The front unit was outfitted with deep tin-lined compartments that held chipped ice for buckets of ice cream and soft drinks. The store was outfitted with two small, white-topped tables with black iron legs, and chairs to match. At the far end of the store was the candy display case. There were rows and rows of various types, bewitching in their color and choices...."[10]

The penny candy attracted countless boys and girls who, with only a penny to spend, agonized over their decision. The soda fountain, with its shiny spigots and board smooth counters, enticed flocks of teenagers into splurging on ice cream cones and sodas. Willehard Karki was good-naturedly patient with everyone. He sold the store in 1938, and it closed in 1944. Ever the keen businessman, while still operating his variety store, Karki bought the building across the street on Savin Avenue, installing a poolroom and later, a bar, causing the quiet neighborhood some concern. In the 1950s the interior was remodeled into a restaurant and remains a favorite spot for locals.

Probably the most unique businesses found in Swedeville were the two commercial steam baths or saunas. A centuries-old tradition in Finland, the sauna held "a simple sanctity" about it for Norwood's Finns. The Savin Avenue sauna, set back from the street on a lot between Karki's poolroom and a multi-family house, stood close to the railroad tracks. It was built in 1910 by August Lehtonen and contained five sauna units, two on the first floor, three on the second. Each unit consisted of three rooms: the dressing room, the shower room, and the steam room. The Cedar Street sauna, located just across the railroad tracks in South Norwood, opened soon after Lehtonen's, and contained six units, all on one floor. It was built by Kustaa Anttila. Less elaborate than the Savin Avenue bathhouse, the steam rooms on Cedar Street also served as the washrooms. Both Lehtonen and Anttila were well-known to the Swedeville enclave; Lehtonen had been involved in the Cooperative Store and Anttila had previously owned a variety store in the neighborhood.

Both saunas were open to the public from 3 p.m. until midnight on Fridays and Saturdays; men, women, sometimes entire families, found the sauna relaxing, meditative, and a means to reduce stress. Often after a good steaming—thought to cleanse both the body and the spirit—friends would gather for coffee and quiet conversation. Still in business more than seventy years later, the Savin Avenue steam baths closed in the 1980s. It was the end of an era.

Despite living in this tiny, bustling, self-sufficient corner of town, insulated from most of Norwood, residents of Swedeville were not isolated from town-wide controversy. While INTO remained the center of recreation and entertainment for the neighborhood, politics occasionally caused upheaval within the Finnish Workingmen's Association. The Norwood Finns had organized within the Finnish Socialist Federation and were committed advocates of the rights of the working man. After the Russian Revolution, however, there were "strong ideological battles" between those who sought to maintain ties to the American Socialist Party and those who, frustrated by the slow pace of change, aligned themselves with the communist-leaning Industrial Workers of the World (IWW). According to local lore the Finns, who were the most ardent about gaining workers' rights and benefits, stood on the side of the IWW, and after many heated arguments and votes, the majority favored an affiliation with that organization. The minority of INTO members then reorganized under the Finnish Federation of the Socialist Party and continued under its auspices until the late 1930s when they joined the Finnish American League for Democracy.

Meanwhile, when word spread that the IWW was moving to take over income-producing enterprises like the Cooperative Store and its nearby dairy , the remaining INTO members cut all ties with that organization. Before that severance occurred, however, trouble came to Finn Hall. In the immediate post-World War I years, civil disturbances and labor unrest throughout the country were blamed on foreign workers, and anti-immigrant sentiment increased. Any people or organization associated with Bolshevism or the IWW bore the brunt of national distrust and political hysteria. In reaction to these troubling suspicions, Finn Hall was raided by police and federal authorities in search of communist sympathizers, subversive materials, and weapons. They found none. As one witness recollected, "They expected to find guns but found only stage make-up and stage properties." And yet, the Sävel Band retained some communist ties. Its musicians performed at the dedication of nearby Lithuanian Hall in 1915—referred to during its early years as "Bolshevik Hall"—and again in 1920 for the May Day celebration of the Lithuanian Bolsheviks of Norwood.[11]

INTO's withdrawal from any association with the I.W.W. put to rest any lingering doubts about the loyalty to America among the residents of Swedeville. Any questions concerning the patriotism of this ethnic community should have been answered during the Great War itself, however, when more than twenty sons of Swedeville enlisted in the military and three lost their lives during the conflict. By the time war was again declared in 1941, Swedeville provided more than its share of not only military recruits but also Red Cross workers and other volunteers.

As time passed, second- and third-generation Finnish-Americans found the passionate ideological debates among their elders perplexing and pointless. Fully assimilated into the American mainstream, they had less enthusiasm for distinctly ethnic activities and associations. Families moved away from the neighborhood, young people married outside their Finnish roots, and the bonds that had united them weakened. In 1959, Finnish Hall was sold to Norwood's American Legion Post No. 70, a transaction people saw as the official end of Swedeville. And yet, even today, if you take the time to walk the loop from Chapel Street around Cedar Street and Savin Avenue, it is not difficult to imagine the welcome refuge this isolated, tight-knit neighborhood must have been for immigrants struggling to survive in a sometimes baffling country. Swedeville was, in many ways, a transition point—from the Old World to the New. It was a place where uncertain, self-conscious, and sometimes ill-prepared travelers found comfort and support for as long as it was needed.

At the close of her memoir of Norwood's Swedeville, *Muisto: Remembrance of Norwood's Swedeville*, Aira Koski Johnson eloquently captures the spirit of the neighborhood:

> Growing up as kids of Norwood's Finnish immigrants, we were given a social life of the best kind.... [It] revolved around INTO activities. For our parents, it was their lifeline, their hold on security in this vast, strange new land. INTO became their extended family. The Hall was a place where, for a few hours, they were not reminded that they were unable to speak proper English or that their jobs were menial.
>
> Every one of the second generation of Finnish Americans interviewed...remembers their youthful days in Swedeville as heart-warming, filled with memorable, and even, at times, blissful experiences... While our parents sometimes struggled to maintain house and home, we children never felt poor or frightened. We were always comfortable in the embrace of our village and its people.[12]

Sources and Notes

In addition to my own research, I was fortunate to find several published pieces in local newspapers about Swedeville. These include: Willie Aho, "Norwood's Finnish Hall Once Beehive of Activity," *Norwood Messenger*, 2 August 1972 (Morrill Memorial Library, clipping, no pagination); Tom Bowman, "They Called It Swedeville," *Daily Transcript*, 28 June 1982, p. 1, 12; Joseph F. Gould, "Racial Survey of Norwood, Scandinavians," *Norwood Messenger*, 9 August 1913, p. 4; Joseph F. Gould, "Racial Survey of Norwood, The Finns," *Norwood Messenger*, 4 October 1913, p. 4; Cheryl MacDonald, "A

New Start in America," *Norwood Bulletin*, 27 May 1999, p. 1, 25. There were also two writings by historian Father William Wolkovich that I consulted: "New England Finlandia and Its Finnish Enclave of Norwood, Massachusetts," *Siirtolaisuus-Migration* (Turku, Finland: The Institute of Migration, 3/1998) and *Lithuanians of Norwood, Massachusetts: A Social Portrait in a Multi-ethnic Town* (Norwood, MA: 1988). Special note should be made of the remarkable memoir about the neighborhood compiled by Aira Koski Johnson, *Muisto: Remembrance of Norwood's Swedeville* (Lulu Press, Inc., 2016). I have relied heavily on these works for an overview of this village within a town, and I have footnoted direct quotations.

1. Bowman, p. 1.
2. Anna Smith Day to Fred Holland Day, letter dated 6 July 1894, Norwood Historical Society archives.
3. "Letters," *Norwood Messenger* (hereafter *NM*), 2 January 1892, p. 3. Rev. Achilles Loder was the same minister who stated that most Irish immigrants were criminals.
4. Koski-Johnson, p. 132.
5. Liisa A. Liedes, ed. *The Finnish Imprint: A New England Experience* (Fitchburg, MA: New England Finnish American Bicentennial Committee, 1982), quoted in Wolkovich, "New England Finlandia," p. 16; "Board of Trade," *NM*, 11 April 1914, p. 2.
6. "Makie Winner Over Owen Daily,"*NM*, 2 January 1915, p.1.
7. Koski-Johnson, pp. 188, 191, 208-209.
8. Koski-Johnson, pp. 213-215.
9. Koski-Johnson, p. 495.
10. Koski-Johnson, pp. 140-141.
11. Koski-Johnson, p. 164; Wolkovich, *Lithuanians of Norwood*, p. 60.
12. Koski-Johnson, p. 556.

Chapter 6

From "Bolshevik Hall" to Butterfly Ballroom: The Assimiliation of South Norwood's Lithuanian Hall

BETWEEN FEBRUARY AND MAY OF 1927, the *Norwood Messenger* printed a series of letters about Lithuanian Hall, located just off Washington Street in South Norwood. Ostensibly debating the merits of Saturday night dances held there, the writers debated the history of the hall and the patriotism of its members. Alluding to the hall's history, Father V. K. Taskunas, pastor of nearby St. George Roman Catholic Church, sought to express his views concerning "the so-called South Norwood ballroom, commonly known among the Norwood Lithuanians as Bolshevik Hall." Denying that an "imaginary inferiority complex" existed among residents of the neighborhood, the priest was more interested in the "moral atmosphere around these dances," an atmosphere that was reportedly dominated by "rowdies and dissolute youngsters" from all parts of town.[1] This brought a vehement response.

The correspondence quickly devolved into a vitriol-filled exchange between parishioners of St. George Catholic Church—who continued to refer to Lithuanian Hall as "Radical Hall" and "Bolshevik Hall"—and members of the newly renamed South Norwood Lithuanian Citizens Association, the owners of the building. In many ways, this exchange was the last gasp of a feud that had its beginnings at the turn of the century. By 1927, South Norwood's Lithuanian Hall had already survived the turbulence of blasphemy, epidemic disease, anarchist rallies, and Palmer's raid. Born on the fringes of an already marginalized community, raised on controversy and activism, and ultimately assimilated, like its neighborhood, into the political and social mainstream of twentieth-century America, the hall and its members provide a telling example of the challenges and mistrust every new immigrant group faces upon their arrival in the United States.

Beginning in the early 19th century, the village of South Dedham, incorporated as the town of Norwood in 1872, began its transformation from agriculture to industry with the opening of tanning, paper, and furniture mills. The first influx of immigrants, primarily Irish and German, built the railroad and later worked in the factories. They congregated in neighborhoods, not surprisingly dubbed "Dublin," "Cork City," and "Germantown." These groups were joined by immigrants from Sweden and Finland, who settled in an area quickly labeled "Swedeville." Between 1860 and 1900, the town's population quadrupled, with foreign-born residents, drawn by industrial expansion, comprising an ever-increasing percentage. Many in the community, including some among the Irish, German, and Scandinavian populations, felt threatened by the rapid influx of immigrants from countries such as Lithuania, Poland, Italy, and Syria. These new arrivals from Eastern and Southern Europe and the Levant began to form a nearly separate community at the southern end of town, known as South Norwood, the South End, or, most commonly, "The Flats."

A roughly triangular piece of land, located at the base of a steep hill that dipped underneath a railroad bridge, South Norwood was a considerable distance from what had developed into the commercial and retail center of town. Virtually contained by the bridge at one end and on two sides by railroad tracks, the area was nicknamed "The Flats" because of the preponderance of multi-family dwellings, each housing several apartments, then known as "flats." The neighborhood almost immediately became congested and overcrowded. Town services, including electricity, sewage, and road paving, were slow to reach South Norwood. Bryant Tolles, in his centennial history of the town, wrote that "this district long remained a shabby, unsanitary, and poorly provided place to live," an area where "the new foreigners had literally been herded together practically as outcasts." Even earlier, local historian Win Everett had described the South End, once populated by farms and small mills, as "a real estate speculator's paradise and the dumping ground of the peasantry of Europe." Uptown residents

The rear of Lithuanian Hall around the time of its dedication in 1914.
At the time South Norwood was still relatively undeveloped.
(Courtesy of Morrill Memorial Library)

made their disdain for the neighborhood quite clear, and viewed South Norwood as if it were a foreign country. According to a 1916 newspaper report, "a great number of people have never visited this section of town," an indication both of how rapidly the area had developed and how isolated and segregated its residents were.[2]

Lithuanian nationals had begun to arrive in South Norwood around 1900. Most took low-paying, unskilled positions at the Bird & Sons plant and the Morrill Ink mill, both within walking distance of their homes. One of New England's first paper manufacturers, Bird's had its beginning in 1795 in Needham, Massachusetts, where George Bird produced mottled and printing paper. In 1803, Bird relocated to Dedham and contracted to make bank note paper for the U.S. Government. Later, the company moved again to a site on the Neponset River in East Walpole, and by 1817 they were manufacturing coarse commercial wrapping paper. Under the innovative leadership of George Bird's grandson, Charles Sumner Bird, the company developed new products, including waterproof wrapping, building, and roofing material. In 1904, Bird constructed a facility in Norwood, about a mile from their East Walpole site, to house its first roofing mill. Seven years later, a floor covering factory opened adjacent to the roofing plant, resulting in a massive manufacturing facility.

Samuel Morrill, a printer and manufacturer of printing inks, took over a small furniture factory site on Pleasant Street in South Dedham in 1856, and concentrated on the development of superior printing inks. By 1884, the plant had expanded from that one structure to a complex that included more than a dozen wooden and brick buildings. Although the manufacture of colored inks began in Norwood in 1905, Morrill's specialty remained Perfecting Press ink, used by the majority of newspapers across the country. By 1913, now incorporated by the family as the George H. Morrill Company, it was one of the largest printing ink works in the world, with customers as far away as Europe, Japan, and Australia. Although they attracted employees from all ethnic groups, both Bird's and Morrill's filled their ranks with Lithuanian immigrants.

Like the Irish, Germans, and Finns who came before them, the Lithuanians formed a mutual benefit association, called the Kęstutis Society, to assist their fellow countrymen in times of sickness and death. Within a few years, though, the society became divided when Lithuanian "freethinkers," atheists with socialist leanings, gained control and expunged all religious references from the organization's by-laws. The religious-minded Catholic Lithuanians incorporated separately as the Lithuanian Benefit Society of St. George and talked of opening a second Roman Catholic parish in town. (St. Catherine of Siena was referred to as "the Irish church.") Meanwhile, across the street, literally and figuratively, the freethinkers wanted to "establish a center for themselves for social, educational, and betterment purposes."[3] Accordingly, on August 10, 1912, the "Hall group" organized a benevolent association of their own. Almost immediately the two societies squared off in competition to see whether a place of worship or a social hall would be built first. Throughout 1913 the churchgoers would announce a fund-raising event only to have a counter-event proposed by the Hall group.

At the same time, the *Norwood Messenger* warned its readers about South Norwood. "This section is a big problem to the town now and will be for some time to come," the newspaper intoned, calling its residents "a foreign element made up of the poorest strata of society." For example, the editor went on, "The town is putting up a splendid twelve room school building for those people and some of them turned around and stole all the lumber being used in its construction, they could lay their hands on."[4] It was not the last time the *Messenger* referred to South Norwood residents as "those people" or made accusations about their lawlessness without evidence to back them up.

By the summer of 1914 the freethinkers had gained the upper hand, and a cornerstone-laying ceremony for Lithuanian Hall took place on St. George Avenue in July. President Anthony Neviackas welcomed the large gathering and described the soon-to-be-completed facility. It was to be a substantial cement block and wooden structure that would hold a classroom, reading room, library, and ladies' room as well as a second-floor hall for meetings and dancing. The primary speaker for the ceremony, Fortunatus J. Bagočius, a popular lecturer and socialist attorney, spoke at length on the long history of persecution in their Lithuanian homeland, first by Germany and more recently by Russia. He reiterated the Benevolent Society's desire to build a hall that they might "have a place to come together, to read the books, to discuss the news, a place for joy and recreation." He thanked several distinguished Norwood citizens for their presence and went on to refute the rumors that the hall would become the headquarters of the socialist Industrial Workers of the World (IWW), Anarchists, and the Black Hand, an Italian criminal organization. "This is no I.W.W." Bagočius shouted. The Boston Lithuanian newspaper, *Keleivis*, a weekly with socialist leanings, also attended the ceremony. In that paper's account, socialist members of the hall were praised for their superior work in building it, and for holding a cornerstone-laying program that did not include "superstitious ceremonies [prayers], and no one sprinkled holy water." It is interesting to note as well that the hall group had actually been incorporated as the "Norwood Lithuanian Benevolent Society and Socialist Association." It was not until 1926 that the name was officially changed to the "South Norwood Lithuanian Citizens' Association."[5]

Four months later, on Thanksgiving Day in 1914, dedication

exercises were held on the hall's own stage. Speakers included James Hartshorn, chairman of Norwood's Board of Selectmen, who offered greetings from official Norwood; businessman and local benefactor George Willett, who opined on the benefits to the community which the hall would provide; and former state representative and venerable Winslow tannery owner Francis O. Winslow, who addressed the audience "not as foreigners or immigrants, but as fellow-citizens." Perhaps to the amusement of the atheists in the crowd, several of the up-town speakers invoked God, apparently unaware that the hall Lithuanians were godless. "We can thank God that He is offering peace and plenty on every hand," Winslow closed his remarks. "May God make of this a place of peace and enjoyment. May God bless you and all you have with you."[6]

From the outset, the hall was busy with meetings and special events. The Lithuanian Literary Society, organized in 1915, kept members informed through monthly book discussions and public lectures. The Norwood Lithuanian Men's Glee Club rehearsed weekly and held public concerts and light operas. In March of 1915, the *Norwood Messenger* announced the first wedding to take place in Lithuanian Hall, a Jewish ceremony performed by Rabbi Eli Kriedberg. Since the small Jewish congregation in Norwood did not yet have a temple, the nuptials of Miss May Berger, a South Norwood resident, and her groom, who came from Chelsea, were performed at the hall. Following the ceremony, the hall was the venue for "a delightful supper and dancing" and the display of "very many beautiful and expensive presents."[7]

It was not long, however, before controversy surfaced. Socialist and radical politicians began to make Norwood a stop on their lecture tours. In December of 1916 John Spargo, a relatively uneducated English stonemason who came to the United States in 1901 and catapulted to fame as a popular speaker for the Socialist Party of America, made an appearance. Speaking under the auspices of the "Norwood Forum," he spoke at Everett Hall in the Civic Center before a crowd of five hundred. The *Messenger* noted that "The Socialist clubs of Norwood were well represented," a reference not only to the Lithuanians but to the socialist elements within the Finnish Workingmen's Association headquartered at Finnish Hall in the Swedeville neighborhood. In July of 1917, after the United States had already entered World War I, an outdoor socialist rally held at the bandstand in Guild Square attracted more than three hundred. Despite the success and relative calm of these gatherings, some in the up-town community were wary of such activities. While the *Messenger* had expressed its opposition to "a flood of undesirables from the darker sections of the Old World," entering the town with "no conception of American ideas," as early as 1914, a few years later, the mood had grown even more somber when the newspaper reported that the birth rate in the Flats "exceeded that of the entire remaining township as a whole."[8]

In March of 1917, as the drumbeat of war echoed in the background, the town held a preparedness parade and rally. They also appointed a General Committee for Public Safety to coordinate all war-related activities. One subcommittee of this civil defense organization was known as the Night Riders. Armed young men sworn in as special police, these "Riders" nightly patrolled the town in automobiles "to guard against possible sabotage to public and industrial property."[11] As in many communities the anti-German sentiments promoted by the government were rapidly transformed into anti-Bolshevik, anti-radical, and anti-socialist crusades. In short order the Night Riders' customary route included not just factories, but known local ethnic gathering sports such as Lithuanian Hall. When the Committee for Public Safety organized a town-wide Patriots' Day parade and rally, the hall Lithuanians were conspicuous in their absence. Suspicion was further aroused when the hall hosted a large socialist gathering on May Day with the Finnish Hall band providing the music. On May 27, Norwood police and agents from the Department of Justice attended another rally at Lithuanian Hall in order to "watch for movements [meant] to interfere with the selective draft."[9]

One week later, a thirty-one-year-old Lithuanian immigrant who lived on St. John Avenue in South Norwood was arrested on a charge of treason. Frank Motchan, identified as "a leader among the Socialists in the south end of town," was reportedly calling his fellow workmen around his machine at the Bird & Son mill and "urging them not to register for the draft." When called into the office and warned, he protested that "he was a Socialist and left his native country because he could not express his opinions and he proposed to say what he thought here." Motchan was turned over to United States Marshals and transported to the East Cambridge jail. He was arraigned and held on bail charged with "knowingly and willfully" attempting to induce men to refuse to register for the draft. He "entered a technical plea of not guilty." Although the adjudication of this case is unclear, Motchan did return to town. His name appears in several newspaper articles during the next few years, although there are discrepancies in the spelling of his name.[10]

The divide between the two Lithuanian factions in South Norwood widened the following year when the groups clashed publicly once again. At a June 1918 rally the hall Lithuanians accused the Lithuanian clergy and their followers of "cooperating in the destruction of Lithuania" by supporting a German government takeover, by which, they contended, Lithuania would be "swallowed up and enslaved." In August, Lithuanian Catholics refuted that accusation and continued to distance themselves from the hall group. They even brought up the freethinkers' failure to participate in the Patriots' Day Preparedness Parade the year before. According to the Catholic contingent, the socialists from Lithuanian Hall "not only did not participate in it, but considered it nearly a humiliating affair. They tried to do their best to induce others not to participate too [and] condemned all the societies who took part in the parade in the most choleric terms."[11]

In the fall of 1918, a frightening epidemic further distressed the Lithuanian population in town. By the end of October more than 100 Norwood residents had lost their lives in the great influenza epidemic that circled the globe. The Committee for Public Safety was put in charge of the official response. When it became apparent that South Norwood's foreign-born laborers were suffering the highest mortality rates, apartments in the Flats were searched, and the sick transported to an emergency hospital, often against their will. As a consequence, apprehension increased, and many immigrant families, fearing deportation, failed to report cases of illness and even deaths. Subsequent statistics showed that just over three-quarters of the deaths in Norwood had been foreign-born adults or underage children of immigrant parentage. The ethnic population hit the hardest was

"Russian," a category that included immigrants from both Lithuania and Poland. During those harrowing weeks Lithuanian Hall was pressed into service as an emergency morgue. When the crisis finally subsided, however, a cloud still remained. The final entry of the Epidemic Committee's minutes read: "The question of the socialistic element, as it exists in our town, was brought up and somewhat discussed." The matter was referred to the Committee for Public Safety.[12]

Postwar and post-epidemic America was an unstable environment. Race riots, political bombings, and civil disturbances terrorized many, and, in a holdover from wartime hysteria, much of the violence and labor unrest was blamed on foreign workers. Although there were no reported incidents in Norwood, fear and xenophobia continued to mount. In October of 1919, Norwood citizens learned from the *Messenger* that the existing social upheaval and violence were "principally fathered by aliens."[13] The paper also informed townspeople that the Russian enemy was sending agitators all over the country to instill their ideas into the minds of the naive and uneducated. Unfortunately, the Norwood Lithuanian Socialist Society chose this same month to invite Michael X. Mockus to speak at Lithuanian Hall.

Mockus was a Lithuanian freethinker who emigrated in 1886 and embarked on his first anti-religious speaking tour around 1910. During his lectures Mockus used lantern slides of well-known sacred artwork as a backdrop for attacks on Christian iconic figures and for his condemnation of "religion, capitalism, and government as an unholy trinity." Although his efforts had been greeted by injunctions and even arrest in several states, Mockus remained on the circuit until a September 1919 appearance in Rumford, Maine, where "he specifically mocked the dove in the Holy Trinity symbol, the Virgin birth, and the nearly nude figure of the crucified Christ." He was arrested and charged with blasphemy. While out on bail awaiting trial, he traveled to South Norwood and conducted a three-night series of talks at Lithuanian Hall.[14]

In his own account of Norwood's Lithuanian community, historian Father William Wolkovich drew on personal interviews to recount the occasion. His informants recalled that at this time Catholics "didn't dare set foot in the Lithuanian Hall," but they made an exception for a visit by Mockus. Armed with eggs, they entered the hall and pelted the speaker; several participants were arrested. That same year a dispute between the socialist and communist contingents within the hall occurred. Just as the socialists had wrested control from the early association of Lithuanian Catholics, now the Lithuanian socialists were faced with a takeover attempt by communist followers. Although repelled by the socialists, a small communist cell persevered, and the gatherings of both groups were held in the hall. By the close of 1919 the town and the hall Lithuanians were not on the best of terms.[15]

Into this volatile mixture of misunderstanding and suspicion came Attorney General A. Mitchell Palmer, who had taken over the U.S. Department of Justice in March of 1919. Believing that most radicals would be found in immigrant ethnic enclaves, Palmer organized a new division within the United States Justice Department to pursue what he believed were violent, communistic atheists. This General Intelligence Division, the forerunner of the Federal Bureau of Investigation, was headed by then twenty-four-year-old J. Edgar Hoover. Under Hoover's direction, agents and operatives infiltrated labor unions and radical groups, issued press releases to feed the public's anti-immigrant hysteria, and assembled files on over two-hundred-thousand alleged radicals. During 1919 a spate of bombings was directed at business leaders and high government officials, including Palmer. Although no proof was ever offered connecting these incendiary devices to any radical group, Palmer and Hoover made the most of the incidents. In the fall, eleven cities were involved in raids of alleged anarchist meeting places. Although there were reports of police violence and the denial of constitutional rights, the general public supported the action and cried for more.

On 2 January 1920, synchronized to begin at 9:00 p.m., police departments and Justice Department officials participated in night raids across twenty-three states. Without warrants or probable cause affidavits, they arrested between two and three thousand alleged radicals. Most of the raids took place in private homes, restaurants, and social clubs. Somewhere between eight hundred and twelve hundred residents were seized in New England alone. Club membership lists, books, papers, and even pictures which hung on the walls were taken as evidence, also without search warrants.[16]

Norwood was one of Palmer's targeted communities. With its large contingent of foreign-born residents, most living in a concentrated area already under the surveillance of the Committee for Public Safety, South Norwood was an ideal location for Palmer's raiders. The chief of police, several patrolmen, and two justice department agents carried out the raids. Ten men were arrested on January 2, and two others were picked up during the following week. All were Lithuanians and all were labeled "aliens." Most of the men were taken from their homes; one, identified as Frank Matchen, was apprehended in Lithuanian Hall. Matchen (previously identified as Frank Motchan) was the same man who had been arrested in June of 1917 for advising fellow workers not to register for the draft.[17]

The *Norwood Messenger* reported that all were seized "on suspicion of being 'Reds' or members of the Communist Party." The police also contended that they had found "large quantities of revolutionary and Communist literature in the men's homes."[21] The men arrested during the Massachusetts raids were marched through the streets of Boston in chains and incarcerated on Deer Island, where they were to be held awaiting deportation. An editorial in the *Messenger* hailed the action. Calling those who were arrested "parlor bolshevists," the writer informed his readers that "these people will mostly be sent back to Russia where they came from...."[18] Ultimately, as courts across the country ruled on the unconstitutionality of the raids, the majority of those who were seized were released. At least some of those arrested in South Norwood, including Frank Matchen, returned to their homes.

Later in 1920, unrepentant Lithuanians gathered at the hall to rally support and financial aid for those arrested during the Palmer raids. Presented under the auspices of the Workers' Defense Conference of New England, the rally was deemed a success by attendees. A second politically-charged incident was the subject of discussion at the hall that evening, according to the *Messenger*. The announcement of the meeting had included the line: "Come and hear the truth about the Sacco-Vanzetti cases and the throttling of civil liberties in America."[19] This infamous cause was revisited later in the decade, but first

Lithuanian Hall was the site of early socialist and communist rallies and lectures; it later became a popular site for weddings and dances. *(Private collection)*

Lithuanian Hall began to expand its mission.

Athletics have long been recognized as a route to assimilation in America, and second-generation Lithuanians in South Norwood quickly embraced a variety of organized sports. These included diving, swimming, track, and eventually football and baseball. But it was Greco-Roman wrestling, a wildly popular sport during the 1920s, which helped to bring Lithuanian Hall into the mainstream. When the hall began to host wrestling matches, it drew an entirely new audience into the second-floor function room. In short order, Wednesday nights became wrestling night at the hall, with up to four bouts offered each week.

For the first time, the local newspaper spoke affectionately about the South Norwood facility. In December 1920, the *Messenger* reported that one match between "an Italian champion," identified only as Rizzo, and Frank Yousko, a six-foot-two, two hundred twenty-pound wrestler billed as "the Lithuanian giant," promised to be "a corking good exhibition." In this instance at least, the "Lithuanian giant" prevailed. Further aiding the hall's cause was one near-legendary Norwood athlete, John Dixon. The son of Lithuanian parents, Dixon excelled in basketball, baseball, and football, and went on to play two sports at Boston College. He also tried his hand at semi-professional baseball and even heavyweight boxing in the 1930s.[20]

If athletic competition and participation helped Lithuanian Hall and its members assimilate, so too did its increasing popularity as a function hall. Although local ethnic radicals continued to hire the hall for lectures and rallies, the building was frequently used for non-political purposes throughout the 1920s and 1930s. It became an accepted site for showers, wedding receptions, anniversary parties, and gatherings of all sorts. Even St. George churchgoers overcame their distaste for the place. Father Wolkovich later confirmed that a truce of sorts had taken place between the church and the hall Lithuanians as "People in wedding parties and their guests began walking the short distance from one street to another after a church marriage." In November 1923, for example, the *Norwood Messenger* ran an account of the celebration of an "old-fashioned wedding in real old country style." Following the religious service at St. George Roman Catholic Church conducted by Father Taskunas, "the party adjourned to Lithuanian Hall where the wedding feast was spread."[21]

And yet, Lithuanian Hall was not without political activism and notoriety in the late 1920s. Anthony Bimba, a Lithuanian communist, who had spoken there on several occasions, was brought in to speak while out on bail awaiting trial in 1926. After a rally in Brockton, Bimba had been charged with sedition and blasphemy, under an ancient Massachusetts law passed during the Salem Witch Trials. Although the speech he gave in Norwood contained much of the same fiery rhetoric, no charges were filed against him. Following a six-day trial, a jury found Bimba not guilty of blasphemy, but guilty of sedition for advocating communism. He was fined $100.[22]

A year later a rally in support of Sacco and Vanzetti was held at the Hall "before a record crowd of sympathizers and curious spectators." The Italian-born anarchists had been convicted in 1921 of the murder of a paymaster and guard during the armed robbery at the Slater & Morrill Shoe Company in Braintree, Massachusetts. By 1927, the pair had become a cause-celebré around the world. According to the *Messenger*, the "protest mass

meeting" at Lithuanian Hall in May of that year was chaired by
Frank Matchian, the same man who had been charged with treason
in 1917 and arrested during the Palmer raids of 1920. The main
speaker, one Jack McCarthy, talked not just about the Sacco-
Vanzetti case but also about "unjust arrests" across the country.
The issue, McCarthy stated, ultimately was the struggle between
workingmen and capitalists. Those in attendance were entertained
by the Finn Hall's band and a children's chorus. Neither the Bimba
nor the Sacco-Vanzetti rallies seemed to slow Lithuanian Hall's
steady march toward respectability, however.[23]

Instead of radical politics, the most controversial topic in 1927
was the contentious debate and temporary ban on the hall's popular
Saturday night dances. The *Messenger* published a sharp exchange
of letters between William Kudirka of the Catholic Lithuanians and
Anthony Neviackas, one of the founders of Lithuanian Hall, about
the acrimonious history between the two groups. But most letter
writers were concerned with the rowdy behavior, illegal drinking,
and "petting" that had infiltrated the Saturday dances, and so
encouraged the selectmen to ban the dance halls. The discussion
also gave voice to South Norwood residents' resentment at being
collectively referred to as "foreigners" by many in the town. "It's
absolutely a joke," one young man protested, that "a man who speaks
Polish, Italian, Syrian, any other language besides English, whether
he has resided here all his life, whether his father and forefathers
were born in the good old USA makes no mark, he's forever branded
as a foreigner." This perceived condescension of the rest of Norwood
remained a sore spot for South Norwood residents for a very long
time; in some respects, it remains even today. Yet clearly by the
time these letters appeared, Lithuanian Hall itself was no longer
considered a stigmatized institution within the neighborhood. It was
now part of the larger South Norwood community and, despite their
past differences, the neighborhood was united in standing up to the
criticism and derision of the "up-towners."[24]

During the 1930s, Lithuanian Hall was the site of moving picture
shows and other entertainments designed to further distance it from
the politics of the previous decade. It also became home to

A renovated Lithuanian Hall still stands on St. George
Avenue, a remnant of the neighborhood's history.
(Private collection)

the men's Sons of Italy Lodge as well as its women's auxiliary and
junior members. The Lodge met at the hall each Sunday morning
and even stored their archives and regalia in space provided by the
Lithuanians. the Junior Lodge used the hall's stage for their annual
song and dance shows for more than five years. Once prohibition was
repealed, the first floor became a clubhouse and tavern. Not long
after, during the big band era of the 1930s and 1940s, the second
floor, once the home of socialist protests, was transformed into the
"Butterfly Ballroom." There, excellent local bands attracted young
people from Norwood and surrounding towns to jitterbug, foxtrot,
and tango.[25]

With the onset of World War II, Lithuanian Hall was used by
Red Cross volunteers assembling surgical dressings, and it became
the site of successful War Bond drives. After the war, returning
veterans were feted with a banquet at the hall—a far cry from the
protests that went on before, during, and after World War I. Also
following the war, many Lithuanian families from both St. George's
Church and the hall sponsored a new wave of immigrants fleeing
their homeland. Two newly formed organizations, the St. Catherine's

Benefit Society and a local chapter of the Lithuanian American Council, alternated their meetings between the church and the hall.

As the decades passed, the most dedicated members of Lithuanian Hall moved away, died, or were too infirm to keep the facility functioning. In 1980 the neighborhood's newest members, a group of Portuguese immigrants, proposed to buy the building and continue its use as a social club. Instead, after some debate, the South Norfolk County Association for Retarded Citizens (SNARC) was allowed to buy Lithuanian Hall and convert it into a community residence for adult citizens with challenges.[26]

Throughout its almost seventy years of existence, South Norwood's Lithuanian Hall held a wide variety of public activities, including political protests, non-religious proselytizing, live theater, movies, sports, ethnic rallies, dances, banquets, and weddings. Its institutional journey from the margins to the mainstream mirrored the same arduous road to acceptance that its constituents traveled. Founded in an attempt to make a community of displaced people feel at home, it outlived its politically unpopular origins to be embraced by the community at large. When the name Lithuanian Hall is mentioned today, most people who remember it smile. It is the memory of dances, weddings, anniversary parties, and social occasions that has endured. It may have taken decades, but ultimately Lithuanian Hall was successfully transformed from "Bolshevik Hall" to "Butterfly Ballroom."

Sources and Notes

An earlier version of this essay was published in *Life on the Streets and Commons, 1600 to the Present*, edited by Peter Benes. (Boston: Boston University, The Dublin Seminar for New England Folklife Annual Proceedings, 2005). The author is indebted to the late Reverend William Wolkovich, historian and former pastor of St. George's Roman Catholic Church, whose historical accounts of the Lithuanian community in Norwood inspired this piece. Much of the material for this essay was found in the *Norwood Messenger*, then a twice-weekly newspaper. All references to that paper will be identified as *NM*.

1. Reverend V. K. Taskunas, "The Forum," *NM*, 11 February 1927, p. 5. Letters ran from 4 February 1927 through 13 May 1927.
2. Bryant F. Tolles Jr., *Norwood: The Centennial History of a Massachusetts Town* (Norwood, Mass: Town of Norwood, 1972) p. 29, 106; W. W. Everett, miscellaneous *NM* clippings, Norwood Historical Society archives, 1936; "Rapid Growth in South End," *NM*, 21 October 1916, p. 6.
3. "So. Norwood Group Will Observe Twenty-Fifth Birthday Thursday," *NM*, 28 November 1939, p. 1.
4. "Editorial," *NM*, 16 August 1913, p. 4.
5. "Lithuanians Lay Corner Stone," *NM*, 25 July 1914, p.1.
6. "Dedication Held on the Holiday," *NM*, 28 November 1914, p. 3. St. George's Lithuanian Roman Catholic Church was dedicated in 1915.
7. "First Wedding in Lithuanian Hall," *NM*, 16 March 1915, p. 1. The first temple was opened in Norwood in 1924.
8. "John Spargo at Norwood Forum," *NM*, 2 December 1916, p. 1; "Socialist Talk at Bandstand," *NM*, 28 July 1917, p. 1; "Editorial," *NM*, 31 January 1914, p. 4; "Rapid Growth in South End," *NM*, 21 October 1916, p. 6.
9. Tolles, pp. 35-36; "Socialists Meet on May Day," *NM*, 5 May 1917, p. 2; "Socialist Meeting Investigated," *NM*, 2 June 1917, p. 1.
10. "Arrested on Charge of Treason," *NM*, 9 June 1917, p. 4.
11. "The Protest Resolution," *NM*, 22 June 1918, p. 3; "Local Lithuanians Answer Letter: Want Everyone to Know They Are Loyal," *NM*, 3 August 1918, p. 3.
12. For all aspects of the epidemic, see, Patricia J. Fanning, *Influenza and Inequality: One Town's Tragic Response to the Great Epidemic of 1918* (Amherst, MA: University of Massachusetts Press, 2010).
13. "Editorial," *NM*, 18 October 1919, p. 4.
14. Rev. William Wolkovich, "Two Lithuanian Immigrants'

Blasphemy Trials during the Red Scare," *Historical Journal of Massachusetts*, 26, no. 2 (summer 1998): 146.

15. William Wolkovich, *Lithuanians of Norwood, Massachusetts: A Social Portrait in a Multi-ethnic Town* (Norwood, MA: William Wolkovich, 1998) p. 17.

16. For discussions of Palmer's raid, see: Robert W. Dunn, ed., *The Palmer Raids* (NY: International Publishers, 1948); Julian F. Jaffe, *Crusade against Radicalism: New York during the Red Scare, 1914-1924* (Port Washington, NY: Kennikat Press, 1972); Robert K. Murray, *Red Scare: A Study in National Hysteria, 1919-1920* (Minneapolis: University of Minnesota Press, 1955); Constantine M. Panunzio, *The Deportation Cases of 1919-1920* (NY: Federal Council of the Churches of Christ in America, 1921); Louis F. Post, *The Deportation Delirium of Nineteen-Twenty* (Chicago: Charles H. Kerr, 1923).

17. "Local Men Are 'Red' Suspects," *NM*, 10 January 1920, p. 6. According to the Norwood Police Department (Logs, 1920), the names and addresses of the men seized during the January 2, 1920, Palmer Raids were:

Benjamin Davadwicz	6 Andrus Place
Paul Krucas	Folan Ave.
Joseph Mackewicz	13 Tremont St.
Frank Matchan	seized in Lithuanian Hall
Lugis Zaykuff	63 Chapel St.
John Geibavicz	13 Tremont St.
Fabian Markiewicz	1182 Washington St.
John Valma	14 St. George Ave.
Kazimier Zuiry	1124 Washington St.
William Miscevicz	seized in Millis
Sergay Haponich	1188 Washington St. (seized on January 8)
Demetri Devorak	12 Oolah Ave. (seized on January 10)

18. "The Justice of Deportation," *NM*, 17 January 1920, p. 3.

19. "Cheered the Soviets of Russia," *NM*, 4 December 1920, p. 1.

20. "The South Norwood Wrestling Bouts," *NM*, 27 November 1920, p. 6. For an account of John Dixon's career, see Wolkovich, *Lithuanians of Norwood*, pp. 80-81.

21. Wolkovich, *Lithuanians of Norwood*, p. 77; "Big Wedding at Lithuanian Hall," *NM*, 24 November 1923, p.5.

22. Wolkovich, *Lithuanians of Norwood*, p. 60.

23. "McCarthy Talks of the Sacco-Vanzetti Case," *NM*, 6 May 1927, p. 1. Despite a series of appeals, Sacco and Vanzetti were executed in August of 1927. (The man's name was spelled Motchan and Matchan and Matchian in various articles. Such carelessness in the spelling of names is an indication of how invisible and unimportant many immigrants were considered.)

24. "The Forum," *NM*, 4 February 1927, p. 5; "Ban Saturday Night Dances," *NM*, 18 February 1927, p. 5.

25. Regarding the Sons of Italy and the "Butterfly Ballroom": Michael Triventi, interview with author, 18 April 2005.

26. As group home: "Norwood debates residence for retarded," *Daily Transcript*, 19 December 1981, p. 1; "Approves home for retarded," *Daily Transcript*, 14 January 1982, p. 1.

Chapter 7

Joe Gould's Norwood

JOE GOULD (1889-1957) SPENT MOST of the last forty years of his life walking the streets of New York's Greenwich Village, where he became the most famous—and infamous—derelict in the city. While sometimes charming, he could also be cagey, scurrilous, and even vicious. He is memorialized in the poetry of E. E. Cummings, the letters of Ezra Pound, *New Yorker* profiles by Joseph Mitchell (1942 and 1964) and Jill Lepore (2015), each of which later appeared in book form, and one movie. Gould claimed to be writing the "Oral History" of his age, a mammoth tome that recorded the conversations and ruminations of ordinary people as they went about their mundane lives.

By the time Gould died in 1957 in a New York asylum, he had been in and out of institutions for decades and was quite insane. Lepore posits a plethora of diagnoses, including autism, syphilis, paranoia, and psychosis, and a succession of horrifying treatments— restraints, sedation, teeth extraction, electric shock, and lobotomy— as Gould fell into the abyss of ever-worsening mental strife.

What, one might ask, does the harrowing tale of Joe Gould have to do with Norwood? Well, Gould's life began in Norwood, and it is in the town that both his ultimately squandered potential and his vain struggle against encroaching instability first appeared. In many respects, the tragedy that befell Joe Gould is a Norwood story.

Joseph Ferdinand Gould was born on September 12, 1889, in a house at 11 Market Street in Norwood, one of a haphazard collection of commercial and residential buildings, already falling into disrepair. By the 1920s these structures had been razed and Market Street eliminated, when today's town common and its eastern boundary,

Central Street, were created. Within a few years, Gould's father, Dr. Clarke Storer Gould, a physician and surgeon, built a large home at 486 Washington Street, the main thoroughfare of the town. As Joe later described it, the house "had three stories and twenty-one rooms, and it had gables and dormers and ornamental balconies and parquet floors.... There was a mirror in our front hall that was eight feet high and decorated with gold cherubim. There were beautiful terra-cotta tiles around the fireplaces. There were diamond-shaped windows at the stair landings, and they had red, green, purple and amber panes." It was a mansion fit for a respected doctor and influential citizen, which was no doubt how Clarke Storer Gould saw himself. According to Clarke's mother, Lydia Lawrence Gould, their branch of the Gould's had been in New England since 1635. Her own Lawrence line could be traced back to 12th century England, and, she cautioned her grandson, "We should never forget it."[1]

Clarke Gould's father, Joseph Ferdinand Gould (for whom his son, Joe, was named) was also a physician. He was a Harvard graduate and a surgeon in the 4th Regiment of Massachusetts Volunteers in the Civil War. Later he had a practice in Boston and taught at Harvard Medical School. For some reason, however, Clarke did not follow his father into academia and a Boston practice; he was, as Joe Gould put it, "prevailed upon to move out and practice in Norwood." In 1888 Clarke had married Amanda Vroom, a Canadian-born immigrant from Nova Scotia. Perhaps the Yankee Goulds did not approve of the match, or perhaps Clarke's own disposition—one source said he "was known to fly into rages"—made his father reluctant to bring him into his own orbit. In any event, Dr. Clarke Storer Gould, who like his father had graduated from Harvard, was encouraged (or "prevailed upon," as his son put it) to relocate to this small town of 3,700 inhabitants some fifteen miles southwest of Boston.[2]

The Gould family—Clarke, his wife Amanda, their son, Joseph, and daughter, Hilda—settled into the same house in which Gould practiced medicine (he held office hours in his home every afternoon and evening). Clarke took little time off but his wife, nicknamed Minnie, took their children to Nova Scotia each summer to visit relatives. Young Joe Gould loved his vacations in Canada. It was there, he said, that he had learned the language of seagulls. For the rest of his life, sometimes for money when he was living on the streets, Gould imitated the birds, cawing loudly, skipping and shuffling about, and flapping his arms and hands. As Lepore notes, such seemingly uncontrollable gestures and sounds are now seen as indicative of certain forms of autism, undiagnosable in the 1890s. "Long ago, long before this distress had a name," Lepore continues, "wouldn't it have been remarkably clever for a boy who couldn't help but flap his hands and walk on tiptoe and screech to make up a story about how he was imitating a seagull, on purpose?"[3] Such a tale could have provided cover and comfort to a child who clearly understood that something was amiss.

As long as he could remember, Gould confided to Joseph Mitchell, he was "perplexed by his own personality." For a time, at least, he blamed his erratic behavior on shyness. "I am introvert and extrovert all rolled in one," he contended, "a warring mixture of the recluse and the Sixth Avenue auctioneer. One foot says do, the other says don't. One foot says shut your mouth, the other says bellow like a bull. I am painfully shy, but try not to let people know it."[4]

What people knew, since he was very young, was that Joe Gould was different. "The truth is," Gould admitted, "I wasn't much good at anything—at home or at school or at play." It was said that he scribbled and drew pictures all over the walls and floors of his bedroom. In elementary school, he was awkward, restless, and sometimes anti-social. He could never keep in step with the two by two lines of children heading to assembly or recess—during which he was known to spit at the girls—and he reportedly "had to be tied in his seat in an effort to keep him from disrupting the classroom." Still, he participated in the customary school and town-based entertainments and events. In 1895, at six years old, he had a role in a dramatization from Kate Douglas Wiggin's *The Bird's Christmas Carol*, and when he was fourteen he presided over the lemonade table during the Universalist Church's Washingtonian Festival. But he never really found friends among his peers.[5]

"To begin with," he recounted, "I was undersized; I was a runt, a shrimp, a peanut, a half-pint, a tadpole. My nickname, when anybody thought to use it, was Pee Wee." Gould remained diminutive his entire life—barely reaching five feet four inches—and was usually referred to disparagingly as "Little Joe Gould" by New Yorkers and tourists who eventually came to witness his antics. As a child, his nose ran constantly. "Usually, when I was supposed to be paying attention to something, I was busy blowing my nose," he recalled, "I was just generally inept" and clumsy with both hands—Gould used the term "'ambisinistrous,' or left-handed in both hands."[6] It's easy to imagine how such a boy would have been treated by other children: isolated, avoided, and teased. Joe Gould knew he was thought of as abnormal and was tormented by that fact.

Even worse, he knew his deficiencies were recognized by his parents. "My father didn't know what to make of me," Gould said, "and I sometimes caught him looking at me with a thoughtful expression on his face." The realization that he was considered inadequate was unmistakable. "I loved my father, and I wanted him to think well of me, but I knew from the time I was a little boy… that I was going to be a disappointment to him." As if to confirm that suspicion, while still a teenager Joe ventured to confide in his father that he was thinking of becoming a doctor, too. "That'll be the day," was Clarke Gould's response.[7]

Joe received similar discouraging signals from his mother. One evening when the family was together after supper, he remembered, "I was studying and I happened to look up and I saw that she was looking at me and apparently had been for some time and that tears were running down her cheeks. 'My poor son,' she said." How must a small, socially awkward child, who already suspected there was something wrong, have felt when faced with such parental reactions? On a bright note, Joe seems to have achieved some respite from his turmoil in the home of a neighbor who later recalled he would lay on his stomach in her parlor reading, so engrossed she "had to step over him."[8]

As Gould reached high school age, his academic path was well established. Although he was rarely absent from school, his conduct fluctuated wildly. His grades varied, with English his best subject overall and math his worst. He joined the Debating Society and presented a paper on "Current Events" in January 1905. Perhaps more telling, when the society elected officers in March of that year, Joseph Gould was chosen "Janitor." The teenaged Gould persevered, however, and was one of fourteen pupils who delivered "High School Declamations" at Village Hall to the community as a whole; his subject was "The Organ Grinder." Finally, on Wednesday, June 26, 1907, Joseph Ferdinand Gould walked across the stage at Village Hall and accepted his diploma. The school's curriculum had offered four types of study: Classical, Scientific, General and Commercial. Gould had completed the Classical Course, which included instruction in Greek, Latin, and German.[9]

By the time Joe Gould graduated from high school, the Winslow and Smith tanneries, the Norwood Press and Plimpton's printing plants, Morrill's ink factory, and Bird's floor-covering enterprise had come to shape the town. These large-scale manufacturing sites, all clustered along the railroad tracks fairly close to or even within the town's commercial center, made Norwood a noisy, dirty, smoke-filled, odiferous but bustling place. The clanging of the presses and the thumping caused by the production of wide rolls of floor-covering, accompanied by the constant arrival and departure of railroad freight cars, echoed throughout the town. The scent of tanning and ink-making vats was beyond unpleasant, and the smoke being spewed from multiple stacks darkened the sky. In addition, the pollution of Hawes Brook was reaching a critical point. The acids, limes, and soup of excrement, grease, and bits of sheep tissue that was dumped into Hawes as it passed Winslow's tannery only worsened the already yellowed brook waters. And, further downstream, even while the workers at the Morrill ink mill complained about the fearful stench of all this waste, that factory added its own combination of dyes and ink remnants, killing every living thing in the river. Choked with organic matter and pollutants, the fouled waters of Hawes Brook poured into the Neponset River and on into Boston harbor.[10]

Norwood had become a hodge-podge of old and new; stately homes, ramshackle sheds and stables stood side-by-side on inadequate, narrow roadways. By 1901, trolley lines crisscrossed the streets and only added to the confusion and din. But Joe Gould didn't mind: "I used to like some of the old buildings downtown, the old wooden stores. And I used to like the smell from the tanneries, particularly on damp mornings. It was a musky, vinegary, railroad smell. It was a mixture of the smells of raw sheepskins and oak-bark acid that they used in the tanning vats, and coal smoke, and it was a characteristic of the town." The young teen would have been quite familiar with these sights and smells. The Gould home—all twenty-one rooms—had been built no more than a block away from the Smith tannery. On a hill between the two sites stood an ancient burial ground. In 1880 Norwood had opened a new cemetery across town on wide-open acreage, its graceful design developed by a landscape professional. After that, the older graveyard, the resting place of the original town settlers, was rather neglected and infrequently visited, except by a certain lonely boy with a vivid imagination. "I used to like to wander around in a weedy old tumbledown New England graveyard that was directly in back of our house on Washington Street," Gould explained. "The weeds were waist-high, and you could lie down and hide in them. You could hide in them and speculate on the rows upon rows of skeletons lying on their backs in the dirt down below."[11]

Following his graduation from high school, Joe Gould reluctantly entered Harvard, writing in one of his later autobiographical essays, "I did not want to go. It had been my plan to stay home and sit in a rocking chair on the back porch and brood." Between his unremarkable high school career and poor entrance exam scores, Joe never would have been admitted at all except that his father and grandfather had been Harvard men. Once there, his attendance was spotty, he did not turn in assignments, and he often failed his classes. As a result, he was on and off academic probation. Finally, he was expelled, and Joe Gould did not graduate in 1911 with his class. There was speculation that he had a nervous breakdown; if true, it was an ominous sign of what was to come.[12]

For once his father came to his defense, although he was perhaps more concerned with the family name than his son's welfare. Clarke Gould wrote a stern rebuke to Harvard's administration. "A college should never become so big or impersonal that it tends to break, rather than make a boy," Dr. Gould contended and he believed that was what the school had done to his son. The excuses were plentiful: "He is left-handed, very near-sighted, and not very strong," Clarke wrote. "He writes slowly because of this so can not take very good notes." Perhaps due to this alumnus' parental pressure, Harvard eventually relented and, after several missteps and setbacks—few professors wanted to work with him—Joe Gould received his degree a number of years later, shortly before he left for New York.[13]

In the years leading up to his departure, however, along with a host of failed schemes to make up his academic credits, Gould sought to carve out a place for himself in his hometown. When asked by his mother what he intended to do, Joe replied, "I intend to stroll and ponder." In doing so, he composed and published a series of articles for the *Norwood Messenger*, the local weekly newspaper. Gould called this nine-part series about Norwood's changing ethnic make-up a "Racial Survey" in keeping with the contemporary convention of identifying ethnic differences as racial. In this extensive work, he offers a surprisingly accurate description and illuminating analysis of the town's rapidly shifting population. It is the earliest, most comprehensive and even-handed discussion of native-born and immigrant residents of the town, written at a time when nativist sentiments were on the rise nationally and locally. Between 1900 and 1910, the town's population grew in size from 5,400 to 8,014, a 48% increase. By 1920, it had reached 12,627, a further 57% increase. Taking into account the decrease of immigration in general with the onset of World War I, the majority of this influx happened just as Gould was making his study in 1913. In his series, Gould discusses the historical, occupational, religious, and social aspects of numerous groups with empathy and clarity. By "strolling" through the streets and neighborhoods of his town with an open mind and a ready pen, Joe Gould provided a remarkable snapshot of Norwood and its citizenry at a crucial point in its history.[14]

"The purpose of this series of articles is to tell about the present inhabitants of Norwood," he begins, "to show where the elements that go to make up the town come from, what manner of life our foreign citizens are now leading and what their future possibilities are." His plan to discuss the immigrants in the order of their arrival was a purposeful one. By doing so, he hoped to alleviate the concerns then

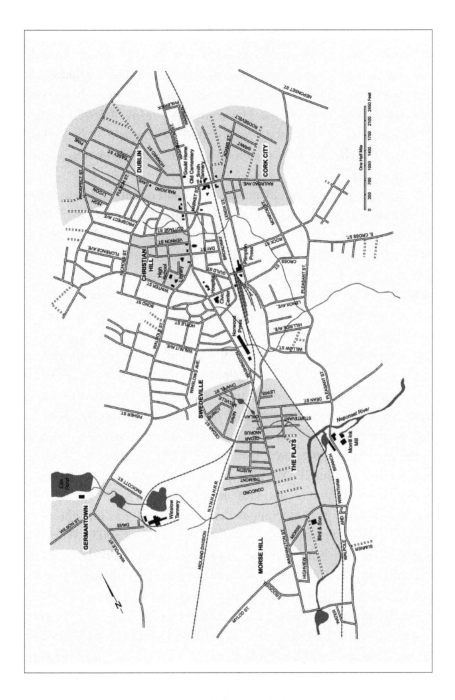

A circa 1912 map of Norwood including the ethnic neighborhoods about which Joe Gould wrote. The Gould home is on Washington Street between Dublin and Cork City, just in front of the old cemetery.

emerging among the town's long-time inhabitants, particularly those of "Yankee" blood. "Seeing that earlier arrivals from foreign strands have become good Americans," Gould states, "will show us that many fears which we have about the new immigration are entirely without foundation."[15] Relying on the Massachusetts census of 1875 through 1905, Gould began with a statistically-based opening article chronicling the dramatic changes in population that were causing unease among the townspeople.

Following this quantitative analysis, Gould opened his discussion of Norwood's people with the "Native-Born" population. Unlike his own grandmother, however, Joe dismisses colonial pedigrees. Although he acknowledged that those whose ancestry went back to previous centuries may feel they have a "sentimental claim of being a little deeper rooted than others in the national soil," he believed this was of no consequence since "the fruit that grows on the branches is more important than the part which is underground." Likewise, he was not concerned with "the history of the ancient parish of Dedham," or "the influences of the old Yankee stock upon local industries and town affairs," asserting that "perhaps they did no better than others would have done." So much for ancestral hero worship. "Human nature is the same everywhere, and we cannot credit our pioneers with most of the successes of the town, without attributing to them most of the failures," he continued. "We all hope that the town will keep only the best heritage of the past, and lose only its inherited defects."[16]

Gould went on to document the institutions—the Daughters of the Revolution, the Grand Army of the Republic post and its Women's Relief Corps, the Sons and Daughters of Veterans, and the recently founded Norwood Historical Society—organized by these "Native-born" residents "to preserve the patriotic memories and ideals" which the early settlers had passed on to younger generations. He stressed, however, that "It is a matter of pride to be an American, and so any one born on our soil considers himself one of us, whatever his parentage may be." Gould referenced Israel Zangwill's 1909 play *The Melting Pot* to declare that "it is not birth but ideals that make the American."[17]

It was a generous and gracious sentiment, but unfortunately it was not shared by the majority of "the old Yankee stock" in town.

Although immigrant labor was welcome in the burgeoning factories of Norwood, the workers and their families were not. Tensions ran high as the most recent arrivals from southern and eastern Europe settled in the southernmost part of Norwood, where multi-family dwellings were rapidly built to house them. Within a month of the start of Joe Gould's series, in August 1913, the editor of the *Messenger* offered his view of that neighborhood and its residents: "This section is a big problem to the town now and will be for some time to come. It is a foreign element made up of the poorest strata of society."[18] A good percentage of Norwood concurred.

Ignoring such attitudes, Gould examined many immigrant enclaves, writing separate articles about the Irish, "Other British" (English, Scots, Canadians), "German-speaking people" (Germans, Austrians), Scandinavians (Norwegians, Swedes, and Danes), "French-Speaking People" (the French and French-Canadians), Italians, Russians, and Finns. With each installment he discussed the reasons for the group's emigration from their homeland, the organizations and social clubs they formed upon their arrival, their occupations, and their affiliation or non-affiliation with organized religion. No matter the group, Gould made a positive assessment. He praised the fact that the Irish "have held office in local government, and performed their duties well" for decades; he found the Swedes exceptionally literate and, along with French-speaking Canadians, they encouraged bi-lingualism which "develops the intellect." Italians were praised for being "courteous and thrifty" and Finns were celebrated for equality between the sexes, their Workingmen's Association that encouraged literacy, athletics, theater and music, and their co-operative store which refunded its profits to customers.

Gould explained that many Lithuanian, Polish, and Jewish immigrants had been mistakenly identified as "Russian" because of their subjugation to the Czar, particularly noting the "religious and political persecution" of the Jews. He made sure to mention as many names as possible in each article; the officers of all the organizations, the best athletes, the most prominent residents. He must have spent considerable time with his subjects in order to obtain the kind of detail he included in these profiles. Perhaps his own status as an outcast facilitated his access to these marginal groups. Each installment captured the history and experiences of his subjects. Of course, some encounters were more fruitful than others. For example, his account of the "German-speaking people" was particularly nuanced.

Two very different businesses—furniture making and tanning—had attracted the Germans to South Dedham. In the mid-19th century, Willard Everett's furniture factory, located in the center of the village, employed skilled craftsmen and wood carvers from Germany. After Everett's burned down in 1865, many of this first wave of Germans followed the business when it was relocated to Boston. A second group of German-language speakers was drawn to Norwood by the tanneries. Gould traced Norwood families back to the districts of Baden, Bavaria, Prussia, Saxony, Scheswig-Holstein, and Württemberg—and Austria, as well as a few of Hungarian and Slavic descent; the common denominator was their ability to speak German. Most of these men and their families settled in the southwestern area of Norwood on and around Wilson Street near the Winslow tannery; the neighborhood became known as "Germantown."

An examination of resident lists in the early 1910s, when Gould was writing, reveals family names such as Eppich, Balduf, Waldheim, Verderber, Schmidt, Schacht, Hauck, and Eckhardt living on the street, the majority of whom were tannery workers. A few, like Wolfgang Waldheim, were lured to town by tannery owner Francis O. Winslow, who sought to organize a town band. Waldheim, a gifted musician, moved from New Hampshire when Winslow promised him a job at the tannery and inexpensive land for a house, which he built at 83 Wilson Street.

The German-speaking immigrants created a tightly-knit community of their own. In 1889 they organized a "Turnverein," or athletic club, to promote good health through physical activity. In 1893 they built the Turnhall for meetings, gymnastics, and German-language classes. At its peak, the Turnverein could boast over 150 members and an even larger number of associate members. When Gould was writing the Turnhall had officially disbanded, but the building still functioned as a neighborhood civic center.

Across Wilson Street stood a second community facility, Arbeiter Hall. Built in 1901, it was the headquarters of the Workmen's Sick and Dead Benefit Fund, which, according to Gould, was "one of the best paying mutual benefit societies in America."[19] Membership dues provided assistance to the sick, widowed, or aged in the neighborhood at a time when Social Security did not exist and few businesses offered insurance or medical benefits to workers. Workmen's Hall, as it came to be known, was a family recreation venue as well, and sponsored entertainments that filled the street with music, laughter, good food, and camaraderie. A short distance away, at 71 Wilson Street, Julius Balduf, a tannery foreman, operated a bowling alley for the amusement and recreation of his friends and neighbors.

Finally, indicative of the community's distance and isolation from the center of Norwood, Germantown had its own medical facility. Located at 95 Wilson Street, it was also the home of Charles and Annie Groote. Under the direction of Dr. Thomas O'Toole, the hospital provided outpatient care for the neighborhood and eventually included in-patient beds, a nursery for newborns, and an operating room.

Gould wrote extensively about the military background of Germantown's inhabitants. Charles Groote, for example, had served Germany in three wars. Laurenz (Lawrence) Kuld, who was eighty-eight and the oldest German in town when he spoke with Gould, had been on the losing side of "a revolutionary wave" in mid-19th century Germany and was a fugitive for several years before emigrating. He then worked at the tannery on Endicott Street for nearly six decades. Gould recounted the Old-World military service of German and Austrian immigrants Karl Kuld, Gustaff Bastian, and Fred C. Messenger, who fought on various sides of the Prussian, Austrian, and German conflicts. Joe Gould may well have been acquainted with Messenger, a tailor who ran a shop on Market Street near the Gould home.

After the Harvard debacle of 1911, Joe Gould also spent time at his uncle's ranch in Canada. By 1914, he was purportedly leading an effort to "free Albania." Subsequently, after a disturbing episode of nerves during which he recalled, "I began to twitch uncontrollably and see double," his interest in Albanian liberation abated. Still, he pondered theories about hatred, inequality of opportunity, and race prejudice; was arrested outside the Tremont Theatre in Boston for protesting D. W. Griffith's film *Birth of a Nation*; and at some point he became enamored of eugenics. In the summer of 1915, he was trained in fieldwork at the Eugenics Record Office at Cold Spring Harbor, Long Island, which, according to *New Yorker* writer Joseph Mitchell, was "making studies of families of hereditary defectives, paupers, and town nuisances in several highly inbred communities."[20]

Had the "Racial Survey of Norwood" aroused Gould's curiosity about eugenics and the ramifications of insular communities—such as the ethnics in Norwood who had an "indisposition for intermarriage"—or was his fascination with these loosely linked subjects merely the symptom of a slowly unravelling mind? Gould's writings about Norwood's ethnic populations was a tour de force by anyone's standards, and startling given Gould's reputation. The disdain residents held for him is obvious in descriptions that survive. Looking back years later, one neighbor recalled that Joe Gould was "a familiar sight to Norwood as he walked down the street chewing a stalk of celery," while another confirmed that even in those early years, he "was an eccentric." And, Gould himself once overheard his school principal refer to him as a "disgusting little bastard."[21] He was, to put it simply, considered the town fool, embodying the incompetence, gracelessness, and irresponsibility that label confers. And yet, he had pulled off the data collection, analysis, and composition of a multi-part survey with confidence and accuracy. Later, he occasionally demonstrated skill as a writer in other venues. Some of his essays, including "Marriage" and "Civilization," and several book reviews, were published; others, both fiction and non-fiction, were not. They are entertaining and cogent but none are as fact-based or evocative as his analysis of his neighbors. "There always was a queer streak in the Gould family," one family acquaintance recalled.[22] Perhaps this deliberative and thoughtful study of his home town helped to stave off the chaos he felt churning inside his head.

Joe Gould made one other attempt to find a useful place in town. For two years (1913 and 1914), he served as the census enumerator for the school department, a post which required him to visit every house and compile a list of the total number of children, with a breakdown of girls and boys. In addition, he had to determine the number of illiterate minors over fourteen years of age. It may well have been this house-to-house canvass that inspired the racial survey, a means to add depth and context to his statistics. And his canvassing of homes likely gave him the access he needed to interview his subjects.

As he strove to hold on to his ever-elusive stability, it is easy to see how his research on Norwood's immigrants brought him under the influence of anthropologist Albert E. Jenks, then studying racial amalgamation; Earnest Albert Hooton, a physical anthropologist known for his work on racial classification; and, ultimately, training at Charles B. Davenport's Eugenics Record Office. In 1916 Gould traveled to North Dakota to measure the heads and classify the skin tone of Native Americans. He documented this excursion in a series of lengthy letters published in the *Norwood Messenger* between March and May of that year. Eventually, a passing grade on an exam from Hooton enabled Gould to earn his Harvard degree, and shortly thereafter he headed for New York.

There was little left for Joe Gould in Norwood. "I used to like a good many of the people," he later explained to Mitchell, "they had some old-Yankee something about them that appealed to me." The feeling had not been mutual. "As I grew up, I gradually realized that I was a kind of fool to them. I found out that even some of the dignified old men that I admired and respected the most made little jokes about me and laughed at me." No matter how hard he tried, Joe could not avoid their cruelty, and he finally concluded, "I somehow just never fitted in. When he informed his father of his intention to go to New York, Dr. Gould reportedly replied, "In that case, son, you've made your bed and you can lie in it."[23]

But Clarke Gould was having troubles of his own. According to Joe, his father had made some bad investments which were ruinous to the family's finances. No wonder Dr. Gould, approaching fifty, was willing to serve in the Army Medical Corps during the World War. By 1918, the Goulds no longer lived in the grand home at 486 Washington Street. Dr. Clarke Storer Gould was now listed in the town's directory

Adapted from a vintage photograph, this portrait sketch of Joe Gould won an award in Norwood's 1972 Centennial Art Contest. *(Courtesy of Charles Fanning)*

(in small rather than the large bold print from previous years) at 623 Washington, a commercial building with offices and housing on the upper floors, much like his first residence on Market Street almost thirty years earlier. A florist, an insurance and real estate office, and a tailor shop shared the building's storefront. Clarke Storer Gould died in March of 1919. Sometime in the 1920s his widow, Amanda, moved to 100 Vernon Street, a house which she shared with three other women.

Joe Gould never forgot his home town. Occasionally, especially after Joseph Mitchell's profile appeared in the *New Yorker* in 1942, people from Norwood would track Gould down at one of his New York haunts (the Minetta Tavern or some other barroom) and make themselves known. By then, he was disheveled and dirty, with his sparse hair and unkempt beard growing gray. He would jump up to greet the visitor with a wide, toothless grin. "You're from Norwood!" he would shout enthusiastically. He still spoke rapidly with a thin, high-pitched voice that retained the remnants of a Boston accent. "Tell them I'm going back," he would say. "Yes, pretty soon I'm going back to Norwood because it's a nice town in which to end one's days."[24] But he never did.

Perhaps it is just as well. Joe Gould's true feelings about Norwood and its citizenry were poignant and complicated. "Little by little, through the years," he had admitted to Mitchell, "I had come to hate Norwood. I had come to hate it with all my heart and soul." It is of little wonder, when one thinks of the way he was treated. "There were days, if wishes could kill, I would've killed every man, woman, and child in Norwood, including my mother and father." But when he left town "with a light heart,"—or so he thought—it was not long before something came over him. "I hadn't gone far, however, before I began having a reaction that took me by surprise. On the train, all the way to New York, I was so homesick for Norwood that I had to hold on to myself to keep from getting off and turning around and going back."[25]

Joseph Mitchell begrudgingly admired Joe Gould because "he had declined to stay in Norwood and live out his life as Pee Wee Gould, the town fool." No matter how discreditable Gould became as mental illness overwhelmed him and he ventured further from reality, he appeared to be a "banished man" to the author. In a way, he was. Gould himself admitted "I was terribly mixed up in my feelings about Norwood." What would have happened if he had stayed? Nothing good, that's for sure. Little Joe Gould had had enough of the ridicule and the abuse and the pity. And so, he left. But, not without learning one more painful lesson: "That's one of the damnedest things I ever found out about human emotions and how treacherous they can be," he said, "the fact that you can hate a place with all your heart and soul and still be homesick for it."[26]

Although Joe Gould never returned to Norwood, he carried the town with him for the rest of his life. And, he may even have had the last laugh; at least it seemed so to poet E. E. Cummings, who wrote:

> and a myth is as good as a smile but little joe gould's quote oral
> history unquote might (publishers note) be entitled a wraith's
> progress or mainly awash while chiefly submerged or an amoral
> morality sort-of-aliveing by innumerable kind-of-deaths
>
> (Amérique Je T'Aime and it may be fun to be fooled
> but it's more fun to be more to be fun to be little joe gould)[27]

৯৵৵৵৵

Notes and Sources

Unless otherwise noted, material related to the general history of Norwood can be found in Bryant Tolles, *Norwood: The Centennial History of a Massachusetts Town* (Norwood, MA: Norwood Printing Company, 1973) and Patricia J. Fanning, *Norwood: A History* (Charleston, SC: Arcadia Publishing, 2002). Many have been fascinated by Joe Gould and his story. There are many editions of Mitchell's biographical essays. I have used Joseph Mitchell, *Joe Gould's Secret* (NY: The Viking Press, 1965) as my source, along with Jill Lepore, *Joe Gould's Teeth* (NY: Alfred A. Knopf, 2016.).

1. Mitchell, *Joe Gould's Secret*, pp. 58, 57.
2. Mitchell, *Joe Gould's Secret*, p. 57; Lepore, *Joe Gould's Teeth*, p. 19.
3. Lepore, *Joe Gould's Teeth*, p. 19.
4. Mitchell, *Joe Gould's Secret*, pp. 19-20.
5. Mitchell, *Joe Gould's Secret*, p. 59; Lepore , *Joe Gould's Teeth*, p. 19; "Norwood's Joe Gould Again Lands in National Limelight," *Norwood Daily Messenger* (hereafter *NM*), 26 November 1947, no pagination, Morrill Memorial Library file; *Norwood Advertiser and Review*, 14 December 1895, p. 4; 22 February 1903, p. 4.
6. Mitchell, *Joe Gould's Secret*, p. 59.
7. Mitchell, *Joe Gould's Secret*, pp. 59, 58, 61.
8. Mitchell, *Joe Gould's Secret*, p. 112 ; "Norwood's Joe Gould Again Lands in National Limelight."
9. *Norwood Advertiser and Review*, 27 January 1905, p. 4; 17 March 1905, p. 4; 31 March 1905, p. 4; *Annual Report, Town of Norwood*, year ending January 31, 1908 (Norwood, MA, 1908).
10. For information on pollution of Hawes Brook, see: Diana Muir, *Reflections in Bullough's Pond: Economy and Ecosystems in New England* (Hanover, NH: University Press of New England, 2000), pp. 95-97.

11. Mitchell, *Joe Gould's Secret*, p. 66.

12. Mitchell, *Joe Gould's Secret,* p. 25; Lepore, *Joe Gould's Teeth*, p. 21.

13. Lepore, , *Joe Gould's Teeth*, p. 21.

14. Mitchell, *Joe Gould's Secret*, p. 25 ; Joseph F. Gould, "Racial Survey of Norwood, Parts I-X," *NM*, July 5, 12, 19, and 26, 1913; August 2, 9, and 16, 1913; September 20, 1913; and October 4, 1913.

15. Joseph F. Gould, "Racial Survey of Norwood, I. Statistics of Population," 5 July 1913, p. 2.

16. Ibid.

17. Ibid.

18. "Editorial," *NM*, 16 August 1913, p. 4.

19. Joseph F. Gould, "Racial Survey of Norwood, V. German-Speaking People," 2 August 1913, p. 4.

20. Mitchell, *Joe Gould's* Secret, p. 26; Lepore, *Joe Gould's Teeth*, pp. 34-37; Mitchell, *Joe Gould's* Secret, p. 26.

21. "Norwood's Joe Gould Again Lands in National Limelight;" "Former Norwood Man Is 'Profiled' In New Yorker," *NM*, 28 December 1942, 1; Mitchell, 60.

22. Lepore, *Joe Gould's Teeth*, p. 19.

23. Mitchell, *Joe Gould's* Secret, pp. 66-67.

24. Patricia Chism, "Joe Gould Vows He'll Return," *NM*, 20 January 1948, no pagination, Morrill Memorial Library file.

25. Mitchell, *Joe Gould's* Secret, p. 67.

26. Mitchell, *Joe Gould's* Secret, pp. 145, 51, 65, 67.

27. E. E. Cummings, poem "39," *100 Selected Poems* (NY: Grove Press, Inc., 1959), p. 48.

Chapter 8

Norwood 1918: The Anatomy of an Epidemic

THE INFLUENZA EPIDEMIC OF 1918 was one of the worst medical catastrophes in modern history, one that ranks with the Black Death in its decimation of populations. It began in March 1918 in the American Midwest and then spread to Europe, probably via troop ships carrying soldiers from the United States. In August 1918, the fall wave hit the United States' East Coast and spread across the country, and it went on to ravage the world. Finally, from December 1918 through March 1919, sporadic "trailer" outbreaks occurred in many locations. The death toll was enormous. There were more than 30 million deaths worldwide; the United States alone lost over 750,000. In my book, *Influenza and Inequality: One Town's Tragic Response to the Great Epidemic of 1918* (Amherst, MA: University of Massachusetts Press, 2010), I wrote of Norwood's experience during this pandemic. The following is an excerpt from this work.

On September 28, as cases of influenza mounted, Norwood created a Special Committee on the Epidemic and rapidly focused on an emergency plan. Since the small local hospital was filled to capacity and its staff already overworked, the town needed another site to send patients. The Norwood Civic Association building was particularly appropriate as an Emergency Hospital; it was near the center of town, close by the existing hospital, and its architecture made the isolation of certain parts of the building possible. The Social Hall, an upstairs room used for dancing lessons and small parties, was proposed as the women's ward. Everett Hall, the largest room in the building, and one often used for plays, graduation

When influenza struck in 1918, the Norwood Civic Association building
was utilized as an Emergency Hospital. *(Courtesy of Robert Donahue)*

exercises, proms and town meetings, was designated for men. The
gymnasium was turned into a morgue. There were also ample rooms for
storage of supplies, rest areas for volunteers, and any other needs that
might arise.

Dr. Lewis H. Plimpton, recently retired from private practice,
agreed to oversee the Emergency Hospital; nurses were to be directed
by the hospital's nursing supervisor. The coordination of the kitchen,
food, housekeeping, and general administration was put under the
direction of Mrs. Marcia Winslow, a member of the prominent Winslow
family. Girl Scouts were set to work scrubbing floors, setting up cots,
and making the beds. The Boy Scouts ran errands around town.

The Committee stated that opening the Emergency Hospital was
advisable because it would enable physicians to handle more cases—
particularly those patients living in the outlying districts. But Norwood
had no geographical "outlying districts." What Norwood did have were
immigrant neighborhoods that many residents viewed as foreign, and,
particularly in the case of South Norwood, dangerous. That attitude
resulted in decisions that changed the course of the epidemic response.

There were other options. For example, the town could have been
divided geographically. Several neighboring towns did just that and
physicians treated patients only in their assigned areas. If Norwood's
emergency plan had followed this decentralized model, the focus
on neighborhoods would have allowed people to be treated in their

homes, not removed to a makeshift, understaffed medical facility
where only rudimentary care could be offered and where crowding
could contribute to the transmission of disease.

In addition, existing community resources could have been
used to alleviate the epidemic's impact. Cots could have been set up
in any number of religious or social halls: Lithuanian Hall, Finnish
Hall, Winslow Hall, Workmen's Hall, and Casey Hall all stood ready.
Columbia Hall at St. Catherine's Church, and meeting rooms in
other churches were available as well. Volunteers drawn from the
neighborhood, those acquainted with the people and the language,
could have been supervised by medical personnel working in each
area. Such a plan would have provided adequate medical coverage
and, in addition, better emotional and social support to patients and
their families. Instead, with an eye towards efficient social control
of the immigrant population, officials opted for a more hierarchical
approach.

On Sunday morning, as troops of Girl Scouts arrived to make up the
cots, stock shelves, and cover the front desk at the Emergency Hospital,
a call for assistance went out. Thirty female schoolteachers responded,
but few others. The final days of September were relatively quiet; only
two residents died on September 30. But as in all instances of epidemic
influenza, a time comes when the disease suddenly spreads exponentially,
sweeping through a community like a firestorm. In Norwood, those
incendiary days began on October 1. A day later there were hundreds of
new cases confirmed and many others likely unreported.

The Emergency Hospital began to fill up with patients, most from
South Norwood. The Epidemic Committee had instituted a house-
by-house canvass by the Home Guard (a subcommittee previously
charged with controlling subversive behavior) in South Norwood.
Even if they wished to remain at home, people with symptoms were
still transported to the Emergency Hospital. Feeling threatened by
the sudden intrusion of town authorities, residents resisted the forced
evacuation, often by denying illness. The *Norwood Messenger* noted
that many of the cases brought to the Emergency Hospital were "in
such an advanced stage that medical attention was utterly useless
when they arrived."[1]

The issues were more complex than the newspaper implied, however. Many residents of South Norwood believed they would get better care at home and might even be neglected or harmed at the hospital. Some were too sick or too frightened to seek assistance. Others remembered the medical inspections they had endured as they entered the United States and, fearing deportation, simply refused to open their door when the Home Guard came. One man later recalled that when officials knocked on their door, his parents hid him in a closet so he would not be found; obviously, it was a traumatic event for the child. Fear was palpable. One couple who lived on the outskirts of South Norwood was taken to the Emergency Hospital on September 29, despite their protestations. Their three children—boys aged four, six, and eight—were left home alone. When the authorities returned for them, they found the children had fled. According to the family, they lived in the woods for days, returning to the house only long enough to eat the soup, bread, and cookies left by neighbors who understood the children's fear of "capture" by officials. The boys' mother died, but their father, after having been mistakenly tagged as dead and moved to the morgue, eventually recovered and returned home.

As can be inferred by such an error, the scene at the Emergency Hospital was more chaotic than comforting. "The first patient I admitted was a young man in his late twenties," one Girl Scout volunteer wrote in a memoir of the crisis, "who was rushed on a stretcher into the men's ward by two members of the Home Guard." She tried to get the patient's name and address from his distraught wife, "who had three frightened children hanging onto her skirt." But the woman only stood there, weeping helplessly. "Since she was a foreigner and couldn't speak English," the observant teenager concluded, "she must live in the 'Flats,' that section south of the town which the hierarchy pretended did not exist." As the volunteer tried to communicate with the woman, she suddenly staggered and fell against the counter. "To my horror," the girl reported, "I saw her lips and ears had turned a dark purple in her ashen face, a sure sign of death." The woman was hurried into the women's ward, leaving her terrified children in the care of volunteers.[2]

During the next seven days, forty-six people died, more than a quarter of the usual annual death toll. The town struggled to cope. On October 2, the Epidemic Committee had opened a well-nursery at the Winslow Elementary School for children whose mothers were too sick to care for them. Sleeping accommodations were set up in the front rooms of the building, and a dining room was installed across the hall. Six teachers immediately volunteered to take charge of the nursery, and by the evening of October 3 three children had already arrived. By the time the well-nursery closed, nearly three weeks later, twenty-six children had been cared for—some for as long as twelve days—by eleven teachers and their assistants.

On October 3, Dr. James McMurray and Dr. David Lepper from the U.S. Shipping Board Service arrived in town. They had been sent to Norwood by the National Health Service Bureau and the State Board of Health. McMurray was assigned to help in the organization and work of the Emergency Hospital itself while Lepper, who spoke several foreign languages, handled the treatment of patients in the community, particularly in South Norwood. There his "tact and courtesy," as well as his language skills, were a great advantage. On that same day, eight more townspeople died.

Alarmed by the sudden spike in cases and the still understaffed Emergency Hospital, the Epidemic Committee called on the services of the Massachusetts State Guard. Twenty members of the Guard arrived on October 5. Housed in the Billiard Room at the Civic, they drove make-shift ambulances, collected laundry, mopped the wards and corridors, and guarded delirious or violent patients. The committee also issued orders that no further patients from adjacent towns would be admitted into the Emergency Hospital unless the towns in question sent nursing or attendant assistance.

How people viewed the events of the week depended on their social status within the community. While the Epidemic Committee was congratulating itself on the swift and effective measures taken to stem the epidemic, immigrant families faced a different reality. Afraid, unsure of themselves, and unfamiliar with the language and customs, the residents of South Norwood felt violated as their homes were entered and their relatives and friends transported to the Emergency Hospital from which they often did not return alive. It was a terrorizing ordeal.

The uncertainty about how the disease was transmitted compounded anxieties for the committee, too. The *Norwood Messenger* began to link the disease to the ongoing war and foreign invasion. An editorial, likely written by owner Alec Ambrose, a member of the Epidemic Committee, noted that there was a "mysterious feature" to the spread of influenza: it had appeared simultaneously in army and navy camps. According to the paper, this fact started "speculation as to the possibility of the introduction of germs by our enemies" and declared that "the closest scrutiny" should be given to the movements of anyone suspected of "disloyalty and malice."[3]

On Monday, October 7, the Epidemic Committee voted to post quarantine signs on every house where disease had been found. It was suggested that officials try to explain the reason for the placards to the occupants "if possible." On many occasions, the message was not adequately conveyed. "I remember them talking about those signs— quarantine signs," one influenza sufferer from Cork City recollected, "It was as if, I don't know, they'd done something wrong. And they were being punished."

Another victim distinctly remembered the posting of the quarantine sign on her door: "I remember Wally Riddell, he was a cop, a big burly guy. He and Joe Curran's grandfather came up to the house with a great big white sign and on the sign it said INFLUENZA in red letters. And they nailed it to the door. I was like quarantined...kind of scary. I'll never forget it." One resident of the Dublin neighborhood was apparently so angered or shamed that he "kept tearing the sign down...[T]he board of health finally came up and said if he tore that sign down again he'd be fined $35." Rather than providing a sense of security and comfort for flu victims and their frightened families, official actions seemed to add to their burden.

Fear began to erode routine interactions. Groceries were left on porches instead of being brought inside and mail was baked in the oven before being opened. Churches were closed, wakes and funeral gatherings were banned; pool halls, barrooms, soda fountains, billiard parlors, and stores were shuttered. Grocery wagons were

This advertisement for Orent Brothers store appeared in
the *Norwood Messenger* during the epidemic of 1918.

commandeered for use as hearses. Children were kept inside: "My
mother wouldn't let me go anywhere," one man recalled. "She
wouldn't let me go out with friends or anything. It was awful. But she
was so afraid I'd get it too." Everyday socializing came to a halt. In the
neighborhood known as Germantown, one resident recollected, "We
stayed by ourselves. No social life." An Irish resident remembered,
"Everything came to a standstill…We couldn't see people. We weren't
allowed out the door."

Still the epidemic persisted. For those unlucky enough to come
down with the flu, symptoms appeared quickly and were severe. All had
the body aches, weakness, and exhaustion that normally accompany
influenza. High fever, sore throat, and delirium were commonplace.
"I remember seeing things crawling up the wall," one patient recalled.
Many had severe nosebleeds and headaches. One survivor, who was a
child during the epidemic, remembered waking up in the Emergency

Hospital "with the pillowcase full of blood. It ran out of my eyes, my ears, my nose and my mouth." One of the State Guard members thought the boy had been stabbed, but the nurse quickly told him it was the fever breaking.[4]

Although most were young and newly arrived in America, the victims did have relatives and friends who mourned them. To publicly affirm the grief that was felt, personally crafted notices of deaths began to appear. Bonaventure Bagnato, a twenty-eight-year old Italian immigrant, received a tribute placed in the *Norwood Messenger* by his friends. The article stated that Bonaventura was "a fine young man, educated in Italy, well known in Norwood, of high principles and excellent character, and very popular with his friends." Employed at the American Brake Shoe & Foundry Company in Norwood as a molder, the young man was survived by his parents and several siblings, all of whom lived in Italy.[5]

News of the epidemic was a topic in the weekly Lithuanian language newspaper, *Keleivis*, published in South Boston. One correspondent from Norwood wrote, "Since September 15 that new disease Spanish influenza has been raging here. It has spread so much that there is practically no home where this unwelcome guest is not paying a visit. There are even some families where each member lies stricken on a patient's bed. Worst of all it's almost impossible to call a physician. If you can find one on the street, rejoice, because you won't get one by phone nor find one at his home."[6] The newspaper also noted the loss of two young laborers, both in their 20s, living in South Norwood, who were members of Norwood's Lithuanian Socialist Alliance.

There were many other tragedies. Emma Maki, forty-two, who had emigrated from Finland and was living in Swedeville, was the sole support of seven children. According to a neighbor's written recollection, she was taken in a horse-drawn carriage to the Civic and placed on a cot. She received minimal attention since the staff was so overwhelmed by the number of patients. Whether delirious from fever or simply concerned for her family, Emma tried to leave her bed to return to her children and fell down dead.[7]

Walter Theall, thirty-six, a worker at the Norwood Press, left a wife and five children. Anna Cvilikas, from Lithuania, a twenty-five-year-old mother of two small boys, and Annie Dicizii, twenty-four, from Italy, were neighbors in South Norwood; both women died on October 5. Tuerson Mowlod and Elsag Mahomed, both tannery workers from Turkey, who lived in the same boarding house on Sturtevant Avenue, died one day apart. On October 7, Rosa Cattarino, an Italian immigrant who had lost her husband and child in late September, died at the Emergency Hospital. When the Lithuanian correspondent wrote to *Keleivis* of the deaths in Norwood, he concluded "Though I send this sad news, I don't know if I will be around to read them in print. We are, as it were, in a field of battle where no one knows what tomorrow will bring…. The streets just resound from undertakers' wagons and doctor's automobiles."[8]

While the Epidemic Committee focused on statistics, Alec Ambrose used his *Messenger* to moralize and indict the sick in South Norwood. An article on October 12 read, "In certain sections of town the authorities are not receiving any cooperation whatever in their efforts to stamp out the dread malady. It is only by their own efforts and inquiries that new cases are located in these sections and when they are finally uncovered by methods rivaling the performances of the celebrated Sherlock Holmes, the cases are so far advanced that the physicians' efforts to prevent a fatality are unavailing. These cases or a portion of them at least, have been festering for perhaps a week or ten days, and in addition to the fact that the infected person is beyond medical aid, has infected a varying number of others."[9]

The death toll continued to climb. In addition to Carl Carlson and Emma Maki, the tiny Swedeville neighborhood lost seven men, women, and children; the oldest was thirty, the youngest two. Across town, Julia Drummy, twenty-four, had been married for eighteen months. In the fall of 1918, she and her husband were eagerly anticipating the birth of their first child. The baby girl was born on September 20, but Julia had contracted influenza. In accordance with the Epidemic Committee's regulations, her husband was not allowed to go into the hospital to visit her. "Sometimes," however, his daughter recalled being told, "they would bring her to the window so he could wave." The new mother died on October 8.

That same day, another young mother succumbed. She was remembered by her husband in a letter printed in *Keleivis* under the heading "Correspondence from Norwood." "Theofila Pakarklis died here on October 8 from that wicked influenza disease," the letter began. "She was an exemplary housekeeper and a friendly woman. You could scarcely find anyone who knew her to criticize her. For that reason, her unexpected death brought grief to many an acquaintance but especially to her husband left with three children." Thanking friends, relatives, and acquaintances for their condolences, her husband, Joseph, closed with the words, "I am left in the deepest grief."[10]

Even with the assistance of the State Guard and teachers, the Emergency Hospital was seriously understaffed, and calls went out to the community-at-large for additional assistance. "It is horrifying, terrible, down there," volunteer Nellie Shumaker wrote in her diary. "Mostly foreigners and so sick." Eventually a Girl Scout was allowed to assist in the women's ward. "Before the day was over, I was feeding patients, rushing bed pans, placing ice bags on fevered heads and obeying the nurses," she recalled. "Late that afternoon I was holding the head of a very sick young woman who was vomiting up a vile black liquid. She turned blue, slumped over my arm and was dead." The young girl quickly learned there was little that could be done for the sufferers; even the physician in charge of the women's ward admitted that if the flu turned into pneumonia, "there was little hope of saving them."[11]

During the peak weeks of the epidemic, sixty-five Norwood residents were interred in town. In the two weeks between October 1 and October 14, there were more than fifty burials. People recalled the seemingly endless stream of undertakers' vehicles rolling along the streets. One resident who came down with the flu remembered her convalescence spent in part watching out the front window of her home as funeral cortege after funeral cortege passed into the nearby cemetery.

Norwood has two cemeteries, both owned and managed by the town. Old Parish Cemetery was established in 1741 when the area was a homogeneous settlement of Congregationalists. In 1880, eight years after the village was incorporated as Norwood, Highland Cemetery on Winter Street was created. It was designed to have a wide, tree-lined avenue leading up to a gracefully shaped and carefully plotted central configuration. As historians have noted, many American towns used cemeteries to further institutionalize existing hierarchies. Winding paths, trees and shrubbery, and the shape and size of family plots were all a purposeful manifestation of social class status and privilege for those who could afford it. Norwood's Highland Cemetery was originally designed to be just such a burying ground. The large lots at the crest of the hill sold quickly to wealthy families who installed impressive memorials to their ancestors and themselves.

Many of those who came to Norwood to work at the ink mill, the tanneries, and the printing companies were immigrants; some of these were Roman Catholic, others had no religion. Until the founding of Highland, Catholics were usually interred in the archdiocesan-owned land of St. Mary's Cemetery in the nearby town of Canton. With an abundance of land now available, Norwood officials wanted Catholic residents to use the town cemetery as well. In the late 1880s, a "Catholic section" was laid out and Catholics began to bury their family members there.

On the outer edge of cemetery land, a section of single graves was designated for Roman Catholics as well. The main entrance, chapel, and central circular drive could not be seen from this location which was obviously intended for more marginal town residents. In addition to the Catholic section, another group of single graves, available for people who were neither Protestant nor Catholic, was allotted at the base of an extremely steep hill behind the main Protestant burial ground. Later, a strip of land on the outskirts of the Roman Catholic single graves section was set aside as the "Catholic Free Lot," an area for the destitute to be buried. There were no markers here. It was a cold and distant place at the far side of the cemetery.

Of the sixty-four flu victims buried in Highland Cemetery (one was buried in a family plot in the Old Parish Cemetery), forty-seven were interred in single graves and three in the Catholic Free Lot. Row after row at the edge of the cemetery quickly filled up: children, men, women, side by side—six on October 5, five on the seventh, six on the eighth, seven on the eleventh—and multiple burials every day for the first two weeks of October.

As the small gravestones appeared, an interesting phenomenon occurred, one that made it difficult to preserve the memory of the victims. The names engraved on the tombstones were different in spelling from those appearing on official death certificates, in newspaper accounts, and in cemetery records. For example, Monica Kiarshis in the Annual Town Report was Monica Karshis in cemetery records and Monika Kiarsienie on her gravestone. Theofila Pakarklis was transformed into Jofile Parkarlis in the cemetery records and to Teofila Parklis on her grave. Sixteen victims, including three interred in the Catholic Free Lot, had no markers at all, confirmation of their low social status and dire economic circumstances. Among those was the Cattarino family, who seemingly had no one to see to their affairs. The child Nojar Cattarino, perhaps at the request of his mother Rosa, was buried on top of his father, Romeo. When Rosa herself was buried twelve days later, she was identified as Rosa Catalina and interred in a single grave some distance away.

The social status of influenza victims in America was often overlooked by later scholars trying to explain why the epidemic did not immediately find a place in the country's social memory. Alfred Crosby, one of the first historians of the epidemic, conjectured that "if the pandemic had killed one or more of the really famous figures of the nation or the world it would have been remembered." But this epidemic "characteristically killed young adults and therefore rarely men in positions of great authority." The remarks of another scholar echo this notion of unimportance: "Despite being the largest epidemic in history, it had little long-term effect," wrote Robert Swenson, "because...the population losses were rapidly replaced."[12]

The haphazard and inconsistent spelling of names in Norwood records, as well the large number in single graves and the free lot who had no grave markers, is a confirmation of these sentiments. This epidemic did not claim many of the wealthy; it had the greatest impact on the poor in the Swedeville, Dublin, Cork City, and South Norwood neighborhoods. The disrespect and disdain implied by the location of graves and carelessness of spelling was recognized by those left behind. When asked where influenza victims were interred at Highland, one resident, who had lost a family member to the epidemic, replied with anger, "On the far side along by the road to the dump. They're all buried together. They're really cheap stones and a lot of the names are misspelled. You go look at them. The farthest right of the cemetery. Up against the dump fence."

Yet Crosby also notes that "if one turns to intimate accounts, to autobiographies of those who were not in positions of authority, to collections of letters written by friend to friend and husband to wife in the fall of 1918, and, especially, if one asks those who lived through the pandemic for their reminiscences, then it becomes apparent that Americans did notice, ...that they remember the pandemic quite clearly and often acknowledge it as one of the most influential experiences of their lives."[13] The sharpness of these memories leads one to ask who writes history and whose experiences count in crafting national memory.

"Nations do not remember spontaneously and collectively," one analysis of social memory explains. "The bearers of national memory are the upper middle classes and the intelligentsia." Social memories are created by the privileged and reinforced over time; eventually they become embedded in the collective consciousness of a nation. Those living on the margins of a culture or a community do not have access to these memory-makers. Consequently, their stories are often omitted in the creation of a history.[14] There is little doubt that the impact of the 1918 epidemic was felt most by those with the least access to the authoritative written word: poor military conscripts, Native Americans, laborers, and immigrants. Thus, they were too marginalized for their experiences to earn a place in America's collective memory. That is, perhaps, why there is no large body of literature or art to commemorate this tragic event.

Sensing that the crisis had passed, the Committee decided that public gatherings might resume on Saturday, October 19, at 6:00 p.m. and that churches could be reopened the following day. The Winslow School emergency nursery was closed on Monday, October 21. The School Committee postponed the reopening of schools until October 28 to allow time for fumigation. Still, the week ending October 19 brought nine deaths, including a husband and wife, Nan and Thomas Holm, whose passing left two children orphaned. They were the third married couple to succumb: Romeo and Rosa Cattarino (along with their son, Nojar) and Catherine and Richard Ryan preceded them. The Ryans had resided in the Cork City neighborhood with their two small children. Catherine had passed away on October 4 and her husband on October 6. Richard Ryan had been a member of the Ancient Order of Hibernians and was employed as a painter at the Readville Car Shops, an early site of contagion. The Ryans were buried in a joint service with the *Messenger* noting that "much sympathy is felt for the little ones now bereaved of both parents."[15] This last full week of crisis also took three of the youngest victims: two boys, a newborn (eight days old) and a six-month old baby from South Norwood, and a two-year-old girl from Swedeville.

The *Norwood Messenger* ran a general review of the epidemic on Saturday, October 19, giving special notice to the "combined speed of preparation, remarkable cooperation and effective management" shown by the Epidemic Committee. For the first time, the newspaper acknowledged that the number of volunteers had not been "forthcoming," a failure which had precipitated the request for assistance from the State Guard. It is not known whether the lack of willing volunteers stemmed from a fear of contracting the disease or disdain for those residents—"mostly foreigners" as Nellie Shumaker had put it—who were stricken.[16]

On October 22, all special epidemic regulations except those regarding quarantine were lifted. At 6:00 p.m. on Wednesday, October 23, the Emergency Hospital closed its doors with the final eight patients transferred to an isolation ward on the third floor of the Norwood Hospital. The Civic was fumigated. To the members of the committee and most uptown residents, the epidemic had been a test of their management skills and organizational aptitude. It had not been so much a personal dilemma as a logistical one, and they were very pleased with their performance.

The fall wave of the epidemic ended on October 27 with the death of Marie Mike, age thirty, a Syrian-born mother of two who had resided in South Norwood. Of the Norwood resident deaths, 66.7% were foreign-born adults, 22.2% were U.S.-born adults, and 11.1% were underage children of immigrants. No children of U.S.-

born citizens died of influenza. The ethnic populations hit the hardest were the Poles, Lithuanians, Italians, and Irish. Over half of the deaths occurred in South Norwood, with Dublin, Cork City, and Swedeville following behind. October 1 through October 12 was the deadliest time period, with fifty-eight residents dying during those twelve days. The incidence of influenza deaths traced a normal curve beginning on September 19, peaking in mid-October and trailing off by the end of the month. The age of the victims also followed the nation-wide indicators unique to the 1918 epidemic: there were fifty-seven deaths in the twenty to thirty-nine-year age bracket.

In December and January, influenza returned. On December 21, the *Messenger* noted that from the beginning of the month twenty-seven cases had been reported, and there had been five deaths. Many people remained absent from work. On December 28, the newspaper acknowledged 150 new cases. By January 4 there were eight deaths and 280 diagnosed cases of influenza. Still, the relatively small number of cases led the Epidemic Committee to decide that reopening the Emergency Hospital was not warranted. As a precaution, public gatherings were banned from January 4 through January 15. The Board of Health requested that funeral attendance be restricted to close relatives only. By January 11, 1919, the influenza situation was clearing up. The Board of Health estimated 389 cases since the end of November, with about 130 active cases left. By January 18, only six cases required daily attendance by a physician. Norwood had weathered the final phase of the Great Epidemic.

The civic response to the 1918 epidemic in Norwood, Massachusetts, was a strikingly modern framework made up of an Epidemic Committee, a rapidly deployed police command, and an overall centralized authority. Because of their refusal to engage local ethnic communities and their social support systems to combat the contagion, many lives that probably could have been saved were lost. In any epidemic event, those most at risk must trust governmental and medical professionals, be educated about the risks and about which interventions are effective. Above all, they must feel supported and safe. In retrospect, the events that took place in Norwood in 1918 help us understand how a global disaster effects a local community. Should another pandemic occur, one can hope that this awareness will result in policies and practices that are prudent, humane, and just.

Postscript: Lessons Learned?

In 2020, a little more than a century after the above-described events, the world again faced a pandemic, this one a novel coronavirus. How did Norwood fare? Despite being blindsided by an early exposure among town officials and serious outbreaks in a nursing home and a long-term care hospital—facilities that did not exist in 1918—which took dozens of lives, Norwood's response overall was inclusive, nonjudgmental, and supportive. Volunteers stepped up to make masks, raise funds and gather supplies for the community's food pantry, and provide meals for food-insecure families. Others supplied funds for restaurants to prepare meals for first responders and hospital employees, a program that assisted eating establishments badly in need of support.

On the medical side, the Norwood Hospital, now part of the for-profit Steward Healthcare System, continued to serve the community with testing and outpatient and in-patient care, until a devastating June 2020 storm caused its closure. Meanwhile, Moderna, a Massachusetts-based biotechnology company with a research and manufacturing facility in Norwood, developed a Covid-19 vaccine. It was given emergency approval by the FDA in December 2020 and distribution began shortly thereafter.

Unlike the *Messenger* in 1918, the local media, both print and cable, informed the public about all aspects of the epidemic. The Town of Norwood website and social media pages posted updated information for residents, and a Citizen Information Center telephone line was made available. Grants were offered to local businesses to help them through the crisis. Through creativity and determination, the school department, the public library and the senior center continued to provide instruction to students, as well as programming and assistance to the community-at-large. Most significantly, the Health Department coordinated outreach, testing, and tracing programs in addition to disseminating accurate, up-to-date public service announcements and press releases. Nonetheless, Norwood was hit hard. The town manager explained the high incidence of cases was due, at least in part, to the number of nursing homes and assisted living facilities in town, the density of the town's population, and pockets of residents in the lower socio-economic brackets.

Throughout the United States, as in 1918, residents of low-income, overcrowded neighborhoods contracted the virus at higher rates and were more likely to be hospitalized and die. Once again, these populations lived and worked in more hazardous environments, had less access to medical care, were more likely to be food-insecure, and yet were deemed "essential workers." Like a century before, marginalized people suffered the most. Former U. S. Health and Human Services secretary Mike Leavitt once stated, "By their nature, pandemics happen across the globe—but their effects are excruciatingly local."[17] The civic response to the 1918 epidemic may have failed the ethnic communities of Norwood, but not so in 2020. This time, deeply saddened by the loss of life, the town made every effort to provide care and support to all its residents.

Sources and Notes

Most of the material in this account came from Town of Norwood Annual Reports; Minutes of the Special Committee on the Epidemic Situation, typescript, Norwood Historical Society (NHS) archives; Jean Stewart Bower, "How One Small Town Saved Its People," a 14-page typescript, 1977, NHS archives; and interviews with residents conducted 1993-1994. Because several interviewees did not wish to be identified by name, none have been so identified. Transcripts of interviews have been retained.

1. "Epidemic Strikes Norwood," *Norwood Messenger* (hereafter identified as *NM*), 5 October 1918, p. 2.
2. Bower, p. 10.
3. "Epidemic Strikes Norwood," p. 3.
4. Thomas Cullinane, typescript memoir, NHS archives.

5. "Death of Bonaventura Bagnato," *NM*, 12 October 1918, p. 2.

6. "Correspondence from Norwood," *Keleivis*, 16 October 1918, p. 3. Translation by Rev. William Wolkovich.

7. Aira Johnson, correspondence with author.

8. "The Willow," in "Correspondence from Norwood," *Keleivis*, 16 October 1918, p. 3. Translation by Rev. William Wolkovich.

9. "Epidemic Fought to a Standstill," *NM*, 12 October 1918, p. 2.

10. J., "Correspondence from Norwood," *Keleivis*, 23 October 1918, p. 3. Translation by Rev. William Wolkovich.

11. Dorothy Shumaker Diaries, NHS archives; Bower, pp. 11-12.

12. Alfred Crosby, *Epidemic and Peace, 1918*, (Westport, CT: Greenwood Press, 1976), p. 322; Robert M. Swenson, "Plagues, History, and AIDS," *American Scholar* 57 (spring 1988), p. 186.

13. Crosby, p. 323.

14. James Fentress and Chris Wickham, *Social Memory* (Cambridge, MA: Blackwell, 1992), p. 127; Geoffrey H. Harman, "Public Memory and Modern Experience," *Yale Journal of Criticism* 6 (1991), p. 242.

15. "Funeral of Mr. and Mrs. Ryan," *NM*, 12 October 1918, p. 1.

16. "Norwood Death Toll Over 100," *NM*, 19 October 1918, p. 3.

17. Mike Leavitt, quoted in news release, "NGA Launches Major State Pandemic Preparedness Project," 1 October 2006.

Chapter 9

Norwood by Design

THE ROOTS OF CITY PLANNING in America emerged at the end of the Civil War when reformers known as "sanitarians" advocated for drastic changes to the physical environment. They sought to raze overcrowded, often rat-infested tenements and replace them with complexes that provided not only clean housing (with running water and public sewage systems) but also conveniently situated outdoor spaces for leisure and exercise. At about the same time, the new field of landscape architecture, led by Frederick Law Olmsted, was attempting to take patches of vacant property and marshes and convert them into urban gardens and parks for public use.

Sanitarians quickly gave way to the "City Beautiful" movement. Founded in England as a public health initiative, it was brought to the United States at the turn of the twentieth century. Proponents sought to provide cities with adequate housing, clean air, safe streets, and a landscape dotted with open spaces, all in an effort to foster an appreciation of nature. In retrospect, however, there was often more social control than social reform built into their designs, since planners promised not only civic beauty but the management of urban centers through efficient municipal services.

In fact, by 1910, the "City Beautiful" essentially became the "City Efficient." That was the year that Frederick Law Olmsted, Jr. who, along with his brother, had taken over his father's firm, urged the audience at a National Conference on City Planning to replace any social reform interests they might have with scientific detachment and pragmatism. As one historian observed, to Olmsted, Jr., "The importance of city planning was its use as a tool for efficient long-range municipal management rather than for the advocacy of reform nostrums."[1] Such a view was in keeping with the beliefs of one local man who envisioned a model New England town with low taxes, a smoothly functioning municipal government, a well-ordered landscape, attractive housing, public services, and plentiful recreational sites and facilities. That man was George F. Willett.

George Franklin Willett casts a long shadow across Norwood's history. And with good reason. Born on August 7, 1870 in nearby Walpole, where his ancestors had settled some 200 years earlier, Willett graduated from high school in 1887 and went on to study industrial chemistry at Boston University. He took additional courses at the Massachusetts Institute of Technology, which was then located in the Back Bay. Impatient with academic work and eager to apply his theories about business in the real world, he left college in the fall of 1890. A chance encounter with Francis O. Winslow, owner of the Winslow Brothers tannery in Norwood, led Willett to enter the wool business in 1891. Within two years, this driven, exceptionally intelligent, and charismatic young man was offered a partnership in the Winslow Brothers tannery. He declined, but by 1897 he had gained control of both the Winslow tannery and Lyman Smith's Sons, Norwood's other tanning factory, and had united them into one corporation, Winslow Brothers and Smith. He had also married F. O. Winslow's daughter, Edith, and built a mansion next to his father-in-law's on Walpole Street. By 1900, George Willett, not quite thirty, was a millionaire.

Willett formed an industrial holding company with Edmund H. Sears and successfully managed businesses in the wool-, felt- and rubber-processing industries. As his business empire grew, he turned his attention, ingenuity, and keen business instincts toward his adopted home. According to Willett, at this point in time, Norwood was "a little dried-up seedy village, homely, inconveniently laid out and miles behind the modern procession."[2] With a population of approximately 5,500 in 1900, the community, which had become an independent town only a quarter-century earlier, did indeed have its problems. Although it had one of the highest property tax rates in the state, there were few public services, only ill-repaired school houses, few recreational areas, no all-inclusive civic organizations or health care facilities, and a

This portrait of George F. Willett hangs in the
Norwood Civic Center on Nahatan Street. *(Photo by Author)*

notably inefficient municipal government. The man from Walpole was
determined to change all that.

With an all-encompassing vision, unmatched brilliance, and a near
messianic zeal, George Willett sought to reform and remake the town.
Often described as a distracted genius whose mind raced from one
complex scheme to another, Willett's arguments overpowered any
audience—whether of one or many—by the force of his personality
and the magnitude of his ideas. George Willett did not simply think
"big;" he thought on a gargantuan scale, the likes of which the residents
and officials of Norwood had never seen. Before he was through,
Willett had pushed, cajoled, harangued, and harassed the majority
of townspeople into believing his dreams were attainable: a low tax
rate, municipal reform, a local bank to serve the community's needs,
a housing association to build homes, a public hospital, and a civic
association dedicated to citizenship and healthful recreation. And he
accomplished much of it!

Willett's ultimate plan went even further, however; he promised
a total physical refashioning of the town. The Norwood that George
Willett envisioned would encompass a revamped downtown business

district, a network of boulevards and parkways that would make destinations from Boston to Cape Cod easily accessible, a system of parks, playgrounds, and fields that would enhance the community, a carefully designed zoning by-law, and a residential development he came to call Westover.

In April of 1912, with the backing of the Norwood Business Association and Board of Trade, Norwood's town meeting approved the formation of its first Planning Committee. Only the second such board established in Massachusetts, the committee's duties were to advise the town on planning matters, make a comprehensive study of Norwood's existing land and buildings, and develop an overall plan for the future. Not surprisingly, this was the brainchild of George Willett, who was appointed to the committee, along with Walter J. Berwick, Francis J. Foley, Patrick J. Lydon, and Mahlon R. Perry.[3] Willett was immediately elected chairman, a post he held for twelve years. Under the auspices of this group—which did not become an official Planning Board until 1918—Willett eventually produced and proposed Norwood's first ever master plan. To that end, shortly after his appointment to this Planning Committee, Willett contracted the services of noted landscape architect and town planner, Arthur A. Shurcliff.[4]

Shurcliff was born and lived most of his life on Beacon Hill in Boston, although he preferred less urban environments and spent his summers in rural New England. From a young age he enjoyed woodworking and craftsmanship. He took courses in carving and design while in high school, and metalwork while attending M.I.T. Graduating from that institution with a degree in engineering, he had already set his sights on a career in landscape architecture. In 1894 Shurcliff interviewed with the pioneer in the field, Frederick Law Olmsted, but it was Olmsted's partner, Charles Eliot, who suggested the young man enroll in classes at Harvard to augment his engineering degree with a familiarity in the fine arts and horticulture. Two years later, Shurcliff joined Olmsted's firm which, by that time, was being run by both Eliot and Olmsted's two sons, Frederick, Jr. and John Charles. Shurcliff became a close friend and protégé of Charles Eliot, and was devastated when his mentor died at thirty-seven years of age of meningitis in 1897.

Although the Olmsted sons were not as visionary or talented as either their father or Eliot, Shurcliff remained with the firm and even helped Frederick, Jr. establish a landscape architecture program at Harvard. When he set up his own practice in 1904, this congenial and collaborative relationship continued. During his career Shurcliff reshaped the public landscape of Boston by creating the Charles River Esplanade. He went on to design the gardens of Williamsburg, Virginia, as well as the landscape surrounding the Quabbin Reservoir in Massachusetts. In addition, as a town planner, a designation he began using in 1904, Arthur Shurcliff consulted on, or developed designs for, over two dozen Boston area cities and towns, including Norwood.

A student of history, Shurcliff had a profound appreciation for the cultural landscapes and historic places of Massachusetts, an appreciation that influenced his approach to planning. As the modern age arrived, however, his engineering background enabled him to balance landscape preservation with highway planning. Better than most, Shurcliff successfully "adapted the 19th century profession of landscape architecture to the new realities of sprawling metropolitan regions, changing urban demographics, and the rise of the automobile."[5]

Shurcliff's ability to visualize and articulate not only green space but also highway design was rather ironic given the fact that he never learned to drive. The planner always lived within walking distance of his office and would bicycle to and from the train station if he needed to visit the suburbs. Infrequently, and reluctantly, he was sometimes forced to use a taxi, hire a driver, or ride with a client. There is no record of his riding with George Willett during the ten years he studied and surveyed Norwood, but if he had, it would have been a harrowing experience for the quiet, understated Shurcliff. The constantly distracted Willett was known for his erratic handling of cars; one associate recalled an occasion when Willett was so occupied in conversation that he drove right through the plate glass window of the Sears store in Copley Square.

In 1913, shortly after he began working with Shurcliff, George Willett delineated a few of his thoughts on Norwood at a meeting of the Board of Trade. He had been an early proponent of Progressivism and the belief that rational business practices were the answer to social problems. He even published a pamphlet titled "Can Business Methods be Applied to the Conduct of Municipal Affairs?" and spoke on this philosophy at venues across the country. Although Progressives did not think, as many did, that the poor were simply unfit, they did claim to know what was best for the disadvantaged. They also felt that their beliefs justified their control of social and economic institutions for the good of all, a paternalistic oppression at best. Even Willett's initial presentation reflected this conceit. As always, his scheme was grand. He envisioned Norwood as a bedroom community for businessmen who would travel via automobile (not streetcar or train) to professional positions in Boston. His aim was to attract these middle- and upper-middle-class residents by creating gracefully winding tree-lined streets for single family houses in developments dotted with parks, playgrounds, and neighborhood schools.

As he was formulating his intentions, Willett had already purchased both open land and developed parcels in residential and business districts throughout town and intended to sell— hopefully through the Housing Association—his acreage to developers willing to implement his vision of a parkway system of prosperity. He was vehemently opposed to allowing more multi-family homes to be built, especially the kind that covered most of South Norwood. Calling these domiciles, which often housed extended families as well as boarders, "objectionable structures," Willett vowed "to stop the three-deckers dead at the railroad underpass" that led from "the Flats" up Washington Street to the town center.[6]

Although not part of this 1913 presentation, Willett's plans for the town's central commercial district were already unfolding. He imagined a dedicated, centralized retail district, a "traditional" town common or square, and an impressive municipal building, believing that these structural changes would attract new residents whose tax dollars would, in turn, pay for future improvements. Willett's aim was to make Norwood "so beautiful and attractive that it would come to be recognized throughout Metropolitan Boston as a suburb which offered unusual attractions as a place in which to live and bring up one's family."[7]

The transformation of downtown Norwood had begun earlier with the Conger Block (1895) (Washington Street at Railroad Avenue) and the Hawkins Block (1899) (at Washington and Hoyle), which were built by the turn of the century. Shortly thereafter, the Norwood Associates Block (1903), the Fisher Block (1907), and the Sanborn Block (1907) went up along Washington Street. Meanwhile, "The Hook," long the spot that marked the town center, disappeared when Willett bought and moved the aging Village Hall and Tiot Tavern buildings. Market Street and Cemetery Street (which had been the route to the Old Cemetery), with their ragtag assemblage of wooden shacks and stores, were wiped from the map. Central Street was straightened and extended parallel to Washington, a configuration that would allow for a new town common and municipal building as well as additional tracts for development.

On the west side of Washington Street stood the former homes of Joseph Day, Joel Baker, Lyman Smith, and L. W. Bigelow, impeccable residences built by the community's leading merchants and manufacturers of the mid-nineteenth century. As town historian Win Everett remembered them, "They were pure white with green blinds and set high on sharply banked lawns. Under the thick shade of the Washington Street maple trees, they gave "The Hook" an atmosphere of solid wealth and respectability."[8] The quartet of houses were the pride of the quaint nineteenth century village, but, to Willett, they were an anachronistic reminder of the past. To make way for a widened, paved main street and new two- and three-story commercial blocks, these once impressive homes were relocated onto side streets.

Throughout the 1910s, substantial commercial buildings rose on both sides of Washington Street, until eventually the First Baptist Church stood alone surrounded by business blocks. Between 1910 and the start of the Great War, for example, the Premier Theater (1911), the Talbot Block (1912), the Odd Fellows Building (1913), the Callahan Building (1914), the Long Block (1915), the National Bank Building (1916), and the Folan Block (1916) appeared, and Willett's plan for a modern retail district became a reality. By this time, while Arthur Shurcliff was translating Willett's fever dreams into an all-encompassing plan for Norwood's overall development, George Willett had found another ally, local architect William G. Upham.

Raised in Norwood, which had been incorporated only eight years prior to his birth, William Gilbert Upham completed high school with the class of 1899. During his graduation exercises, held in Village Hall, he was part of a debate on the question "Should the United States Own the Railroads?" Upham took the negative stance while classmate Fred James Kiley spoke in the affirmative.[9] There is no record of who won over the audience. Upham's father, George, and his mother, Anna Maria Pratt Upham, both had roots in New England going back to the seventeenth century, a family lineage that no doubt piqued his interest in history and genealogy. Eventually Upham served as president of both the Norwood Historical Society and the Upham Family Society. During his tenure in the latter role, he supervised the restoration of the society's headquarters at the Phineas Upham House in Melrose. Long before he embraced these volunteer positions, however, this son of Norwood was an earnest, hard-working young man seeking a career.

George Upham had been a blacksmith and later a machinist at the American Tool and Machine Work Company in Hyde Park. On the occasion of George and Anna's Golden Wedding Anniversary in 1923, it was noted that George Upham still rose each morning and commuted to his job at the age of seventy-five.[10] But William did not follow in his father's footsteps. An early interest in drawing—likely passed on to him by his grandfather, Elias Pratt—led him to take a position as a draftsman and enroll as one of the first students in Harvard's School of Architecture. For a time, he worked for Clarence H. Blackall, known for designing the Copley Plaza Hotel, several theater buildings, including the Colonial and the Wilbur, and, according to historian Walter Muir Whitehill, the first apartment house in any city along the east coast. Blackall also reportedly built the first steel-framed structure in the city of Boston.

In 1912, while still working for Blackall, Upham designed the new headquarters of Norwood's Independent Order of Odd Fellows. This local fraternal organization had been founded in 1886 and had met at various locations, most recently in the Tiot Tavern, one of the anchors

Norwood native William Upham was the architect of many
public and commercial buildings in Norwood.
(Courtesy of Nancy Bailey)

of "the Hook." Upham designed an impressive three-story Classical
Revival building of yellow brick, finished with a limestone façade and
granite trim. There were storefronts on the street level, while portions
of the second and third floors held meeting rooms and a banquet hall.
A two-story ceremonial lodge room completed the structure.

In 1914, just as he was completing the design of the three-story
Callahan Building at 726 Washington Street, which housed both the F.
W. Woolworth 5 & 10 Cents Store and Callahan's Norwood Furniture
Company, Upham officially registered as an architect. A few years
later, however, when he signed up for the draft, he was employed
by Stone and Webster, an engineering and construction company
in Boston. For most of the next ten years Upham concentrated on
the construction and renovation of private homes in Norwood and
adjacent communities, with the exception of commissions to design
masonic temples in Providence and East Providence, Rhode Island,
and Waltham and Norwood in Massachusetts.

Located on Day Street, one block up from the center, the temple
was the first built solely for Norwood's Orient Lodge of Free and
Accepted Masons, which had been organized in 1861. The group had

met in Village Hall until 1915, when George Willett purchased that building as part of his downtown modernization effort. They then convened in the Conger Block's hall until the new temple was fully constructed in 1918. Still in use, the building is made of Harvard brick with Indiana limestone used for both the trim and the two Greek Ionic columns at its entrance.

William Upham was a member of the Orient Lodge and Norwood's Board of Trade, and he was appointed to the Town Affairs Committee of that Board in 1915. His participation in these organizations brought him into a close acquaintance with George Willett, since Willett was also a member of both groups. Willett and Upham naturally became good friends, as they shared a dedication to Norwood and a determination to make the town into, as Willett put it, "the biggest, busiest, and best suburban municipality in New England."[11] When Norwood's Planning Committee became an official town board in 1918, George Willett was elected for the first time by his fellow citizens, and he continued as chair. William Upham was a successful candidate to the Planning Board in 1920. Together these two men, along with Arthur Shurcliff, developed, designed, and presented to the community its first ever comprehensive town plan.

Willett had faced his share of setbacks as he sought to re-create Norwood. Although his municipal reform—tax restructuring and new system of government—was successful, he had already run into resistance over his notions about residential development and building codes. In April of 1913, at a Norwood Business Association and Board of Trade meeting, Massachusetts Civic League member Elmer S. Forbes had warned of the dangers inherent in the proliferation of three-deckers. Emphasizing that such houses were often shoddily built, he also criticized not just the developers but the residents: "Those from parts of Southern Europe and Asia, with their disregard of sanitary regulations, have produced conditions which are bad and growing worse.... Such tenants as occupy [these] poor houses will cost you more for schools, for police, and fire protection."[12] Willett shared Forbes' opinions and had attempted to stop the construction of these triple-deckers at that time, but after a public hearing on the matter nothing had been resolved.

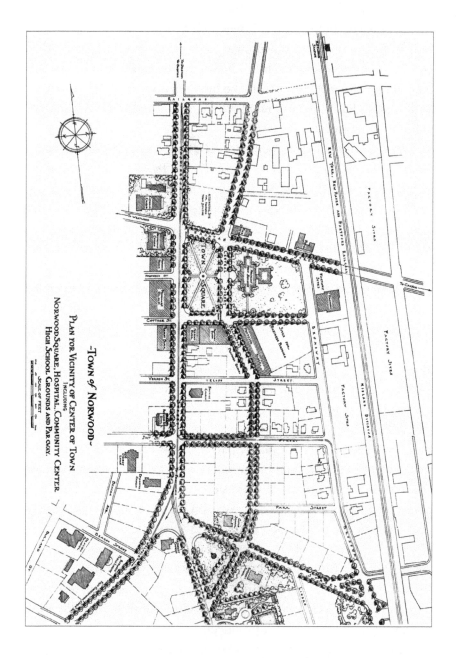

Arthur Shurcliff's 1923 drawing of a proposed town common for Norwood was
included in Willett's Master Plan. The depiction has the town hall
located where the Norwood Theatre was later built.

Other elements of Willett's ambitious plans had met opposition as well. By 1918, with the United States now at war, anti-immigrant sentiment was on the rise, and the country was beginning to look inward. As a result, Willett's singular civic aspirations were no longer popular. Even worse, after spending the early part of 1918 in Washington, D.C., he returned to find his financial affairs in jeopardy. By September, he had lost control of the Norwood Housing Association, the main source of funding for the hospital and civic. At a public meeting, over Willett's objections, town officials and businessmen convinced those in attendance to separate the housing association, hospital, and civic, essentially dismantling Willett's dream. As one local historian put it, "If Willett still believed that his vision for Norwood had the support of the Board of Trade and town officials, this meeting put an end to such illusions."[13] The Norwood Hospital was incorporated as an independent entity in 1919 and, although Willett managed to salvage the Civic Association, the organization was never the same. It remained in debt throughout the 1920s and, following a string of destructive fires, Willett finally sold the property to the town in 1930.

The entrepreneur and industrialist retained his enthusiasm for town planning, however. Willett, like Shurcliff, believed that the automobile would become the preferred method of transportation, especially among the middle- and upper-classes, the constituency he wanted to attract to Norwood. The two men were prescient. Most early city planners did not comprehend the impact cars would eventually have, and thus failed to incorporate the need for vehicular traffic into their proposals. But, for Willett, improving the condition and layout of the town's roads was vital.

Until 1915, even Washington Street was a dirt road. Uneven, potholed, and muddy after a rain, it had trolley tracks running down its center. That year, after Willett razed dilapidated buildings situated on inconvenient lots, Washington Street was broadened and paved, just in time for the proliferation of concrete and brick business blocks to continue. Finally, Willett insisted a town square and municipal building should be created, one that was impressive enough to complement this new modern commercial district. By the end of 1922, he was prepared to unveil his grand plan for Norwood.

George Willett personally financed the publication of the forty page "Report of the Planning Board to the Citizens of the Town," which was supplemented by maps and drawings. In an introductory essay, Willett emphasized that this was a "scientific" and "intelligent" plan for the development of Norwood, as well as an egalitarian one. Pointing out that "Formerly, places of beauty were owned entirely by a few wealthy persons in the community," with the general public allowed to enjoy them only "on gala occasions," Willett assured the townspeople that under this plan, "Parks, playgrounds, and advantages of this sort, together with good streets, are now looked upon as essential to the normal, healthy growth of every community" and "it is agreed that these improvements must belong to the people." After outlining the history of the Planning Board and a few key points in the plan, and thanking all those involved, he urged Norwood's residents to give the proposal "thoughtful attention."[14]

Arthur A. Shurcliff wrote the bulk of the report, which explained historical population and tax valuation increases, descriptions of existing roadways and recommendations for new through and diagonal streets, and an elaborate system of open space and recreational fields. There were detailed proposals for improvements of the streets surrounding the railroad station, and the development of the Lenox, Nahatan, Monroe Street district that included a community playground and park. Shurcliff also included recommendations on ways to ameliorate the junction of street, railroad, and trolley tracks at the High Bridge at the intersection of Washington and Prospect Streets.

Perhaps most importantly, Shurcliff observed that, at this point in time, although Washington Street had ample width, paving, and lighting, the center of town "lacks a square which would distinguish it from other area communities."[15] He included a bird's-eye-view drawing of his proposed town square design. It was the centerpiece of the proposal, and the only part of the plan that came close to implementation. The tree-lined parkways, boulevards, and elaborate parks and playground system were never constructed.

After being met by a less than enthusiastic response to his grand scheme, George Willett resigned from the Planning Board at the close of 1923. William Upham replaced him as chair and led the defense of both the Town Plan and the even more contentious debate about Zoning Regulations.

The first comprehensive zoning ordinance in the United States was developed for New York City in 1916 and it sought to delineate specific areas for housing, commerce, industry and leisure. Such designations were designed to enable a community to take shape in a calculated, rather than a random, manner. Initially, townscapes had grown informally and, until 1910, Norwood had both benefited and suffered from this lack of overall planning.

Originally an outlying village within Dedham, industries, such as tanning and milling, had arrived first, and since they required power and a means of transportation for their goods, they tended to be located along the waters of the Hawes Brook and Neponset River. They were soon joined by the ink mill, which did the same. Before long, an informal village center emerged. A tavern was built at a crossroads convenient to travelers, followed a few years later by the addition of a blacksmith shop and dry goods store. Homes were located on widely separated agricultural and dairy farms. Eventually, houses filled in the gaps in areas convenient for laborers to walk to the factories until, by the first decade of the twentieth century, an upsurge in immigration led developers to erect streets of triple-deckers on what had once been flat farmland in the southeast part of town. Meanwhile, successful factory owners built expansive estates in the southwestern district. None of this happened with any design in mind. The industrial plants had been lucrative for the community, but the influx of workers needing shelter had resulted in a hastily-built, unplanned neighborhood. The Planning Board now wanted to impose a method and purpose to any future development.

"The aim of zoning," according to John P. Fox, a professional consultant to the Planning Board, "is not to restrict buildings, but rather to get the right buildings in the right place." Factories required enough land for expansion without encroaching on neighborhoods, retail businesses should be concentrated together in order to succeed, and areas for single-family, two-family, and tenement (anything over two-family) housing would be better off in distinctive geographical areas as well. Fox's "Draft of Zoning By-Laws" within Willett's overall Town Plan, detailed the establishment of districts, their use-regulations, construction regulations, and general provisions.[16]

When this Zoning By-Law proposal was brought before the Town Meeting in May of 1925, after a year of discussion, the debate—at an extraordinarily well-attended town meeting—primarily pitted George Willett and the town's wealthier citizens against a coalition of working-class residents led by Martin F. Lydon of Railroad Avenue. The plan, Willett stated, would restrict large open tracts of land, mostly on the west side of town (near a proposed golf course), for single-family housing only. Lydon voiced the opinion that such a development would be out of reach to the working man and his family, who could only afford to live in an apartment or a two- or three-family home. And, Lydon concluded, "I don't want to see a law adopted that will make it any harder for these people."[17] This initial Zoning By-Law was soundly defeated. A year later, a second zoning plan that made almost all housing districts "general residential" instead of "single-family," again failed to pass. A third proposal was finally approved in May of 1927. These new zoning regulations, as one writer summarized, "served to reinforce many of the neighborhood divisions that had existed for more than two decades: the immigrants [would live] near factories in South Norwood, the Irish in two-family and small single-family homes, [and] the wealthy in single-family areas."[18]

George Willett's goal of turning Norwood into a model community virtually ended with the rejection of his initial 1923 Master Plan. Although he tried repeatedly to build Westover—a 1934 brochure advertised "the planning and building of a complete village of small estates, where every home shall have a perfect setting and a protected privacy, in harmonious and artistic surroundings,"—his development never became reality.[19] Additionally, there were acrimonious exchanges between Willett and the town throughout the 1930s and beyond; they clashed over the development of Westover, the use of Willett Pond, and the site of a new town yard, among other things. And while the legend of George Willett continued to grow, he was never again as influential as he had previously been.

Willett is, however, still recognized as Norwood's greatest benefactor, one who poured his personal fortune into an attempt to better the community. He is rightfully credited with creating the Civic, bringing a health center to the public, essentially remaking the downtown business district, and envisioning the town square and municipal building. In 1969, a few years after his death, an elementary school was dedicated in his memory and his portrait hangs in the Willett Room of today's Civic Center.

Although Arthur A. Shurcliff completed his most noteworthy commissions elsewhere, he was consulted on the development of Charles W. Eliot Park, behind the Balch School, in 1924, supervised the landscaping at Shattuck Park in 1927, and was employed to make preliminary plans for the development of "White Mike's Field" (the area surrounding Father McAleer's) and the Wilson Street Playground in 1936 and 1937. Also, in 1937, as part of a Works Progress Administration (WPA) project, his plans for improvements to Highland Cemetery were begun.[20] Thus, Shurcliff, too, left his imprint on Norwood.

In many ways, it is the legacy of William G. Upham that is the most visible and substantial. Unlike his friend, George Willett, Upham was never a controversial figure. Remembered as being public-spirited, and a thoroughly "good guy," he designed or renovated dozens of public buildings and private homes. Like Arthur Shurcliff, Upham sought to maintain the beauty of natural landscapes. He loved to garden, was chairman of the Trees and Parks Committee of the Norwood Board of Trade, and even published a brochure to encourage residents to beautify their own property by adding trees, shrubbery, and plantings.

And it is William Upham's architectural vision that still dominates Norwood's streetscape. Alongside his private commissions for the Odd Fellows Building and the Masonic Lodge, his public commissions included a distinctive Colonial Revival high school building (Norwood's third) which stood on Nichols Street from 1926 to 2011, the Federal Post Office on Central Street, the castellated Neo-Gothic railroad bridge that enabled the extension of Nahatan Street, and the municipal water purifying station on Route One. Upham described the latter with its red brick Colonial Revival façade as "a very good illustration of how a factory building...can be made to beautify the surroundings."[21] The two fountains that stood in front of the completed station served not only to enhance the design but to aerate the water.

William Upham is best known, however, for the design of the buildings that anchor the town square: the Norwood Theatre and the Memorial Municipal Building, both constructed using Massachusetts granite and Indiana limestone as complements to one another. The nearby State Armory building (today's Civic) and railroad bridge used a similar unifying façade. The theater and town hall—one a modern adaptation of Spanish Romanesque architecture, the other a neo-Gothic cathedral-like monument to veterans—provided permanence and solemnity to the then newly-constructed central town common. Bryant Tolles, the author of Norwood's centennial history, described the Memorial Municipal Building with its soaring carillon tower as "perhaps the best work that its architect, William G. Upham, ever achieved," and concluded that "It is probably the town's most famed material possession."[22] Nearly fifty years after Tolles' assessment, and nearing a century since its dedication, the building remains as significant to the community as ever.

In 1917, Norwood resident Patrick J. Pendergast wrote and self-published a book of poetry called *Selected Gems*. It is doggerel, to be sure, but provides insight into one man's sentiments about his hometown. Many verses are steeped in local lore with recognizable names and places, such as Father Troy, the first resident pastor of St. Catherine's Catholic Church, Rev. Arthur H. Pingree, the heroic Congregational minister who lost his life trying to rescue drowning children, Hartshorn's Market, the Civic Association, and Willett's Pond. One ode, titled "The Great White Way,"[23] is a tribute to Washington Street, and begins:

> On Sunday morn in Norwood, the people they do stray,
> From their pleasant homes through the town and go to
>   church and pray,
> Then they join the throng, and they move along, upon
>   the great white way.

To townspeople, like Pendergast, the then recent metamorphosis of Washington Street from a rutty, dirt and gravel road to a wide, smoothly-paved avenue was a dramatic indicator that this "little dried-up seedy village" could become, as George Willett predicted, "the biggest, busiest and best suburban municipality in New England."

Within a decade, however, the resolve of officials and residents had faltered, and the town George Willett imagined was not to be. Still, although not all of their plans came to fruition, there are remnants of Willett's vision, Shurcliff's landscapes, and Upham's architecture scattered throughout Norwood. In the end, they deserve to be remembered for their efforts.

Sources and Notes

Norwood's history can be found in Bryant Tolles, *Norwood: The Centennial History of a Massachusetts Town* (Norwood, MA: Norwood Printing Company, 1973) and Patricia J. Fanning, *Norwood: A History* (Charleston, SC: Arcadia Publishing, 2002). For information on sanitarians and the City Beautiful Movement, see Jon A. Peterson, "Impact of Sanitary Reform Upon American Urban Planning, 1840-1890," and Jon A. Peterson, "The City Beautiful Movement: Forgotten Origins and Lost Meanings," both in *Introduction to Planning History in the United States*, Donald A. Krueckeberg, ed. (New Brunswick, NJ: Center for Urban Policy Research, Rutgers University, 1983).

1. Stanley Buder, *Visionaries and Planners, The Garden City Movement and the Modern Community* (NY: Oxford University Press, 1990), pp. 161-62. See also: John Fairfield, "The Scientific Management of Urban Space," *Journal of Urban History* 20 (2) (Feb. 1994), pp. 179-204, and Peter Batchelor, "The Origins of the Garden City Concept of Urban Form," *Journal of the Society of Architectural Historians* 28 (3) (Oct 1969), pp. 184-200.
2. George F. Willett, quoted in "Late George Willet[sic] Was Norwood's Benefactor," *Norwood Transcript Anniversary Edition, 1970*, p. 92.

3. *Annual Report of the Town of Norwood*, year ending January 31, 1913, p. 37. With the exception of Patrick J. Lydon, who was a machinist, all members of Norwood's first Planning Board were manufacturers or professionals, part of the "professional-managerial class," the kind of men usually involved in early city planning. See: Marina Moskowitz, "Zoning the Industrial City: Planners, Commissioners, and Boosters in the 1920s," *Business and Economic History* 27 (2) (Winter, 1998), pp. 307-317.

4. Born Arthur A. Shurtleff, he changed his surname to Shurcliff as an adult. For biographical information on Shurcliff, see Elizabeth Hope Cushing, *Arthur A. Shurcliff* (Amherst, MA: University of Massachusetts Press, 2014).

5. Cushing, *Arthur A. Shurcliff*, p. ix.

6. "Board of Trade Regular Meeting," *Norwood Messenger* (hereafter *NM*), 6 December 1913, p. 1; George F. Willett, quoted in W. W. Everrett, "5 Frontiers of Tyot, Part 4: The Settlement of the Third Frontier," *NM*, 18 August 1936, p. 1.

7. George F. Willett, "People Are Misled by Industrial Fallacy," *NM*, 11 December 1931, pp. 1, 5.

8. W. W. Everett, "5 Frontiers of Tyot, Part 4," *NM*, 18 August 1936, p. 1.

9. *Annual Report of the Town of Norwood*, year ending January 31, 1900.

10. "Golden Anniversary in Norwood," *Boston Globe*, 2 May 1923, p. 12.

11. *Norwood Civic Herald*, November 1916, p. 16, quoted in Heather S. Cole, "Progressive Era Municipal Reform in Norwood, Massachusetts, 1900-1920," (M.A. Thesis, Salem State College, 2006), p. 1. For biographical information on Upham, see: Heather S. Cole, "Transforming Norwood: Architect William G. Upham's Contribution to Early 20th Century Norwood, Massachusetts History," (privately printed, 2012). For information on Upham's relationship to George Willett, Nancy Bailey (Upham granddaughter), email to author, 2020.

12. "Board of Trade Meeting," *NM*, 5 April 1913, p. 1.

13. Cole, "George F. Willett," p. 104.

14. George F. Willett, "Report of the Planning Board to the Citizens of the Town, 1923," (published by George F. Willett), p. 5.
15. Arthur A. Shurtleff [Shurcliff], "Report of Arthur A. Shurtleff, Town Planner," in Willett, "Report of the Planning Board, 1923," p. 23.
16. John P. Fox, "Report of John P. Fox, Consultant on Zoning," in Willett, "Report of the Planning Board, 1923," p. 29; proposed By-Law, pp. 30-37.
17. "Zoning By-Law Defeated by Large Vote in Town Meeting," *NM*, 2 May 1925, p. 1.
18. Cole, "Progressive Era Municipal Reform," p. 115.
19. George F. Willett, "Westover: A New England Village of the Twentieth Century," (Norwood, MA: Plimpton Press, c. 1934), Norwood Historical Society Archives.
20. *Annual Report of the Town of Norwood*, year ending December 31, 1924, p. 154; *Annual Report of the Town of Norwood,* year ending December 31, 1927, p. 131; *Annual Report of the Town of Norwood*, year ending December 31, 1936, p. 11; *Annual Report of the Town of Norwood*, year ending December 31, 1936, p. 41.
21. William G. Upham, quoted in Cole, "Transforming Norwood," p. 14.
22. Tolles, p. 45.
23. P. J. Pendergast, "The Great White Way," *Selected Gems* (privately printed, 1917), p. 19.

Chapter 10

Win Everett's Fables

Parson Weems' Fable (1939) by Grant Wood alludes to the nostalgic and inaccurate view of history Weems promoted. *(Collection of the Amon Carter Museum)*

IN SEPTEMBER OF 1931, Robert E. Costello, editor of the semi-weekly *Norwood Messenger*, printed a reminiscence piece about Old Norwood by Win Everett. Born in Golden, Colorado, in 1878, the son of Francis Everett and Clara (Hoyle) Everett, both of whom could trace their roots to South Dedham, Willard Winthrop "Win" Everett came to Norwood at the age of seven with his mother after his father's death. He graduated from Amherst College in 1901 with a degree in biology, worked for a time at the Natural History Museum in Rochester, New York, and then turned to journalism. He held positions in Springfield, Massachusetts, and then New York City (where he was a reporter for the *New York Sun*) before joining the staff of the *Boot and Shoe Recorder*, a trade publication, for which he wrote advertising copy.

Returning to Norwood in 1918, Win took up residence in the Everett family homestead on Winter Strèet with his wife and two daughters. While he continued to earn his living in the advertising business (although he apparently left the *Boot and Shoe Recorder* in 1928), his avocation was community history. He joined the then fledgling Norwood Historical Society and began to collect stories and material pertaining to Norwood. In 1931, the article titled "Have a Drink of Deacon Tinker's Choklit Sody!" was seemingly Everett's first foray into history writing.

Composed in an informal "folksy" style, a tone he likely mastered while producing volumes of magazine copy, the article described the streetscape of the center of Old Norwood— known as the Hook— including both the Tinker Building and the personnel found working at its drugstore, especially the "dear, kindly, gentle-voiced Deacon Tinker, with his black skull-cap on his pure white locks." It was an entertaining account, from a child's perspective, of the store and its stock, most of all Tinker's "choklit sody." Everett then described the offices in the municipal building next to Tinker's: "One large, grimy room—a long old fashioned 'stand-up' bookkeeper's desk and a noble iron stove. Tax office, clerk's office, selectmen's office, and all other town offices handily rolled into one space and practically one official."[1]

Within a matter of days, the locals responded to Everett's recollections and Win found himself "almost waylaid for getting a few items twisted." A week later, corrections and pertinent details were updated in print. It was obvious that Everett and editor Costello, a local man who had been at the *Messenger's* helm for seven years, were on to something. While the paper had always kept up with local news, births, deaths, weddings, retirements, and sporting events, this trip down memory lane had prompted unusual interest. By the beginning of November, when a former resident, living in Marlboro, submitted his own account of the Market Street businesses and a remembrance of the devastating fire that destroyed the Universalist Church in 1884, Costello was requesting that readers "send us a line" with their own anecdotes of the past[2]

The following year—1932—the *Messenger* published a series called "Reminiscences of Norwood Pioneers" which celebrated the lives of leading businessmen and clergy. Although unattributed, these may well have been written by Win Everett, who was fast becoming the unofficial town historian. As such, he helped spearhead the community's participation in the bicentennial celebration of the birth of George Washington, a recognition that included parades, costume balls, sermons, and public events across the country. The principal purpose of this nation-wide commemoration—to promote an understanding of and pride in George Washington's life as a farmer, soldier, and statesman—was only enhanced by the trials of the Great Depression. In this decade of crisis, the country as a whole was united in celebration of its beginnings. Norwood's participation was twofold. In April, school children presented a pageant that included dramatic readings, historically-based tableaux, and a one act play. In October, the Norwood Historical Society sponsored an "official" program that featured political speeches and stirring patriotic music.

Somewhat ironically, in the months between these two events, in June of 1932 tens of thousands of military veterans had traveled to Washington, D. C. by train, automobile and on foot seeking long-promised bonuses for their service in the Great War. They set up tent cities in and around Washington. President Herbert Hoover, aware that the money to pay the bonuses could not be procured without raising taxes,—something he was not willing to do in the midst of a deepening economic downturn—refused to support the participants (although he did secretly approve the acquisition of tents, supplies, field kitchens, and personnel to assist the protestors, as well as the use of government property to house them, and even a transportation loan bill to help them get home). As the discouraged veterans reluctantly disbanded at the end of July, a near riot ensued. U.S. troops, led by General Douglas MacArthur, who ignored Hoover's orders to stand down, made matters worse by using tear gas and physical force to clear the encampments. Needless to say, it was an awkward interlude for those seeking to honor George Washington, the man who had led the nation's first army.

Norwood's Washington Bicentennial Pageant, held in the Junior High School auditorium on Washington Street in autumn, was a rousing success. The American Legion Post 70 Band, the award-winning pride of the town, opened the festivities with the Washington Bicentennial March. After the invocation by St. Catherine's pastor, James Doherty, a chorus of fifty school children performed the George Washington Cantata, composed especially for the event by Jean V. Dethier, music supervisor for the Norwood Public Schools. Master of Ceremonies, Thomas B. Mulvehill, a popular selectman and well-known businessman, guided the evening of music and tributes, all of which culminated in a keynote address by prominent Brookline lawyer and George Washington expert, Melvin M. Johnson. The benediction was given by the Rev. Walter Crane Myers of the First Baptist Church. Norwood townspeople left feeling proud.

In 1933 and 1934, Win Everett occasionally submitted "little yarns," as he called them, to the *Messenger*; chiefly stories and legends picked up from acquaintances and old-timers. On July 20, 1934, however, a letter from Everett addressed "To the citizens of Norwood and the Editor of the Norwood Messenger" appeared in the paper announcing his intention to gather historical and genealogical data as part of a Norwood Historical Society-endorsed project funded by the Massachusetts Division of the Federal Emergency Relief Administration.[3]

One of the two federal job-creating agencies that preceded the Works Progress Administration (WPA)—the other was the Civil Works Administration (CWA)—the Federal Emergency Relief Administration (FERA) funded a number of projects in several states. Originally enacted under the Hoover Administration's Emergency Relief and Construction Act of 1932, this program was state-controlled and required demonstrable need on the part of each applicant. Beginning in 1933, Norwood benefited from a CWA program aimed at public school buildings and grounds that paid for carpentry, electrical, painting, and plumbing projects, most of which would have been left undone without the funding. In 1934, the town received over $160,000 Federal CWA and FERA dollars, expending a mere $21,000 of its own money to complete various maintenance and construction projects. Among them were road extension and cemetery expansion work, school and municipal building repairs, and the construction of a reading room in the previously unfinished portion of the local library's new wing. All of these projects employed hundreds of unemployed, needy residents.

Two unique projects were funded by FERA as well: a sewing program that paid local women to make clothing and bedding for distribution to families in need, and Win Everett's proposal to collect and record historical material pertaining to the town of Norwood. From August 1934 through August 1935, Everett received approximately $1,500 to support the research he called an "historical survey of the town's history." The project was three-pronged. First, with the cooperation of long-time residents and descendants of former Norwood people, Everett planned to collect photographs, tin-types, daguerreotypes, oil and watercolor paintings, crayon portraits, amateur sketches, even rough drawings by children of "old time people and things." Second, he would assemble genealogical information about the first Irish- and German-born settlers in South Dedham. Finally, Everett was keenly interested in putting together a complete history of old post roads and stage-coach routes that ran through the village of Tiot, as South Dedham was colloquially known, in the 18th and 19th centuries, including the sites of tollgates and taverns along the routes.[4]

Although the project was technically funded by a state-sponsored FERA grant, by the time Everett commenced work the Roosevelt administration and its "New Deal" had already established the Public Works of Art Project (PWAP) which hired painters and sculptors in forty-eight states to embellish government buildings and courthouses. During its eighteen months of existence, PWAP employed nearly 3,600 artists and produced 16,000 pieces of art. The success and results of these two experimental programs (FERA and PWAP) cleared the way for a much broader relief program, the Emergency Relief Act of 1935. This legislation created the ambitious Works Progress Administration (WPA). Although initially it appeared that the WPA would be devoted exclusively to construction work, a small clause buried in the bill authorized a federally-controlled program that would provide assistance to jobless writers, artists, musicians, actors, and entertainers. Shortly after the WPA's inception, the grant-in-aid program of FERA, which had functioned under state administration, was abandoned, and the WPA emerged as the funding authority with complete jurisdiction in the United States.

There is no indication that Everett sought WPA funds to continue his "historical survey," but the twelve months he was given by FERA was more than enough to supply him with mountains of data and historical information. Rather than present his findings in a statistical report as he had promised, however, Everett decided to use the acquired material in newspaper articles, with the caveat that the information contained in his writings should only be considered "source material" for later historians.[5] Thus, although he authenticated the tales told to him whenever possible, the stories published in the *Norwood Messenger* were not to be taken as fact, but as fable. Any subsequent historians or writers would be wise to confirm the accuracy of the material. As such, the work of Win Everett was in keeping with historical, artistic, and cultural trends prevalent in the United States during the 1930s.

With the first signs of the Depression, Americans had begun to reconsider their collective past, evaluating their own history and reconfiguring their cultural sense of self. What did it mean to be an American? Could past traditions and people provide a road map out of the current uncertainty toward a more stable, prosperous future? As Alfred Haworth Jones summarized in his 1971 essay, "The Search for a Usable American Past in the New Deal Era," this "national rediscovery" of history was manifested in various ways: novels, films and theater with historical settings, scholarly biographies of notable figures from America's past, documentary photographs (such as those taken by Dorothea Lange and Walker Evans), the purposeful research into folklore and folk customs, and regionalism in painting.[6] After Franklin Delano Roosevelt's election, government-sponsored cultural projects continued to propel this agenda forward through WPA guides and historical surveys.

Jones also noted that after the Armistice of 1918, peacetime prosperity had allowed people to live "primarily in the present" as the generation of the 1920s found heroes among their contemporaries.

Henry Ford, Charles Lindbergh, and Herbert Hoover were admired for their individual achievements, attainments that set them apart from the mainstream. But as many sociologists have contended, communities unite during a crisis; they want to be part of something larger than themselves. Driven by a critical need to defeat the growing panic and pessimism surrounding them, Depression-era populations searched for assurance. Focusing on a shared past gave the majority of the nation a unifying purpose, a history and culture that could be called upon to overcome the present and shape the future. As John Dos Passos put it, people of all walks of life needed "to know what kind of firm ground other men, belonging to generations before us, have found to stand on" and then begin to build on that.[7]

The Colonial Revival of the late nineteenth century had broken some of this ground. Proponents of the movement argued the significance of Colonial-era furniture, mementoes, and even antique clothing and recipes as a means to preserve the early roots of American culture. At least part of this interest in the collective history of the nation's ancestry, however, could be traced to a growing concern that an influx of immigrants was a threat to national identity. Thus, in the early decades of the twentieth century, the results of this anxiety were the rise of nativism, calls for immigration restriction (Southern and Eastern Europeans were particular targets), and an emphasis on assimilation through education. By the 1930s, folk art, tales of America's forefathers (chiefly associated with sought-after qualities of simplicity, honesty, and self-sufficiency), and indoctrination in a universal origin story were seen as the best kind of social cement.

In addition, this era gave rise to both public and private collecting of early American artifacts, and helped develop an historic preservation movement. Historic restoration projects at Williamsburg, Virginia (aided by John D. Rockefeller) and Greenfield Village in Dearborn, Michigan (advancing the legacy of Henry Ford), as well as Old Sturbridge Village and Historic Deerfield in Massachusetts, were all founded and funded by wealthy entrepreneurs who aimed to salvage and, in some cases, re-create, examples of the nation's beginnings. Cloaked in nostalgia for a supposedly simpler, more heroic past, these "restoration" projects presented to the twentieth century's urbanized and diverse populations a heritage that embraced the values of community, hard work, and self-reliance, qualities seen as fundamental to the national character.

In keeping with this trend, at the peak of this historical resurgence, in June of 1934, about eight months after the death of famed photographer and community historian Fred Holland Day, the Norwood Historical Society acquired the Day family's mansion and his collection of documents, photographs, and artifacts pertaining to Old South Dedham and Norwood. Since its incorporation in 1907, the society had functioned in a modest way with occasional meetings and few members. But certain provisions in the wills of both Fred Day and his parents, Lewis and Anna Day, prompted the society to increase its visibility and obtain both the house and an invaluable assortment of archival material.

As an acquaintance of Fred H. Day's and a fellow aficionado of historical subjects, Win Everett understood the significance of this acquisition. A member of the Norwood Historical Society's board of directors, he was a central figure in the transactions that brought this remarkable collection to the society. The procurement could not have come at a more opportune time for Everett. It may well have played a part in his decision to apply to the Federal Emergency Relief Administration for funding. While Everett conducted his proposed "historical survey," he was not only able to encourage those he contacted to donate photographs, papers, and objects to the society, which now had a place in which to house them, but he was also able to use Day's archive as a source for his sketches. Although Everett's FERA grant ran for only one year—from August 1934 to August 1935—this wealth of data enabled him to continue to write his "Tales of Tyot" (according to Everett, "Tyot" not "Tiot" was the proper spelling) throughout 1936 and into 1937.

Introducing his newspaper articles, Everett noted that some sixty years after its incorporation in 1872 Norwood had no published volume about its origins and history, only disparate anecdotal accounts "widely scattered in old newspapers, official reports, pamphlets and other sources." In fact, he noted, much of the town's history could be found only "in the minds and memories of elderly people."[8] Under the FERA's auspices, Everett intended to collect and collate whatever information he could find. His interviews and scavenging of records, coupled with the material in Day's collection, resulted in more than 100 stories, legends, yarns and recollections. Many dealt with the development of the town and its neighborhoods, its roadways, schools, and churches. There were ghost stories, tales of mayhem and murder, the coming of the railroad, and the lives of significant individuals, including Lemuel Dean, George Willett, and James Fisher.

Between June and September, 1935, Everett ran seven articles about Norwood's fire department history. Along with a description of the founding of the Washington No. 7 and the America No. 10 Engine Companies, he published a directory of as many early company members as he could compile. The familiar names would certainly have sparked many conversations around town. The following year Everett devoted four consecutive "silhouettes" to Henry O. Peabody, his gun-making fortune, his unexpected bequest to build a school for girls in Norwood, and the strange machinations surrounding the sale of his property to Cameron Forbes. As might be expected, Everett appeared confident relating events that occurred in the not too distant past, subjects for which he was most likely to find documentation and witnesses.

In addition to the Peabody saga, his description of Norwood's response to the great influenza epidemic of 1918 was grounded in first-hand reporting. Similarly, his profile of Walpole metal craftsman, J. B. Crosman, known as "Peter the Smith," appeared in *Leisure* magazine and was reprinted by the *Messenger* in August of 1936. Visiting Crosman at his forge in the Walpole Town Forest, Everett composed one of his most poetic pieces, writing in part, "Genuine, unretouched romance hangs heavy over Peter the Smith's dark, spark-spattered barn, and his rambling 18th century home is still redolent of the days when Walpole belonged to King George." He described Crosman himself as a man who "is not the dreamy, impractical type you would expect. Far from it. He thinks straight from a store of hard experience and equally hard reading. His words are both winged and frequently barbed."[9] Win Everett, the skilled journalist, could conjure up both an environment and a personality with just a few well-chosen words.

Willard Winthrop "Win" Everett, journalist and editor for the *Norwood Messenger,* chronicled legends and tales of South Dedham and Norwood during the 1930s.
(Courtesy of the Morrill Memorial Library)

When Everett reached back in history for some of his tales, the results were varied. In one story, he relates the (probably apocryphal) story of the Marquis de La Fayette spending the night in Moses Guild's home while on his way to the dedication of the Bunker Hill Monument in 1825. In Everett's retelling, however, the wife of Moses Guild, using a rather odd dialect, urges La Fayette to "put up your beasts and chaise over in Col. Fiske's stable over to the steam mill 'cross the street," when, in reality, Guild's barn was not leased to Fiske until well into the 1840s. According to Everett, this tale was "vouched for by one of the oldest men in Norwood," but did admit that "a yarn which dates from 1825 must naturally have some cracks in it."[10] Other similar early legends included a story of a lunar eclipse terrifying native people and the local militia in 1675 at King's Bridge on Pleasant Street, and an introduction to Native American William Ahautun, who Everett identified as the namesake for Norwood's "Nahatan" Street, a fact substantially corroborated by subsequent research.[10]

But Everett's favorite topics were related to travel; turnpikes, railroads, stagecoaches, and even automobiles inhabited many of his sketches. Several of his tales focused on the history of roadways—from the Old Roebuck Road (Pleasant Street), to the Wrentham Post Road (Walpole Street), to the Norfolk and Bristol Turnpike (Washington Street)—and the stagecoaches that traversed these early highways. And, in another batch of articles, Everett told the story of the railroad coming through town. His enthusiasm for these subjects breathed life into what might easily have been dry, dusty narratives.

One of the most interesting—and undoubtedly reliable—articles related to the 17th and 18th centuries, however, was Win Everett's own archaeological exploration at the Norwood-Walpole town line. Everett playfully recounted the "expedition conducted by the archaeological division of the Norwood Federal Emergency Relief Administration" during which he and his daughters, Carol and Bettina, traveling in the "good ship Chevy 28," docked just off Washington Street near Water Street.[11] Everett's tone may have been light, but his exploration was in earnest. He had been directed to the site by Walpole historian Frank M. Larrabee, who had "discovered" five ancient round Indian mortars—each with a unique size and depth—pot holes he believed were created by indigenous people grinding corn with heavy stone pestles. Beside them, authenticated by a curator from the Peabody Museum at Harvard, were two saucer-shaped indentations reportedly used as whetstones to sharpen implements and weapons. Larrabee and other locals had heard the legend of these mortars, but it took the removal of a mill dam to verify their existence.

According to Everett, as early as 1734 Simon Pettee and John Bullard had planned to build a saw mill and iron works at the crossing of the Neponset River on this site. Whether that happened is unknown. However, generations of the Morse family lived on the land and operated saw and grist mills at Water Street for over one hundred years, until a fire destroyed both the mill and their residence in 1897. The family carried on for a time in a small shop until the property was sold to Hollingsworth and Vose.

While "The Indian Mortars of Tiot," which appeared in the *Messenger* on September 25, 1934, were substantially verified by deeds, visual evidence, and a professional archaeologist, many of Everett's historical tales remained in the shadowy space between unconfirmed reminiscence and speculation. Everett was perhaps at his best, however, when he described the sights and sounds of nineteenth century village life: days spent loitering around "the Hook," or at local swimming holes, playing sports (including sleigh racing down Washington Street), recollecting holiday traditions or unusual events, like the day an angry steer broke loose and terrorized the village. Many of these sketches were nostalgia-laced word-pictures designed to amuse as much as to impart knowledge, to let his readers relate to the early town residents and colonial-era "heroes" on a human level.

Win Everett was not the only writer engaged in spinning tales of enhanced lore, however; nostalgia and myth-building was a cottage industry among American writers and artists in the 1930s. Historical fiction writers—Margaret Mitchell (*Gone With the Wind*), Walter Edmonds (*Drums Along the Mohawk*), and Kenneth Roberts (*Northwest Passage*), to name only a few—attracted avid audiences. Despite the diversity of time, location, and characters, protagonists of most of these works possessed the admirable "American" traits of strength, determination, and self-reliance. Many scholars and cultural observers have analyzed the role that myth and material culture played in the reimagination of local and national identities in this decade. For example, in her essay, "Reviving the Old and Telling Tales: 1930s Modernism and the Uses of American History," Annelise Madsen notes that during this era, "Artists revived the old in a variety of ways, marshaling diverse origin stories and historical artifacts to shape an array of American modernisms. The inclination to look backward was a broad cultural phenomenon."[12]

This phenomenon was thoroughly supported by the Roosevelt administration's funding of projects with historical components. The activities of architects, artists, writers, collectors, museums, hereditary societies, and preservationists uncovered a host of material that could be utilized to counteract a shaken sense of national pride and confidence. Through interviews with Southern sharecroppers, recordings of African-American jazz and blues musicians, and the study of Appalachian folk arts and crafts, project scholars and artists sought to preserve the remnants of a receding culture. Others traced and documented ethnic and racial migrations from around the globe and across America. In this vein, one of Everett's early tales tells of an Irish family who in 1851 "sailed away from County Waterford for the great, legendary land of free America" and Norwood.[13] In addition, the Federal Music and Writers' Projects also embraced the artifacts of primitive environments, like Everett and his expedition to view ancient pot holes.

Likewise, the visual arts celebrated farmers, industrial workers, and everyday Americans. Regionalism, a type of art that focused primarily on small town life and extolled the virtues of hard-working, patriotic citizens, became popular. Acknowledging significant geographical differences, these murals, paintings, etchings, and drawings emphasized the unifying commonalities within a diverse population. Among American artists, Grant Wood epitomized this movement.

Taking as his subject the landscape and people of his native Iowa, Wood's aim was to use the local to tell stories that were timeless and universal. Along with his Midwestern masterpieces *American Gothic* (1930), *Arbor Day* (1935), and *Spring Turning* (1936), Wood captured a wider view of the American experience with his *Midnight Ride of Paul Revere* (1931), *The Birthplace of Herbert Hoover* (1931), and *Parson Weems' Fable* (1939). The artist's goal in creating these works was not to ridicule or discredit the tall, clearly fictitious, tales commonly taught in classrooms across the nation, but to reawaken an interest in American legends. "As I see it," Wood stated, "the most effective way to do this is to frankly accept these historical tales for what they are now known to be—folklore—and treat them in such a fashion that the realistic-minded, sophisticated people of our generation can accept them."[14]

The three historically-based paintings (*The Midnight Ride of Paul Revere*, *The Birthplace of Herbert Hoover*, and *Parson Weems' Fable*) are clearly parodies into which Wood has embedded comical imagery: the tiny nightgown clad figures gawking after Revere, the miniature guide seemingly pointing more at Hoover's underwear on the clothesline than his home, and the axe-carrying child-Washington with the Gilbert Stuart head. And yet, while playing upon each myth's deceptions, there is an element of pride in these images. As Parson Weems holds back the curtain and points to his apocryphal tale, Wood is acknowledging that, though an illusion, there is value to be gained by embracing shared legend and lore.

Remarkably, Win Everett, wielding his pen instead of a brush, established in print this same kind of gently ironic depiction of history. Everett's contention that Deacon Nathaniel Sumner was "undoubtedly Norwood's outstanding Revolutionary figure" is a good-natured one. Drawing parallels with Revere's famous ride, Everett assured his readers that on April 19, 1775 at the age of fifty-five, Sumner dropped what he was doing and headed out to protect his home: "Leaping on his horse, with flint-lock in hand, he thundered down Sumner Street to the Old Roebuck Post Road [today's Pleasant Street]. Northward! Northward! With his white-hair flying in the breeze of his speed, he passed many another son of the South Parish and many another parishioner as they rushed towards Dedham.... Perhaps he even passed Major Aaron Guild, and never knew that he was the gentleman who was to grace our town seal!"

After this amiable jab at Norwood's future historical fable, Everett continued, "At last the Deacon galloped into the green of Dedham Village—mud-splashed and breathless—but still game to go onward to Lexington." Because of their advanced age, Sumner and other veteran militia men like him (including Aaron Guild), were held back at Dedham and, only later in the day, allowed to follow their younger brethren into the skirmish. Among these volunteer forces, Everett declares that Sumner—who was a graduate of Harvard, Deacon of the South Parish Church, and Dedham selectman—was the "most respected of the citizens."[15]

Everett's depiction of the wild-haired Sumner galloping Revere-like along village roadways to Dedham is both inspirational and humorous. Here was, after all, one of South Dedham's most esteemed residents, armed and ready to enter battle against the Crown. But, at the same time, the image of the breathless, disheveled deacon pulling up to Dedham square "with flint-lock in hand" is an amusing and unverifiable one. It is, after all, a long way to ride while waving a fifteen-pound rifle over one's head. The reader can sense the twinkle in Win Everett's eye as he wrote.

He used the same kind of humor in his attempt to sort through the contradictory accounts of just which Ezra Morse built a saw mill on the Neponset River and, thereby, supposedly became the first resident of Norwood—or at least of South Dedham, the village that later became the town. Everett lamented that it was "a dim, crabbed story," one which had puzzled many historians before him. Some gave the mill and "founding" rights to Ezra Morse (1644-1698) while others handed the honors to his son Ezra Morse (1671-1760), but the "truth" of the matter, according to Everett, was lost in "the misread, misquoted, or misinterpreted old records in the Dedham archives." That did not stop him, however, from proposing Norwood's official float in Dedham's Tercentenary parade of 1936 "portray Ezra Morse's saw mill with Ezra himself engaged in sawing the lumber for Norwood's first houses." After all, Everett writes, "Ezra Morse was *probably* [emphasis added] the first settler in the territory which is now the town of Norwood."[16] But, the year, the location, and exact identification of which Ezra Morse it was, remained a mystery to Everett.

In other articles, Win Everett attempted to "right an ancient wrong" or two, contending that various places have been misnamed: that the well-known "Pettee's Pond" actually belonged to the Ellis family, and the adjoining mill was Tisdale's, not Pettee's. Likewise, he declared that "Guild's Pond" and mill were actually built and owned by one James R. Fisher. Not surprisingly, the erroneous names continued in common usage.[17] Whether his advice was taken or his theories accepted, Win Everett brought the then 15,000 residents of Norwood, many of whom were on the brink of ruin during the Depression, an entertaining connection to their shared past. If debating place names, or learning about the history of the now defunct stage coach routes, or hearing the tall tales of the town's origins brought his fellow townspeople some pleasure, or a brief diversion from their very real woes, then so be it. It was all in good fun.

In November of 1936, Robert Costello, the long-time editor of the *Norwood Messenger*, died, and in January of 1937, Willard "Win" Everett was appointed to the post, just as the *Messenger's* owners decided to make the leap from a semi-weekly paper to a daily. "Being editor," Everett declared, was "a new adventure."[18] The *Daily Messenger* tried to cover the world. In February 1937 there were articles about a West Virginia coal mine disaster, the Dionne quintuplets of Canada, and a Flint, Michigan auto workers' strike alongside news of a WPA grant to aid the nearby Canton airport, among other strictly-local news. At the same time, the headlines became a bit more lurid, no doubt to attract subscribers. After a few years, Everett resigned from the *Messenger* but, by 1945, he had returned as its feature editor. He continued the work he loved best by preparing commemorative editions for celebrations such as Roxbury's Centennial and Westwood's 50th Anniversary. And, drawing on his sketches from the 1930s, he assembled the historical sections for the *Messenger's, Official Commemoration and Chronicle of Norwood's 75th Anniversary* in 1947. Win Everett died in November of that year after a brief illness.

In August of 1935, Willard Winthrop Everett, assigning himself the title "Connoisseur of Historical Data," presented bound copies of some of his sketches to the Commonwealth of Massachusetts, the Morrill Memorial Library, and the Norwood Historical Society to confirm the completion of his FERA project. In the attached cover letter, he indicated that he was "glad to state these little stories have admirably served the purpose for which they were designed." The interest they aroused in Norwood, and among the town's former residents who were scattered across the country, delighted and gratified Everett. Readers' editorial comments, story ideas, and additional historical material had poured into the newspaper office. "Old friendships have been renewed," he wrote, "and new ones made."[19] What is more, Everett's resurrection and assemblage of both the verifiable data and the unconfirmed tales bound Norwood's townspeople to an identifiable and previously unrecognized history. It was Everett's hope that this shared heritage might serve as a comforting reminder, during a social and economic crisis, of how

far Tiot village and its inhabitants had come in the preceding two
centuries, and, perhaps, an indication of how much further they
might go if they continued to support their community and one
another.

∾❧∾❧∾❧

Sources and Notes

Biographical information about Willard "Win" Everett came from
his lengthy obituary, "Death Claims 'Win' Everett" in the *Norwood
Daily Messenger*, 10 November 1947, p. 1. The 1932 veterans' march
on Washington was covered in T. H. Watkins, *The Great Depression,
America in the 1930s* (Boston: Little, Brown & Co., 1993). Other
aspects of the Depression were found in *The Great Depression,
America, 1929-1941* by Robert S. McElvaine (NY: Times Books,
1993). Norwood's Washington Bicentennial Pageant was described in
detail in the *Norwood Messenger*, 11 October 1932, p. 1. A history
of the federal works projects can be found in Victoria Grieve, *The
Federal Art Project and the Creation of Middlebrow Culture* (Chicago:
University of Illinois Press, 2009) and Jerre Mangione, *The Dream
and the Deal: The Federal Writers Project 1935-1943* (Boston: Little,
Brown & Co., 1972). The Town of Norwood's Annual Reports, 1934
and 1935, covered specific detail regarding Norwood's FERA and
CWA projects. For 1930s American culture, including regionalism, I
relied on Alfred Haworth Jones, "The Search for a Usable American
Past in the New Deal Era," in *The American Quarterly*, vol 23, no. 5
(December 1970) pp. 710-724 and Annelise K. Madsen, "Reviving the
Old and Telling Tales: 1930s Modernism and the Uses of American
History," in *America After the Fall, Painting in the 1930s*, Judith A.
Barter (ed.), (Chicago: The Art Institute of Chicago, 2016) pp. 88-115.
Barbara Haskell's *Grant Wood, American Gothic and Other Fables*,
(New Haven, CT: Yale University Press, 2018) was also extremely
helpful. Win Everett's tales appeared in the *Norwood Messenger*
throughout 1933 to 1937. The Norwood Historical Society and the
Morrill Memorial Library each have a bound collection of the stories

donated by Everett; included in that volume is an introductory cover letter titled "Tales of Tyot."

1. Everett, "Have a Drink of Deacon Tinker's Choklit Sody," *Norwood Messenger* (hereafter *NM*), 18 September 1931, pp. 10,11.
2. Everett, *NM*, 25 September 1931, p. 3.
3. Everett, *NM*, 20 July 1934, p. 4
4. Everett, *Tales of Tyot*, introductory letter.
5. Ibid.
6. Jones, p. 710.
7. John Dos Passos, quoted in Jones, p. 715.
8. Everett, *Tales of Tyot*, introductory letter.
9. Everett, "'Peter the Smith' and his Forest Forge," *NM*, 7 August 1936, pp. 1, 12.
10. Everett, "La Fayette Stayed at Old Norwood Home," *NM*, 4 May 1934, p. 1.
11. Everett, "The Indian Mortars of Tiot," *NM*, 25 September 1934, p. 1.
12. Madsen, p. 89.
13. Everett, "An Irishman Looks at Liberty," *NM*, 14 August 1934, p. 1.
14. Barbara Haskell, "Grant Wood Chronicles," in *American Gothic*, p. 240.
15. Everett, "Silhouette of Old Tyot, #4," *NM*, 21 April 1936, pp. 1, 2.
16. Everett, "5 Frontiers of Norwood, Part 1," *NM*, 4 August 1936, p. 1; Everett, "Ezra Morse Was the Founder of Norwood," *NM*, 15 September 1936, p. 1. Win Everett did make an error in his identification of Ezra Morse. F. H. Day's genealogical notes indicated the father and son were: Ezra (3) Morse and Ezra (4) Morse. These numbers are a reference to the generational position of the individuals, i.e., the third and fourth generations of Morses in America, *not* Ezra Morse, III and Ezra Morse, IV. This confusion persisted, and Bryant Tolles in his book, *Norwood: The Centennial History of a Massachusetts Town*, incorrectly identified the two as Ezra Morse III and Ezra Morse

IV; they were, in fact, Ezra Morse and Ezra Morse, Jr.

17. "Righting an Ancient Wrong," *NM*, 23 July 1935, p. 1.

18. Everett, "Editor Looks at New Paper," *NM* 4 January 1937, pp. 1, 11.

19. Everett, *Tales of Tyot*, introductory letter.

Chapter 11

A Matter of Conscience

THE 1950s WAS A DECADE of contradictions. Often hailed as the apex of America and the American family—the gross national product increased by 250%; per capita income grew 35%; the rates of marriage and births rose dramatically; and, by 1960, 62% of American families owned their own home—reality was far more complicated. Twenty-five percent of Americans were poor, with one third of the nation's children living in poverty; 60% of the elderly had incomes below $1,000 annually. The Great Migration had brought thousands of black citizens northward, where they were welcomed with racism, segregation, and systemic discrimination in hiring and housing. Women's educational parity with men dropped sharply, and, although more women were working outside the home than ever before, they had been purged from the better paying positions. Women were excluded from most professions and often found themselves beinig offered primarily "mothers' hours." While the economy surged around them—chiefly driven by government subsidies in highway and housing construction; education, employment and home-ownership programs for veterans; and the rise of the military-industrial complex as factories which once served the war were re-tooled to participate in the burgeoning defense industry— huge swathes of Americans were losing ground.

What is more, although World War II may have ended, the Cold War had just begun. While the United States' mainland had emerged from the war unscathed, America found itself at odds with the Soviet Union as Europe began to rebuild. The Soviets supported dictators and communist regimes in the territories which they controlled, while the United States encouraged free elections and democracies. Locked in a philosophical and political battle with the Soviets, and prompted by the fear that there were those who sought to spread communism in the states, Cold War anxiety overwhelmed common sense. Irrational fears led to political repression and coerced conformity. Loyalty oaths became part of American life, particularly for those seeking employment in the public sector. Politicians sought to ferret out communists among labor unions and government contractors, academic freedom in colleges and universities was threatened, and in 1954, the words "under God" were added to the Pledge of Allegiance. All of these economic and political trends had a direct impact on the town of Norwood.

Because of the dominance of a handful of major industries—tanning, ink-making, and printing—the Depression had hit the town hard, and by the 1950s an economic shift was well underway. Labor unrest affected the owners of Winslow Brothers & Smith, with strikes in 1933, 1938, and again in 1949. After this last disturbance, the Smith tannery on Railroad Avenue was closed, followed three years later by the Winslow Brothers facility on Endicott Street.

The early 1950s also brought the demise of the Norwood Press. Operating deficits and a gradual decline in production, along with a labor dispute in 1952, silenced the Berwick and Smith presses, followed by the C. B. Fleming bindery and the J. S. Cushing composition and electrotyping plants in 1954. Meanwhile, the George H. Morrill Company and the Plimpton Press, once powerful businesses employing a large local workforce, succumbed to buyouts and mergers. Morrill's had become part of the General Printing Ink Company in 1929 and had experienced a gradual dissolution. Beginning in the mid-1950s, the controlling interest in the Plimpton Press passed through various investors and corporations, until it too disappeared from town. Although other business concerns and light manufacturers, many receiving government contracts for manufacturing or development work, filled the physical spaces, they could not replace the employment potential of these departed industrial giants.

Finally, beginning in the 1950s, the construction of Route 128, which provided a circumferential route around Boston, and the long-postponed development of "Westover" transformed Norwood into a bedroom community. White collar workers who commuted to the city or industrial parks along the highway began to populate the town. No longer would laborers walk to work at the mill or the factory or the tannery. The suburbanization of Norwood had begun, and yet, the events that unfolded in the spring of 1953 echoed the scandal of an earlier decade—another Red Scare was grabbing headlines. Perhaps ironically, just as their influence and power seemed to be receding, it was three women who took center stage. They came from diverse backgrounds and had vastly different life experiences but, Maude Shattuck, Edna Phillips, and Mary Knowles were brought together by a timely yet historic set of circumstances.

Maude Alice Shattuck (1880-1962) was born into privilege. Her mother, Emma Louise Morrill, was the eldest child of George H. Morrill (1829-1909) and his wife, Sarah Bond (Tidd) Morrill (1833-1864). While finishing his formal education in Europe, George Morrill acquired a printing ink formula. Upon his return to the United States in 1856, he moved the family's business from Andover, Massachusetts to Pleasant Street in South Dedham. By 1869, when it was reorganized under his name, the firm was already considered one of the most important ink producers in the country.

Edmund J. Shattuck (1853-1903), Maude's father, arrived in town from Northfield, Vermont, in 1872, just as the former South Dedham village was being incorporated as the town of Norwood. For a time, he worked for the Hartford and Erie Railroad but after his marriage to Emma Morrill, he joined the family firm. Here his intelligence, business acumen, and integrity set the company on the path to worldwide success and his family to great wealth. The Shattucks and their five children (four daughters and a son) lived on an estate at the corner of Walpole and Winter Streets. Perched on a gentle slope, Shattuck's enormous mansion had peaks and gables, multiple porches on the first and second floors, and was topped by a widow's walk. A staff of servants, including a cook and a laundress, kept the estate, house, and carriage house in efficient running order.

As a teenager, Maude Shattuck attended Dana Hall, a boarding and day secondary school for girls in Wellesley. She was there for three years, from 1895 until her graduation in 1898. The curriculum, which included Latin, French, and courses in the classics and history, provided an excellent foundation for college; Maude chose

Smith College in Northampton, Massachusetts. By the time she arrived at Smith, the small women's college, populated primarily by white, Protestant students of means, was bursting from its original cluster of residential cottages into Northampton itself. More than half the student body lived in off-campus boarding houses—often grand mansions with marble-encased public rooms and expansive suites for students—leading inevitably to social and economic cliques. Shattuck, who chose to live on campus in Hatfield House, perhaps avoiding the cruel practice of exclusion and self-selection in the highly competitive environment, seems to have enjoyed her time at the school. After graduation, in 1902, she kept in touch with classmates, was active in the school's alumnae association (attending "Smith luncheons" while traveling), and welcoming the daughters of alumnae into her Norwood home.[1]

In October of 1903, a little more than a year following Maude's graduation, her father Edmund Shattuck died; he was fifty years old. The *Norwood Advertiser and Review* ran a lengthy obituary detailing the accomplishments of Shattuck noting his political and social influence. According to the newspaper, Shattuck's "cool, calm, business judgment was relied on, his opinions were fair and impartial and he acted as one who had the town's interest at heart." Although he never sought public office, he had served on several committees and as a water commissioner for over a decade. More important, this "quiet man who made little noise in the world," attained his status in the community by "the sheer force of his prestige as a businessman and by personal trustworthiness."[2] His was a legacy his daughter Maude took seriously.

Financially secure due to her family's wealth, Maude Shattuck traveled widely—often with her widowed mother or a sister as a companion—to Bermuda, Honolulu, Japan, the Far East, Europe, and across America. A tall woman (according to her passport application, she was 5'9" tall), Shattuck was athletic—she played competitive tennis and enjoyed boating—as well as intelligent. She served the community for decades on the Norwood Hospital board of trustees, as chairman of the local branch of the Red Cross, on the Playground Committee, and the Women's Division of the Public Safety Committee. She was

The Morrill Memorial Library was built and presented to the town in 1898 by George H. and Louise Morrill in memory of their daughter, Sara Bond Morrill.
(Courtesy of Robert Donahue)

active in the First Congregational Church and the Norwood Civic Association. Maude Shattuck was most devoted, however, to the town's public library.[3]

Norwood's Morrill Memorial Library, the town's first dedicated library building, had been a gift from Maude's grandfather, George H. Morrill, and his second wife, Louisa (Tidd) Morrill in memory of their daughter Sarah Bond Morrill, who had died of typhoid fever in 1896 at the age of twenty-three.[4] Grieving over the loss of their child, the Morrills erected the public library as a permanent memorial to her. The town accepted this philanthropic gesture, and the Romanesque-Revival building was dedicated in February of 1898. Twenty years later, Maude Shattuck, who had been sixteen when her aunt died, was elected to the library's Board of Trustees. From that position she oversaw the building of the Plimpton wing in 1928, an addition made possible by the bequest of another of George H. Morrill's children, Shattuck's aunt, Mrs. Alice Morrill Plimpton.

There was, to be sure, a bit of noblesse oblige in Maude Shattuck's volunteer endeavors. Self-assured and confident of her status within the community, Maude was a practical Yankee who eschewed controversy but stated her opinions without hesitation. Her voice and straight forward manner can be inferred from the statement of her candidacy for re-election to the library board in 1935: "Editor, *Messenger*: Running for the Library Board is a habit I cannot overcome. I have served several terms. There are doubtless many better qualified than I. Frankly, I enjoy the work. Maude A. Shattuck."[5]

Four years later, in 1939, Jane Hewitt, who had been the librarian since 1898, retired. Maude Shattuck, along with the rest of the board of trustees, hired as Hewitt's successor Miss Edna Phillips (1890-1968).

Born in Newark, New Jersey on January 13, 1890 to Edward L. and Letitia (Macy) Phillips, Edna never received a college degree but rose to the top of her chosen profession with an impeccable reputation at the local, state, and national level. She first studied at the New York School of Applied Design and the Art Students' League of New York but, in 1913, after receiving library training through the Public Library Commission of New Jersey, and passing a civil service examination, she became a librarian in Edgewater, New Jersey. Desiring to participate in a meaningful way when World War I broke out, under the auspices of the Y. M. C. A., Phillips operated canteens for U.S. military personnel in Europe from April 1918 through May of 1919, and was among the first six women to serve with the army of occupation in Germany.[6]

In 1921, she took a position as librarian in East Orange, New Jersey, an industrial community with a large foreign-born population, much like Norwood. It was here that Phillips first sought to aid immigrants in their quest to speak, read, and write English, and to become citizens of the United States. Phillips believed a librarian was not a social worker, but an educator. She saw her work with the foreign-born as a three-pronged mission: to facilitate their mastery of English, to prepare them for citizenship, and, perhaps most important, to help them preserve their own distinctive cultural heritage. Two years later, her combination of library experience, international travel, and dedication to service led her to become the Secretary for Library Work with Foreigners, a position within the Division of Public Libraries, then part of the Massachusetts Department of Education.

While her primary responsibility was to assist small towns with limited resources to provide literacy and Americanization education to immigrants, once in the position Phillips extended her influence by reaching out to larger cities and towns where substantial enclaves of foreign-born populations resided. As a result of her experience, by 1925 she had become chair of the American Library Association's (ALA) Committee on Work with the Foreign-Born. She spoke frequently at conventions and to smaller groups of librarians and educators on Americanization-related topics. She vigorously advocated for bringing the culturally-diverse populations of immigrants into the mainstream of American life without depriving them of their inherited culture. To that end she rejected the then popular eugenically-tinged racial theories that categorized and stratified the foreign-born according to presumed mental or physical attributes.

Phillips encouraged the ALA to offer programming on issues related to immigrants and literacy. She also made lists of suitable books for librarians to purchase and contacted foreign-language newspapers, bookstores, and organizations that might assist in book selections and collection development. She felt that it was vital that the children of immigrants take pride in their own history. One way to encourage that was to ensure that children had books which they could bring home in their parents' native language. She agreed with another early advocate of cultural diversity who wrote, "It would be absurd for America to scrap the magnificent contributions which her immigrants have brought not only to our industrial and agricultural productivity, but more important still, to the spiritual and cultural life of America." Although Phillips did not limit her efforts to any one ethnic group, her work on behalf of Italian immigrants garnered her the Dante Medal from the city of Ravenna, Italy, for her "interest and actions in caring for Italian immigrants and in promoting a sympathetic understanding between Italy and the United States."[7]

The passage of the National Origins Act of 1924 drastically reduced the number of immigrants arriving from Europe and, by the early 1930s, although illiteracy among native-born adults remained a problem, the need for literacy education for the foreign-born diminished. This fact, coupled with the economic hardships and budgetary constraints brought on by the Great Depression, forced the Massachusetts Department of Education to eliminate her position.

Phillips spent the next few years as an archivist. She was awarded a fellowship in adult education at Columbia University and then, along with a colleague, received a grant to study adult beginner readers among black, native-born whites, and immigrants across the country. They found that few satisfying books for the adult beginner were available, and thus opened a market for materials aimed at adults with limited reading expertise. From this point on in her career, Phillips focused on the importance of literacy training for adult Americans, both foreign- and native-born.

Returning to Massachusetts, from 1934 to 1939 Phillips was librarian of the Sawyer Free Library in Gloucester, and in April 1939 she accepted the position of librarian of the Morrill Memorial Library in Norwood, a town undoubtedly familiar to her from her work with the Massachusetts Division of Public Libraries. Her impact on the library was immediate. Her initial annual report to the town included not only the customary statistical report on circulation, registered borrowers, and book purchases, but also a six-page "Narrative Report" with sub-headings on "Building a Live Book Collection," "Bringing Book and Reader Together," and "Youth and the Library."[8] She authored a pamphlet to explain the library's mission and goals to the public and coordinated library services to the schools. She continued her affiliations with regional and national library organizations as well as membership in the local Women's Club, Camp Fire Girls, Historical Society, and Literary Club. A gracious, good-humored, and professional presence wherever she went, Phillips worked tirelessly to promote Friends of the Library groups throughout the state and to improve relations between and among racial and ethnic populations in local communities. National periodicals regularly published her views on integrating the foreign-born into the library and her recommendations for staff development and assessment.

In 1944, Edna Phillips began a second term with the ALA's Committee on Work with the Foreign-born, and under her leadership the association supported the efforts of the United Nations. As the chair of the newly-formed Committee on Intercultural Action, Phillips coordinated the shipment of food, clothing, supplies and books to libraries and their staff across Europe. Closer to home, she continued to advocate for adult education, literacy, and the extension of library services to often overlooked populations, while at the same time helping to make the Morrill Memorial Library the center of Norwood. She wrote articles for the local newspaper, spoke at community and library meetings across the state, and offered a wide range of exhibits and programs for adults and children.

Perhaps most significant to the library and its patrons, in 1941 she had spearheaded the opening of a branch library at 1163 Washington Street in South Norwood. It began as a two-day-a-week experiment and was enthusiastically embraced by a grateful neighborhood. From its inception, the South Norwood branch flourished. Its circulation skyrocketed, and meetings of neighborhood groups, exhibits, and special programs drew large audiences. In November of 1948, the South Norwood branch librarian resigned to take a position as head librarian in another community and Mrs. Mary Knowles was hired.

Born to a working-class family in Maine, Mary Gardner Knowles (1910-1997) was raised by an older married sister due to the early death of her mother. Mary entered Bates College, a small liberal arts college in Lewiston, Maine, in 1930. In addition to working at the college library during the academic year, she was employed at a hotel on Chebeague Island during the summer. She was a popular young woman who joined various student organizations, and was elected vice president of her class. It was at Bates that Mary met Clive Knowles, a serious young man from Roxbury, Massachusetts, who was on the editorial staff of the student newspaper. His interests included religious studies and issues relating to class and status.[9]

After their marriage in 1933, Mary Knowles left Bates, received a professional librarian's certificate from the State of Massachusetts, and worked at the Watertown (Massachusetts) Public Library. During that time, Clive Knowles traveled to the University of Chicago Divinity School to study social ethics, and eventually became a labor organizer. In 1948, after a marriage plagued by frequent separations, Clive and Mary separated for good, leaving her the sole support of their young son. It was her work at Watertown that earned her the position of the South Norwood branch librarian.

The South Norwood branch of the Morrill Memorial Library occupied
this storefront on Washington Street during Mary Knowles' tenure.
(Courtesy of the Morrill Memorial Library)

Knowles was a positive influence in South Norwood from the outset. Edna Phillips noted in her 1949 annual report that Knowles' "enterprise, ability and charm" were definite factors in the marked development of the branch. Participation in children's Saturday morning story hours doubled, the collection of foreign language books expanded to include Arabic, Finnish, Lithuanian, Polish and Russian volumes, and classes from the Balch Elementary School (located across the street from the library) made regular visits. Knowles' programs and outreach to children, teachers, and townspeople attracted the entire neighborhood, which soon embraced her as one of their own. Adult patrons flocked to join the newly named "Covi Club" (Club of Various Interests) which met at the branch library. Meeting at least monthly, members of the group shared their expertise on a wide range of subjects. For example, Victor Babel answered questions about interior decorating, and Nellie Pazniokas led a workshop on baking and cake decorating.[10]

In the summer of 1950, due primarily to Knowles' efforts and popularity, the South Norwood branch maintained full-time hours for the first time. On May 14, 1951, a gala well-attended Open House, hosted by the Board of Trustees, Head Librarian Edna Phillips, and

Edna Phillips (standing left) and Mary Knowles (standing right)
inside the South Norwood branch with three patrons.
(Courtesy of the Morrill Memorial Library)

Branch Librarian Mary Knowles, commemorated ten years of direct library service to the people of South Norwood. Six months later, on November 9, 1951, the Federal Bureau of Investigation (FBI) came to call on Mary Knowles.[11]

Concern about communism had increased since the end of World War II, and in 1947 the U. S. House Committee on Un-American Activities (HUAC), which had been designed to surveil labor unions during the 1930s, began to investigate rumors of communist cells in the film industry, the government, and academia. HUAC was subsequently joined in their investigations by the Senate Internal Security Subcommittee (chaired by Senator William Jenner of Indiana) and the Senate Government Operations Committee (chaired by Senator Joseph McCarthy of Wisconsin). Although these committees failed to uncover any major conspiracy or communist activity, many reputations were ruined and careers ended.

Meanwhile, in Massachusetts, several bills aimed at communists and their sympathizers were introduced, and three of these became law. Beginning in 1949, public employees were required to take an oath of allegiance to the state and federal Constitutions; in 1950, the Massachusetts legislature created their own HUAC; and, in 1951, the communist party was outlawed. While some attributed these actions to the state's regionalism and anti-elitism, Massachusetts was also the home of Herbert Philbrick, a man who had turned his stint as a paid FBI informant into a career. He testified before a number of House and Senate subcommittees, wrote a popular memoir, *I Led Three Lives*, and appeared on a television series by the same name. During testimony before an HUAC executive session in July of 1951, Herbert Philbrick had mentioned Mary Knowles.[12]

The FBI was already aware of Knowles because of her association with Harry Winner and the Samuel Adams School for Social Studies in Boston, a "labor school" which provided free education for the working class and was known to have communist affiliations. In fact, Clive and Mary Knowles had both worked at the school. Clive taught collective bargaining and shop stewardship training for trade union representatives; Mary led a children's story hour and later became the school's secretary. After Clive left both the school and his wife, Mary Knowles and her son had lived with the Winner family until her move to Norwood in 1948.

Because of this association, the FBI knew that Mary Knowles had been familiar with, and likely a member of, the communist party, but were unconcerned, believing that Clive Knowles had been more involved in party activities than she. In November of 1951, the FBI hoped that an interview with Mary would enable them to remove her name from their files altogether. But things did not go smoothly.

When FBI agents arrived, they asked Mary Knowles to provide information about the Samuel Adams School personnel, especially Harry Winner, who was then under indictment. She declined to discuss her friends, family, or acquaintances, or any of her own views. Dismayed at her responses, in April of 1952, the FBI informed Norwood town manager, John B. Kennedy—in the strictest confidence—of the situation. Kennedy contacted the chair of the Board of Trustees, Maude Shattuck, and the librarian, Edna Phillips. Neither was surprised by Kennedy's disclosure.

Immediately after the November visit from the FBI, Mary Knowles had spoken with Edna Phillips, informed her of the interview, and offered to resign. Knowles admitted that she had not disclosed her work at the Samuel Adams School prior to her hiring in Norwood, feeling it would hinder her job prospects. Phillips consulted with Maude Shattuck, and both women agreed that Knowles, whom they believed was a fine woman and excellent employee, should not resign. In fact, both Phillips and Shattuck believed Knowles to be "a model employee" who "did her work very well." Given that information, town manager Kennedy agreed that the branch librarian should remain in her position. He informed the FBI that Norwood officials would "keep [Knowles] under close scrutiny" and report any disloyal or suspicious behavior. Finally, Kennedy and Shattuck instructed Edna Phillips not to inform the full Board of Trustees about the matter. The town manager agreed that Knowles' "good record" since arriving in Norwood demonstrated "she was now trying to live in the right way" and they should keep the matter "from being known around town."[13] And there the matter remained for more than a year, although Herbert Philbrick continued to testify before congressional committees naming dozens of alleged communists in the Boston area.

On May 8, 1953, Herbert Philbrick gave public testimony in Boston in front of the Jenner Committee. During his testimony, broadcast live on local radio and television, Philbrick discussed the Samuel Adams School—which he stated was "communist-controlled"—and identified Secretary Mary Knowles as a communist. Blindsided by the testimony and ensuing press frenzy, Knowles once again offered to resign "to relieve the library of any possible embarrassment." Maude Shattuck called a special meeting of the library's trustees for the following evening, but when questioned by the press, she defended the librarian. "I have complete confidence in Mrs. Knowles," Shattuck emphatically declared. "She is one of the loveliest persons I know...." Trustees Martin Curran, Rachel Martin, and Mary Dunn each declared their willingness to listen to Knowles before drawing any conclusions. (The remaining trustees, Vern Richards and Eugene Nelson, were not available for comment; Richards was ill and Nelson was out of town.) Shattuck's resolve to defend Knowles remained steadfast, even when confronted with Philbrick's insistence that Knowles participated in an underground communist cell. "Well," Shattuck tartly replied, "lots of perfectly nice people have become involved with the communists in an innocent way," adding "even Philbrick himself did."[14]

On May 9, 1953, five trustees (Nelson had returned to town and attended), Miss Phillips, and a representative from the Massachusetts Library Commission remained behind closed doors for almost four hours while reporters from the Norwood and Boston newspapers were kept at bay by Norwood police and library custodian Ben Pearson. Phillips and Shattuck offered their account of events—including the admission that they had left the trustees uninformed for nearly a year—and reiterated their support of Knowles, insisting they had seen no evidence of "subversive action or tendencies" during her five years of employment.[15]

Mary Knowles then appeared before the board and stated "it was her conviction that freedom of thought and belief, guaranteed by the Constitution of the United States, should be inviolable," and, therefore, individuals should be free from any obligation to state their personal political beliefs. Board members expressed regret that Mrs. Knowles was unwilling to confirm or deny her current or past status as a communist. In rebuttal, Knowles declared "her belief in brotherhood, in service to others, [and] in efforts to do away with inequalities, racial and economic." In answer to questions by the trustees, she "expressed an unqualified love for the United States," and affirmed that "in the event of war between Russia and the United States she would have unqualified allegiance to this country." Knowles left the meeting via the back door. With the assistance of the police, Ben Pearson escorted Mrs. Knowles through the phalanx of waiting reporters for whom she had no statement.[16]

Two board members wanted to accept her resignation, believing that "the case against Mrs. Knowles in regard to Communism was clear." But Maude Shattuck and Edna Phillips put on a defense. Shattuck stated that accepting Knowle's resignation would mean that they had "pre-judged the case;" Phillips agreed, and "expressed strong support" for Knowles. When a vote was taken, however, four trustees voted to suspend Mrs. Knowles without pay "until additional information" could be received. Shattuck continued to insist that Mary Knowles was "a woman of positive principles" who simply saw no reason that the "political beliefs of a person should be investigated."[17]

Both Norwood newspapers—the *Tribune* and the *Messenger*—gave front page coverage to the events. John J. Cook, the proprietor and editor of the weekly *Norwood Tribune*, wrote that if Knowles was not willing to "disavow communism, she must take the consequences." But he did express his hope that the trustees' action had been based on fact, not just Herbert Philbrick's accusation. Cook saved his sharpest criticism for the library board, however, who had let Knowles "escape" out the back door and avoid the press. Always more sanguine than J. J. Cook at the *Tribune*, the *Messenger's* editor, George Sherlock, made only one reference to the matter editorially. On May 12, he cautioned that there had been "a great deal of guilt by association" since the war and "Norwood residents might do well to reserve their opinions until the serious allegations are either substantiated or proven false." (A week later, on May 19, Sherlock called Senator McCarthy the "Wisconsin windbag" and pondered whether President Eisenhower had had enough of the Senator's tactics.)[18]

This was not Norwood's first encounter with a "Red Scare" or alleged communist threat. In 1920, the South Norwood neighborhood, where the branch library was located, had been one of the communities targeted by the infamous Palmer Raids. Eleven residents had been swept up in a government action ordered by then Attorney General A. Mitchell Palmer and his young assistant, J. Edgar Hoover, who by 1953 was FBI Director. All had been released, but not before being paraded through the streets of Boston in chains. Many recalled the fear those raids had engendered in South Norwood, and the neighborhood was still home to a large population of immigrants. When the *Messenger* reported that "at least three other Norwood residents are being watched in the belief that they have communist tendencies," vulnerable residents, who had learned to avoid controversy, grew silent. Unsurprisingly, trustee Mary Dunn, a vocal critic of Knowles, reported that she had obtained "a sampling of South Norwood reactions" to the situation and "everyone was in favor of immediate dismissal."[19] For those in South Norwood to say otherwise, if confronted by Dunn, would be to invite closer scrutiny.

On May 21, 1953, Mrs. Mary Knowles appeared before an open session of the Jenner Committee and declined to answer questions regarding her activities or associations; she had done the same at a closed-door hearing the day before. Her supporters in Norwood were left with few alternatives. At a special meeting called for June 1, 1953, the library's Board of Trustees voted to accept her resignation. In a final twist, however, Knowles, who said she had previously offered to resign because of her "regard for Miss Phillips" and her hope to avoid negative publicity for the library, had changed her mind. The board would have to fire her. A short while later, Edna Phillips telephoned Mary Knowles to inform her of her immediate dismissal. Although newspaper accounts stated that the vote had been unanimous, that was not the whole story. Only five of the six trustees were present—Vern Richards was unable to attend due to illness—and Maude Shattuck refused to vote. Although it was customary for the chair to refrain from voting unless breaking a tie, in this instance, Shattuck could easily have voted in a show of solidarity with her fellow board members. She chose not to do so, and the official statement on the matter was issued by trustees Mary Dunn and Martin Curran.[20]

Maude Shattuck and Edna Phillips remained unmoved by the arguments of the trustees, townspeople, or media. John Cook ominously predicted in the *Tribune* that because of Shattuck's continued praise of Mrs. Knowles and her "failure to vote" on her dismissal, "the voters are not likely to look kindly upon her re-election." She was re-elected, however, and retained her seat on the board until her resignation due to illness in the fall of 1956.

Coincidentally, Shattuck's beloved Smith College was tainted by the Red Scare as well. Following a series of rumors about communist activity at the college, a few influential graduates mailed a letter to alumnae accusing Smith of employing "Reds," and naming five faculty members as communists. The correspondence, and subsequent investigation by the Massachusetts HUAC, was met with the overwhelming condemnation of alumnae. There is no need to wonder on which side of the controversy Maude Shattuck stood.[21]

It seems Edna Phillips went even further in her support of Knowles. Phillips was a practicing Quaker, among the few religious

Librarian Edna Phillips and the Board of Trustees in 1953 during the
Mary Knowles crisis. Standing (left to right): Rachel P. Martin, Eugene
A. Nelson, Mary L. Dunn. Seated (left to right): Martin B. Curran, Edna
Phillips, Maude A. Shattuck, Vern H. Richards.
(Courtesy of the Morrill Memorial Library)

organizations that lobbied against required loyalty oaths and provided
assistance to individuals and families caught in the panic surrounding
HUAC actions. Known for their temperance and tolerance, Quakers
consistently adhered to the principles of pacifism, equality,
and conscience. Edna Phillips, a member of the Cambridge
(Massachusetts) Friends' Meeting, and Henry J. Cadbury, professor
of divinity at Harvard and a highly respected member of the American
Friends Service Committee, each wrote letters of recommendation
for Knowles. She was hired by the William Jeanes Memorial Library,
which was operated by Quakers, in Lafayette Hill, Pennsylvania,
and began work in October, 1953. Knowles remained at the Jeanes
Memorial Library until her retirement in 1979.[22]

Edna Phillips retired from the Morrill Memorial Library in October
1962. At that time, and again upon her death in 1968, Miss Phillips was
universally praised as "a person of strong convictions and high ideals,"
a woman who "worked toward excellence in all things" and remained
committed to literacy and "reading as a means to individual growth,
intercultural relations, and world peace."[23]

On the night she was fired from the Morrill Memorial Library, at

Maude Shattuck's request, Mary Knowles provided a five-page written statement explaining and defending her position. In it she declared her "commitment" to the Declaration of Independence and the Constitution and its guarantees of freedom of speech and thought—and even the freedom to "refrain from speaking." She reiterated her opposition to "all forms of discrimination and censorship" and her belief "in the basic goodness of men and in the limitless potentiality for good in the human race." It was, she repeated, her belief in the founding documents of the United States that had led her to take this stand.[24] In 1953 Norwood, at the height of the scourge that was McCarthyism, she did not stand alone. Maude Shattuck and Edna Phillips, two other women of conscience, stood with her.

Sources and Notes

General information on the 1950s came from a variety of sources, including: Stephanie Coontz, *The Way We Never Were* (NY: Basic Books, 1991); Charles A. Willis, *America in the 1950s* (NY: Facts on File, 2006); Eugenia Kaledin, *Daily Life in the United States, 1940-1959, Shifting Worlds* (Westport, CT: Greenwood Press, 2000). Material pertaining to Norwood's history can be found in Bryant Tolles, *Norwood: The Centennial History of a Massachusetts Town* (Norwood, MA: Norwood Printing Company, 1973) and Patricia J. Fanning, *Norwood: A History* (Charleston, SC: Arcadia Publishing, 2002).

1. Maude A. Shattuck file at the Smith College Archives. My thanks to Amy Hague, Special Collections, for this information. Also pertinent to Smith's history was Helen Lefkowitz Horowitz, *Alma Mater: Design and Experience in the Women's Colleges from Their Nineteenth Century Beginnings to the 1930s*, (NY: Alfred A. Knopf, 1984). I also thank Dorothy DeSimone for sharing material on Shattuck's Dana Hall years.
2. "Edmund J. Shattuck," *Norwood Advertiser and Review*, 9

October 1903, p. 8.

3. Biographical information on Maude A. Shattuck comes from her obituary, "Miss Shattuck, 81, Dies; Was Library Trustee for 37 Years," *Norwood Messenger* (hereafter *NM*), 14 August 1962, p. 1.

4. Sarah Bond Morrill was named for Louisa's sister who had been George H. Morrill's first wife. She had died in 1864 at the age of thirty-one.

5. "Candidacy Statements," *NM*, 15 January 1935, p. 5. This was the only time Maude Shattuck offered a campaign statement in her nearly four decades as a trustee. The circumstances were unusual. It was a contested election (three candidates for two positions) but all three failed to obtain the required number of valid signatures on their nomination papers. Thus, the outcome was determined by write-in votes. The other two candidates submitted lengthy statements. Shattuck received the most votes.

6. Biographical information about Edna Phillips: "Town Loses a Gracious Lady…Miss Edna Phillips, Librarian Emeritus, Passes Away at 78," *NM*, 6 November 1968, pp. 1, 8. And from: Plummer Alston Jones, "American Public Library Service to the Immigrant Community, 1876-1948: a biographical history of the movement and its leaders: Jane Maud Campbell (1869-1947), John Foster Carr (1869-1939), Eleanor (Edwards) Ledbetter (1870-1954), and Edna Phillips (1890-1968)" (Ph.D. dissertation: University of North Carolina at Chapel Hill, 1991, especially pp. 442-447, 456-465.

7. Charles M. Herlihy, quoted in Jones, p. 450.

8. *Annual Report of the Town of Norwood*, year ending December 31, 1939 (Norwood, MA: Norwood Printing Co.), pp. 80-88.

9. Biographical information about Mary Knowles: Allison Hepler, *McCarthyism in the Suburbs* (Lanham, MD: Lexington Books, 2018), especially pp. 1-37.

10. *Annual Report of the Town of Norwood*, year ending December 31, 1949 (Norwood, MA: Norwood Printing Co.); Miscellaneous clippings from Morrill Memorial Library (MML) files on Edna Phillips, Mary Knowles, South Norwood branch, including

clippings on the Covi Club, no pagination.

11. Invitation to Anniversary Celebration, 14 May 1951, MML, South Norwood branch file.

12. On McCarthyism: Ellen Schrecker, *Many Are the Crimes: McCarthyism in America* (Boston: Little, Brown & Co., 1998) and M. J. Heale, *McCarthy's Americans: Red Scare Politics in State and Nation* (Athens, GA: University of Georgia Press, 1998) as well as Hepler, *McCarthyism in the Suburbs*.

13. Minutes of the MML Board of Trustees, Special Meeting, 9 May 1953. It is interesting to note that the Norwood Board of Selectmen's Minutes during this time period make no mention of the controversy.

14. "Norwood Board To Act Tonight," *Boston Post*, 9 May 1953, pp. 1 ,3.

15. Minutes of the MML Board of Trustees, Special Meeting, 9 May 1953.

16. Ibid.

17. Ibid.

18. John J. Cook, "It Seems to Me," *Norwood Tribune*, 14 May 1953, p. 1; E. V. McLean, "Suspended Librarian May Face Jenner Committee," *NM*, 12 May 1953, p. 1, 2; "Town Talk," [editorial comments], *NM*, 12 May 1953, p. 2; "Town Talk," *NM*, 19 May 1953, p. 2.

19. McLean, "Suspended Librarian," p. 2; Minutes of the MML Board of Trustees, 1 June 1953.

20. Minutes of the MML Board of Trustees, 1 June 1953; "Trustees Fire So. Norwood Librarian On 4 to 0 Vote," *NM*, 2 June 1953, p. 1.

21. John J. Cook, "It Seems to Me," *Norwood Tribune*, 4 June 1953, p. 1. On Smith College's experience: Jacquelyn Dowd Hall, *Sisters and Rebels: A Struggle for the Soul of America* (NY: W. W. Norton, 2019). I thank Amy Hague, Special Collections, Smith College for the entry in "Smithipedia:" https://sophia.smith.edu/blog/smithipedia/smith-and-politics/mccarthyism-at-smith/.

22. October 1953 letters from Phillips and Cadbury in support of Knowles recorded in HUAC Hearing documents; draft letter

from Mary Knowles to Henry Cadbury mentions hearing from him through Phillips: MML, Mary Knowles file.

23. "Town Loses a Gracious Lady…," *NM*, 6 November 1968, p. 1.

24. Mary Knowles, "Statement to the Board of Trustees, Morrill Memorial Library, Norwood, Massachusetts," May 1953. My thanks to Allison Hepler for providing a copy of this document. Mary Knowles was convicted of contempt of Congress; in 1960, her conviction was overturned by the U. S. Court of Appeals. For information on Mary Knowles' subsequent career and legal difficulties see: Allison Hepler, *McCarthyism in the Suburbs: Quakers, Communists, and the Children's Librarian* (Lanham, MD: Lexington Books, 2018).

Chapter 12

Pioneer Families of Color

IN HER MAGISTERIAL NARRATIVE, *The Warmth of Other Suns*, Isabel Wilkerson documents what has become known as the Great Migration, the movement of black citizens who left their southern homes to start new lives in northern and western cities. While Wilkerson chronicles the migration of these domestically-displaced persons between 1915 and 1970, there was an earlier generation of exiles, those who came north in the 1870s and 1880s. Among these black pioneers were members of the Diggs and Tanneyhill families who found their way to Norwood.

Ann Tanneyhill and Henry Diggs were born in 1906, just as the twentieth century was beginning to take root.[1] They were first cousins, their mothers being sisters. But there was also a familial association that went back decades and miles to Frederick, Maryland, where their respective fathers, Alfred Weems Tanneyhill and Charles Tanner Diggs, were born.

Situated in north central Maryland, at the easternmost edge of the Blue Ridge Mountains, the town of Frederick was laid out in 1745. Despite its small size (6,000 by 1850 and 8,000 in 1860), Frederick's location and status as the county seat created a busy and diversified business district. Because of this, religious pluralism became a feature of the community. By the mid-nineteenth century, the main thoroughfare already housed at least six substantial church buildings. One of these spires belonged to the Asbury United Methodist Church, the oldest African-American church in town, founded as a mixed congregation in 1818. It is where the Diggs and Tanneyhill families were likely congregants and, by 1860, free men and women.

Aaron Tanneyhill and Richard H. Diggs—the grandfathers of Ann

Tanneyhill and Henry Diggs—do not appear in the 1850 census, but by 1860, Tanneyhill was a married day laborer and Diggs, married with a child, was registering for the draft in Washington, D.C. Like many free blacks, Aaron Tanneyhill chose to remain close to home. He married Mary Elizabeth Weems sometime prior to 1860 and the couple had two children: a daughter, Arianna, born in 1861, and a son, Alfred, born around 1864. In 1870 Aaron was a laborer on the local Fout farm but, along with Richard Diggs, was on the committee for Frederick's gala 15th Amendment Celebration. Organized to commemorate the ratification of the amendment that gave all men the right to vote, the day's activities included a procession of delegations from across Frederick County, as well as distinguished speakers. The previous year, when Richard Diggs had been an officer of the celebration, the renowned orator Frederick Douglass had taken part.[2]

While under the protection of the federal government immediately after the Civil War, black men were able to exercise the rights, including the right to vote, that had previously been denied them. But, within a few years white populations throughout the South began a campaign to reinstitute restrictions. As a result, one scholar reflected, for blacks "the world got smaller, narrower, [and] more confined with each new court ruling and ordinance."[3] Perhaps because of these circumstances, sometime in the early 1870s, Richard Diggs left Frederick and headed north to Walpole, Massachusetts.

Why he chose Walpole is unknown but, by 1874, when their two-year-old daughter died, Richard and his wife, Sarah Lyles Diggs, had made a home there. The couple already had four other children, all born in Maryland between 1862 and 1869: Nettie, Henry, Charles, and Ida. While in Walpole, the family lost two more children, Joseph in 1876, and William in 1880, but celebrated the birth of twins, Fanny and Frank, in 1877. A carpenter by trade, Richard Diggs may have worked at any number of small-scale manufacturing establishments in Walpole, but around 1885, at the age of forty-six, he brought his family to Norwood, which then had a population of around 3,000. He was employed at the New York & New England Railroad Car Shops as an upholsterer, and shortly thereafter, his eldest son Henry, then twenty, joined him there.

The "car shops," as the complex erected on Lenox Street simply came to be called, had arrived in 1875, just three years after Norwood's incorporation, after the railroad's repair and maintenance facility situated in nearby Readville had been destroyed by fire. Initially, the facility built and repaired passenger and freight cars, but in 1880 the steam locomotive maintenance unit was brought to Norwood as well. More than 300 mechanics and skilled artisans, like Richard Diggs, were employed there, making the facility a vital component of the new town's industrial base.

Richard Diggs apparently kept in touch with the Tanneyhills back in Frederick, even after his relocation to Massachusetts. In 1898 he joined with Aaron Tanneyhill and others to incorporate the Workingmen's Stock Company, described as "a corporation of colored people owning and controlling Greenmount Cemetery," a small 3-acre burial ground adjacent to the Frederick City Hospital.[4] Even earlier, however, around the time the Diggs family moved to Norwood, Aaron Tanneyhill's only son, Alfred, perhaps dissatisfied with his prospects in Frederick, came north to join them.

Alfred Tanneyhill and his contemporary, Charles Tanner Diggs, each in their 20s, found employment as coachmen for two of the wealthiest families in Norwood. Diggs was hired by Francis O. Winslow, the owner of the Winslow Brothers tannery, who lived in a Second Empire mansion on a large estate on Walpole Street, and Tanneyhill found a position at the home of Lewis and Anna Smith Day and their son, Fred Holland Day, whose substantial home overlooked the center of town. Tanneyhill remained with the Day family for more than forty years. Employed first as a coachman, and later as a butler, he eventually managed the entire household, hiring and supervising staff (which included a succession of maids, cooks, gardeners, and nurses), and overseeing routine household purchases. By all accounts the epitome of professionalism, Alfred Tanneyhill was thought of more as a confidant than an employee. Being about the same age, Tanneyhill and Fred Day maintained a close personal relationship and, when he died in 1933, Day left instructions that Tanneyhill was to be consulted on all aspects of the disposal of the estate.

In 1903, when Alfred married Adelaide Olivia Grandison, the

Alfred Weems Tanneyhill and Adelaide Olivia Grandison were married
on October 14, 1903. *(Courtesy of Judith Diggs Potter)*

newlyweds moved into 32 Day Street, a house owned by Anna Day; she
later deeded the property to Tanneyhill. A few years earlier, Charles
Tanner Diggs had married Sarah Elizabeth Grandison, Adelaide's
younger sister, thereby solidifying the ties between the two families.
Adelaide and Sarah were the daughters of William Grandison, a printer,
publisher, and entrepreneur who had a unique history of his own.

Born in 1848, William Grandison was the namesake and only son of
William Grandison, a native of the West Indies, and his wife Margaret
Hazzard Grandison of Maryland. After their marriage in Louisiana,
according to family lore the Grandisons made their way to Canada
sometime in the 1840s and their son was born in Halifax, Nova Scotia.
Educated in Halifax, young William learned the printer's trade and
emigrated to Cambridge, Massachusetts in 1869 at the age of twenty-
one. He applied at Rand, Avery & Company, printers specializing in
travel and sightseeing guides, and, after demonstrating his ability as a
compositor by setting an error-free "proof," he was hired. Grandison
worked at Rand, Avery for a year before acquiring a position at the
Riverside Press, a firm well-known for the artistry and accuracy of its
work.

While at Riverside, Grandison joined the Typographical Workers
Society, but not without an internal debate over electing a man of

Charles Tanner Diggs and Sarah Elizabeth Grandison
were married on October 20, 1897. *(Courtesy of Judith Diggs Potter)*

his race into the union. According to a later *Boston Globe* account, Grandison was "the first colored man admitted to a trade union" in the city, perhaps even the nation. Highly respected for the quality of his work, Grandison was praised for his gentlemanly but frank manner as well as his "undoubted intelligence, his modesty [and] his integrity." By the early 1890s, Grandison was employed by J. Stearns Cushing, who owned a composition and electrotyping concern in Boston. In 1894, Grandison moved his family to Norwood when Cushing brought his business to the town.[5]

Mindful of the unstable commercial landscape in the 1890s, the Norwood Business Association, later called the Board of Trade, sought to attract new industries to the community. One of its first achievements was to bring to Norwood three independent firms—J. S. Cushing and Company, Berwick and Smith Company, and E. Fleming Company—which formed the printing conglomerate known as the Norwood Press. Lured by the offer of free land and other inducements, J. S. Cushing and Company, founded in 1878 and still under the watchful eye of its sole proprietor, J. Stearns Cushing, was first to relocate from Boston. With the addition of the press rooms of Berwick and Smith, and the Fleming book bindery, the Norwood Press enabled all processes of book-making to be completed in one large interconnected plant. It was located in a series of strikingly handsome brick buildings at the intersection of Washington Street and Walnut Avenue.

William Grandison was held in high esteem by the press workers and was elected president of both the printers' union and its relief society. He also served several terms as the Grand Chancellor of the Grand Lodge of Colored Knights of Pythias, a state-wide fraternal organization, and beginning in 1895 held the office of Supreme Keeper of Records and Seal for the organization's National Order. In 1885, along with an acquaintance, he founded, published, and printed the *Boston Advocate*, a weekly periodical "devoted to the interests of the colored people of the United States and Canada." Grandison sold his interest in the *Boston Advocate* prior to his move to Norwood. As with most distinguished residents of the town, the *Norwood Advertiser and Review*'s "Talk of the Town" column followed Grandison's activities, reporting on his vacations, and his and his children's accomplishments.[6]

During the years he was employed at Norwood Press, Grandison lived at 473 Washington Street, quite near the Richard Diggs family, who resided at 368 Washington in a home built for them in 1894 by local contractor Forrest M. Douglass. After his marriage to Sarah Grandison in 1897, Charles Tanner Diggs left the employ of Francis Winslow and began working at Norwood Press as an assistant shipper. Charles and Sarah purchased a house at 439 Washington Street, in the same neighborhood. Alfred Tanneyhill and his wife, Adelaide Grandison Tanneyhill, resided less than a mile away on Day Street, and the two young couples began to raise their families. Charles and Sarah Diggs had four sons: George, Henry, Highland, and Charles. Another son, Melvin, died in 1905 at only eleven months of age. Alfred and Adelaide Tanneyhill were the parents of four children as well, two boys and two girls: Alfred Clayton, Anna, William, and Gertrude. Meanwhile, Charles Diggs' brother, Frank, along with his wife, Louise, raised their family at 368 Washington Street. All of the cousins were naturally close.

As an adult, Ann Tanneyhill reminisced about what it was like "growing up as a child in a small New England town with no other blacks except your cousins around." Although involved in the Norwood community, the families were, in fact, quite isolated. But, Ann, at least, remained unaware of that isolation for years. "We went to church, we went to the movies, did all the things kids do," she explained. While her siblings and cousins were always nearby, she remembered playing and going to school with other boys and girls as well. She especially enjoyed ice skating on local ponds and eating the ice cream which her father made for all the children. "I had a very happy childhood," she continued. "I did not realize that I was different from anybody else until I was about thirteen years old." That was the age at which one of the girls she played with greeted her with a racial epithet. "I didn't understand what she was saying and what it meant," Ann said, and even after her mother explained it to her, "it still had very little meaning for me, very little meaning." Gertrude, the youngest Tanneyhill child, born a dozen years after Ann, recollected a more nuanced view of the family's distinctiveness: "In many ways," she stated, "we were brought up white, that is until it came to dances and other such social activities where you quickly learned there were lines to be drawn."[7]

William Grandison left Norwood Press around 1900 and returned to Cambridge, where he opened his own general printing business. He was the family's connection to the larger and more cosmopolitan black communities of Boston and Cambridge. Gertrude Tanneyhill characterized her maternal grandfather as "a real race man," one who believed in being politically active. She recalled traveling to the city to attend civil rights meetings, dance lessons, social gatherings, and other events—"anything to help us understand that we weren't white"—was how she put it. Through these contacts, the family became acquainted with activists including Archibald Grimké (whom the Tanneyhills knew as a friend of the Day family), William Monroe Trotter (a publisher like Grandison), and others. Ann especially remembered a story told by her great-great-aunt Mary Ann Taylor, who lived in Cambridge and operated a hand laundry patronized by university students. Taylor, who was William Grandison's aunt by marriage, also boarded Harvard students of color in her home. W. E. B. Du Bois, who described Taylor in his autobiography as "a colored woman from Nova Scotia, a descendant of…black Jamaican Maroons," remembered renting her "second story front room" for four years.[8]

Adelaide Grandison Tanneyhill, Ann and Gertrude's mother, had grown up in Cambridge. When she came to Norwood with her father at the age of twenty, she became a typesetter and proofreader at Norwood Press. In 1896, she worked at the University Press of Cambridge, one of the most prestigious firms of its kind. As was customary, Adelaide did not work outside her home after her marriage, but she continued to belong to "The Golden Rule Club of Cambridge," one of countless literary groups populated by middle-class black women at the turn of the century. Considered fundamental to racial equality and social reform, reading and discussing literature provided practical knowledge, an introduction to different ways of thinking, and a means to direct social and political conversation.[9]

While a teenager in the early 1920s, Ann Tanneyhill became a secretary and assistant for her father's employer and friend, Fred Holland Day, who was engaged in historical and familial research. The after-school job entailed consulting records at local libraries and cemeteries, writing, and later, typing, correspondence, and occasionally attending lectures or exhibitions and reporting back to a bedridden Day. Her decision to attend Simmons College was influenced by him, and it was a choice that changed the course of Ann's life.[10]

At Simmons, Tanneyhill joined the Alpha Kappa Alpha (AKA) sorority. For the first time in her life, she was able to attend meetings and parties "where we were all black." Her interactions with students of color from colleges across the city and beyond raised her awareness even more, especially since she had recently faced discrimination. Having taken the state civil service exam, Ann was repeatedly denied employment. But she said her father "knew what was happening"—she was being rejected after each in-person interview because of her race. Alfred Tanneyhill visited the Norwood office of then State Senator (later Governor) Frank G. Allen. Norwood was still a small town and everyone knew Frank Allen; he was the President of the Winslow tannery and had started his political career as a local selectman. Tanneyhill explained the situation to Allen. That very same day, Ann received a call to come for a job at the Massachusetts State House, a position she held for almost two years. But the experience left an impression and helped focus her career ambitions. Upon graduation from Simmons in 1928, she worked at a Springfield, Massachusetts affiliate of the Urban League, a position which quickly led her to New York City and the headquarters of the National Urban League. She remained a staff member there for more than fifty years.[11]

For his part, Henry W. Diggs graduated from Norwood High School in 1924 and followed his father to the Norwood Press. By 1925, older brother George had left Norwood, and when their father, Charles Diggs, died a few years later, Henry, at age twenty-three, became the chief support of his mother and two younger siblings: Highland, just turning eighteen, and Charles Winston, only seven years old.

As Ann Tanneyhill and Henry Diggs began to make their way in the world, the elder generation was passing away. Aaron Tanneyhill died in 1911 in Philadelphia, where he had gone to live with his daughter, and he was buried in Greenmount Cemetery back in Frederick, Maryland. William Grandison, the admired and talented grandfather to the Tanneyhill and Diggs children, died in 1928. And, Richard H. Diggs, who had moved north from Maryland in the 1870s, died at his Washington Street home in 1933. At the time of his death, Diggs was the oldest man in Norwood and holder of the *Boston Post* cane, an inscribed ebony and gold commemorative stave. Distributed by the *Post* to seven hundred New England towns as a promotional gimmick, the walking stick was to be given to each community's oldest resident and upon his death, was to be transmitted to the next oldest survivor. When he died, on November 22, 1933, Richard Diggs was three weeks shy of ninety-five.[12]

Throughout the decades, Ann Tanneyhill worked tirelessly for the Urban League. From 1931 until 1955, she directed the League's Vocational Opportunity Campaign, creating and promoting innovative educational and career-oriented programs. Gracious, yet determined, she faced challenges and struggles with calm perseverance, declaring later that she "was not deterred by the obstacles. They were simply there to be overcome." She became known for her creativity, organizational skills, and her professional demeanor. Along the way she earned a master's degree in vocational guidance and personnel administration from Columbia University's Teachers College.[13]

Gertrude Tanneyhill followed in her older sister's footsteps. After graduating from Norwood High School in 1935, she initially entered

Both Anna Tanneyhill (class of 1928) and Gertrude Tanneyhill (class of 1939) graduated from Simmons College in Boston. These are their yearbook photographs. *(Courtesy of Simmons University)*

the Simmons College's nursing program. Upon learning that the only hospitals available to her for a practicum were black institutions in Washington, D.C. and St. Louis, Missouri, she explained, "I politely told them what to do with that" and transferred to social work. In 1940, she earned a master's degree at the University of Pittsburgh and spent more than a decade with the National Urban League, first in Pittsburgh and later in Brooklyn. Then, for no apparent reason, she recalled, "Something said—Come home" and she returned to Norwood.[14]

The hometown of her childhood had changed. Both her parents, Alfred Weems Tanneyhill and Adelaide Grandison Tanneyhill, had died; her father in 1947 and her mother, three years later. Norwood's population had risen from 15,000 in 1930 to almost 22,000 in 1955, and it had been transformed, as had countless communities across the country, by the Depression years of the 1930s, the war years of the 1940s, and the post-war era. Privately-owned businesses and industries had given way to corporate conglomerates, while the blue-collar workforce had declined in the face of an expansion of the white-collar middle class. At the same time, towns like Norwood were becoming residential suburbs—bedroom communities for commuters. Gertrude returned to a town undergoing a near total industrial and residential reconfiguration.

The large-scale industries that had come to be relied on for working class employment security had disappeared, and had been replaced by light manufacturers, laboratories, and wholesale businesses. The tanneries had all closed by 1952, and were quickly followed by the Norwood Press. Berwick and Smith dissolved that same year, with C. B. Fleming and J. S. Cushing doing the same in 1954. George H. Morrill Company and the Plimpton Press managed to continue until the early 1970s, when they too closed their Norwood operations.

It was the demise of the Norwood Press that most affected the extended family, however. In 1954, just as Gertrude Tanneyhill returned to Norwood and accepted a position within the Massachusetts Division of Youth Services, Henry Diggs lost his job, after being employed at Norwood Press for close to thirty years. Diggs had married the former Irma Thompson, a teacher with a bachelor's degree from Tufts, in 1937. The wedding, which took place in the Tufts College Chapel, was officiated by Irma's father, Elmer E. Thompson, a Baptist minister who had been the first black graduate of Springfield College in Massachusetts in 1904. Irma and Henry Diggs had two daughters, Judith and Jacqueline. After the close of the press, Henry worked at Codex Corporation, a small printing firm on Central Street in Norwood, and at Wellesley Press in Wellesley. But he remained the Norwood anchor for the two families. It was, perhaps, Henry's constancy and dependability that allowed his younger brothers, Highland and Charles, to take on other challenges.

From an early age, Highland Diggs was drawn to music. "I made a lucky choice in picking my parents," he jokingly said in one interview. "My dad, Charles Diggs, was a music lover and my mother, Sarah Grandison, was definitely artistic." There was also "the piano that was gathering dust in my grandfather's parlor." By the age of eleven, although he was studying classical music and opera (his father's favorites), he found the jazz sounds of Duke Ellington and Louis Armstrong irresistible. Soon he was performing jazz piano in neighboring towns with local Norwood bands, after which he began playing swing dance music with a host of groups at venues from Boston to Cape Cod. And his career began to take shape.[15]

Although he had plenty of opportunities to tour nationally, Hi, as he was called, chose to remain local and raise a family. He became a mainstay in Boston's Scollay Square at such spots as the Imperial Café and the Crawford House. According to jazz historian, Richard Vacca, the city was "a prominent place on the jazz map," especially in the 1940s and 50s. "Boston was an incubator of musical talent, a training ground for jazz journalists, a magnet for music education, and a proving ground for new approaches in jazz presentation," in Vacca's estimation, and Hi Diggs was a well-regarded figure at the center of it all. He worked regularly at the Hi-Hat, one of Boston's most important jazz night spots where he encountered such luminaries as Miles Davis, Dizzy Gillespie, Charlie Parker, and Thelonius Monk, whom Diggs called "a genius" when he first heard him play.[16]

A journeyman musician's life is never easy, and Diggs kept up a hectic schedule. Sometimes he was forced to find non-musical employment to support his family, but he would teach, coach, and pick up gigs whenever possible. For one stretch of time, after a divorce, he was doing double-duty at the Hi-Hat and the Pioneer Club, a legendary after-hours club that attracted musicians, entertainers, journalists and night owls. "I was at that time a single parent with four teenage daughters," Hi recalled. "I worked until closing at the Hi-Hat, then went to the Pioneer Club, which got me home in the morning just in time to get my children up for breakfast and to drive them to school." After a few hours' sleep, he would work on arrangements, then fix supper and help with homework before returning to the Hi-Hat. "I was exhausted but can honestly say that it was one of the most pleasurable times of my life," Diggs concluded. Among the jazz greats who found the Pioneer Club in a well-hidden side street off Tremont and sat in with Hi's band were Nat "King" Cole, Count Basie, and Billie Holiday.[17]

In the 1980s, after working at a bank for eight years, Diggs remarried and moved to the South Shore where he continued to pick up gigs and compose. Highland Diggs died in 1992. He was remembered as a talented pianist, creative composer, and generous teacher who shared his musical skill and vision with countless others. A few years after Diggs' death, a three-dimensional "music fence," created by metal sculptor John Tagiuri, made up of a staff with notes corresponding to Hi's composition, "Black Nairobi Moon," was placed in the Dudley Town Common, South Park, in Boston. It provides a unique and fitting tribute to a world-class musician.[18]

Charles Winston Diggs, the youngest of the Diggs brothers, enlisted in World War II. As an airplane mechanic, he became part of the lesser known but indispensable ancillary staff of the famed Tuskegee Airmen, the renown squadrons of black and Caribbean-born military pilots. Trained at Fort Thomas in Newport, Kentucky, Diggs deployed along with those units, many of whom painted the tail, nose, or rudder of their planes red and were nicknamed "Red Tails." The Tuskegee Airmen, who faced considerable discrimination, were the first black aviators in U.S. Armed Forces history, and their actions contributed to the decision to integrate the military. Decades later, in 2006, the Tuskegee Airmen were awarded a Congressional Gold Medal as a group for "their unique military record," a record "which inspired revolutionary reform in the Armed Forces." Charles Diggs did not attend the ceremony in Washington but, on Veterans Day in 2007, Massachusetts Governor Deval Patrick presented Diggs with his award at the State House, an acknowledgment of and gratitude for his service with this ground-breaking military unit.[19]

Back in Norwood, during World War II Henry Diggs became an Air Raid Warden and member of the town's Committee on Public Safety, service that perhaps prompted his subsequent community engagement. In 1950, he was elected as a town meeting member and remained so for more than fifty years. In 1957 he was appointed to the Elementary Schools Building Committee. This committee oversaw the construction of two new elementary school buildings, a project that was successfully completed with the opening of the Charles J. Prescott Elementary School and the Frederick A. Cleveland Elementary School in November and December of 1958. The following year, Diggs was elected to the Norwood School Committee where he served with distinction for some twenty years.

Upon her return to Norwood in 1954, Gertrude Tanneyhill worked as a supervisor for young female parolees with the Massachusetts Division of Youth Services; she was reported to be a "no-nonsense but compassionate" agent. She also took her place alongside her cousin,

The Norwood School Committee in 1959, the first year Henry Diggs was elected to the Committee. Standing (left to right): John F Kelly, Eugene Nelson, Lincoln D. Lynch (Superintendent of Schools), Henry W. Diggs, John F. Reynolds. Seated (left to right): Elizabeth Syverson (clerk), Mary H. Hemman, Frances L. Blanchot. (Not pictured, John J. Cavanaugh, Chair.)

Henry Diggs, as a town official when she was elected to the Board of Trustees of the Morrill Memorial Library, one of only a handful of boards, like the School Committee, that required town-wide election. The duties of the library board were primarily policy making, but records do indicate that through the early 1960s its trustees screened "questionable" adult material for appropriateness prior to placing books on library shelves. The most consequential vote the trustees took during Gertrude's tenure was the hiring of a replacement for long-time and beloved librarian Edna Phillips. When the new director was hired in 1962, he immediately became controversial by labeling the library building "in general better suited to be a monument than a library." He lobbied for the granite edifice to be razed and called for a new, more modern facility instead of the addition that was being planned. He also publicly disparaged the skills and qualifications of the library staff.[20]

In 1964, just as the building program and the personnel reorganization were coming to a head, Gertrude Tanneyhill became chair of the library board. That same year, she left the Division of Youth Services for the Action for Boston Community Development (ABCD), the city's first anti-poverty agency, and became its inaugural director. Also in 1964 she married Charles Cuthbert, whom she had met a quarter century earlier in Pittsburgh. It was the first marriage for each. Cuthbert, who was fifteen years older, retired shortly after they married. Gertrude, 46, continued her career but resigned from the board of library trustees prior to the January 1966 election. In that year's annual report, the director wrote that she "was chair during the critical period of 1963-64" when the board "faced issues which could have broken the Library but which instead will make possible the highest standards of service for years to come." He went on to say it would be "difficult to overestimate Mrs. Cuthbert's role" in the successful resolution of these matters.[21]

In 1972, Governor Frank Sargent appointed Gertrude Tanneyhill Cuthbert to the Massachusetts Parole Board. Five years later, Governor Michael Dukakis appointed her to a second term and named her chairman. She was the first black woman to hold that position. Cuthbert's diverse career of community organizing, direct case work, and Urban League experience, made her a welcome and well-qualified addition to the seven member board. As the former chairman confirmed, Cuthbert enjoyed "a high reputation among the correctional, security and treatment personnel, parole personnel, inmates, and community groups." She enjoyed the difficult work for a number of years. In 1979, however, she went public with her belief that incarcerated women were lacking appropriate services in the Commonwealth, and in a *Boston Globe* "Spotlight" team article examining the Massachusetts prison system, Cuthbert flatly stated her opinion that "there was, indeed, harsher sentencing of blacks and Hispanics than whites."[22] A few months later, then Governor Ed King replaced her. She and her husband left Norwood and retired to Mashpee, Massachusetts where they eventually built a home next to Gertrude's sister, Ann Tanneyhill.

Ann Tanneyhill's career with the National Urban League was filled with remarkable achievements. As Director of Vocational Guidance, she visited high schools and traditionally black colleges throughout the South and played a pivotal role in the league's work toward broadening employment opportunities for both men and women. She wrote radio scripts about employment and training that were broadcast in the United States and abroad, and organized career conferences that brought major corporations to black college campuses. As Vie Kaufman wrote in the Urban League's *Equal Opportunity Journal*, "There is hardly any aspect of the work of the League Ann Tanneyhill did not enhance during her career, nor individual involved in League affairs she did not meet—and help mold." Officially retired in 1971, she was asked to continue with occasional special projects by Vernon Jordan, then League president.

Most of her time in the 1970s and beyond, however, was spent in Mashpee, a town that had been her home since 1948, when she and her brother became partners in a service station and general store business located at the Mashpee rotary. Active in community affairs, Ann became a member of the Mashpee Historical Commission and led the campaign to collect material pertaining to the original Native American settlers of the area, and to renovate the old town library as an Archive Building for the collection.[23]

Henry Diggs, too, continued to devote his time to his community. Although still a tiny minority in Norwood—there were reportedly only twenty-six black residents living in the town of 29,000 in 1968—Diggs stated in a *Boston Record American* profile that he "never felt that his color placed him at a disadvantage in the eye of his neighbors."[24] Norwood was the only home he had ever known, and he participated in all aspects of the community. A member of the United Church, the Rotary Club, and the local Elks Lodge, he was also an avid ham radio operator, and an accomplished woodworker, a skill he may have inherited from his grandfather, Richard Diggs.

A dedicated member of Norwood's School Committee for nearly twenty years, Henry Diggs left that post only when a particularly acrimonious budgetary dispute led to the recall of three of the committee's members, Diggs among them. While chairman of that board in 1970, at the height of the Vietnam War, he delivered an address to the high school's graduating class cautioning them that, "Never before has there been such a polarization, between the young and their elders, urban and suburban societies, and between the races. Discontent, discrimination, prejudice, fear and violence seem to have overtaken the world." Nevertheless, ever hopeful, he enjoined the graduates to "build a bridge" to one another so that "walls of suspicion, fear, prejudice, and hate will disappear."[25] In 1983, Diggs was named to a committee charged with developing a Fair Housing Plan for Norwood. It was adopted in 1984, and accepted by the Massachusetts Commission Against Discrimination (MCAD). He was appointed Norwood's first Fair Housing Director and remained on that board for ten years.

Henry Diggs' wife, Irma, died in 1990 and he began to spend more time on Martha's Vineyard. The history of the black community on the island is a long one. Sometime during the 1930s, the Grandison sisters—Sarah Grandison Diggs and Adelaide Grandison Tanneyhill—purchased property in Oak Bluffs, even before writer Dorothy West began to chronicle the African Americans who vacationed on the Vineyard." Henry always relished his time on the island and, in fact, had met Irma there while she was a college student holding down a summer job. Diggs grew as fond of Martha's Vineyard as his cousin Ann Tanneyhill did of Mashpee.

On a September Sunday in 1996, Henry Diggs, Ann Tanneyhill, and their extended families all gathered at the home on Day Street in Norwood where Alfred Tanneyhill had been employed for forty-five years. By then the house was the headquarters of the Norwood Historical Society, which had purchased the property after Fred Day's death. Through Ann Tanneyhill's generosity, a third-floor room in the mansion had been restored to its original splendor and was dedicated as the Tanneyhill Room over a century after the Tanneyhill and Diggs families arrived in Norwood.

Ann Tanneyhill, ninety, and Henry Diggs, who would celebrate his 90th birthday later that year, had chosen distinct but equally satisfying paths. Having left her hometown, as many young people do, Tanneyhill had embarked on a notable career with the National Urban League but had kept her family and Norwood roots close to her heart. Her cousin, Henry, had remained in Norwood. He had worked hard, married, raised a family, and devoted his life to the betterment of his own community. Fittingly, each received well-deserved recognition for their efforts. Ann Tanneyhill was called "one of the great figures of twentieth-century Black America" by the National Urban League, which established an award in her name given annually to an employee with at least a decade of distinguished service. Meanwhile, Henry Diggs' "wry sense of humor and quiet dignity endeared him to everyone he met" in Norwood, and, upon his death, the Board of Selectmen dedicated the town's annual report to "Henry Diggs, a true friend, citizen and colleague, who we all will miss…[his] many, many years of service…is an example to us all."[26]

With the deaths of Ann Tanneyhill in 2001 and Henry Diggs in 2003, both interred at Highland Cemetery, the more than century-long association between this remarkable family and the town of Norwood came to a close. Both had savored their time in this community, however, and one can only hope that all residents might echo Henry Diggs' opinion of Norwood: "It's a nice town," he had once said. "I don't know of another one where I'd want to live."[27]

Sources and Notes

For general history of Norwood, see Bryant F. Tolles, Jr., *Norwood: The Centennial History of a Massachusetts Town* (Norwood, MA: Town of Norwood, 1972) and Patricia J. Fanning, *Norwood: A History* (Charleston, SC: Arcadia Publishing Co., 2002). Annual Reports of the Town of Norwood, vital statistics contained therein, and census records were consulted. Information regarding the relationship between the Day and Tanneyhill families can be found in: Patricia J. Fanning, *Through an Uncommon Lens: The Life and Photography of F. Holland Day* (Amherst, MA: University of Massachusetts Press, 2008).

1. Ann Tanneyhill's given name was Anna. She was named after her father's employer and friend, Anna Smith Day. Tanneyhill preferred to use Ann.
2. "Emancipation Celebration," *Frederick (MD) Examiner*, 28 July 1869, p. 2; "15th Amendment Celebration," *Frederick Examiner*, 25 May 1870, p. 2.
3. Isabel Wilkerson, *The Warmth of Other Suns* (NY: Vintage Books,

2011) p. 38.

4. "Came Far to Attend," *Frederick (MD) News*, 17 May 1912, p. 3. This article concerns the sale of cemetery property, but mentions both Aaron Tanneyhill and Richard H. Diggs among the founders of Greenmount Cemetery in 1898.

5. "First Colored Union Man," *Boston Globe*, 11 June 1905, p. 24.

6. Ibid.

7. Ann Tanneyhill, interview in Black Women Oral History Project Interviews, Radcliffe College, Schlesinger Library, July, 1974, pp. 1-5; Ann Tanneyhill interview with Verna Curtis, Library of Congress, and Anne Havinga, Museum of Fine Arts, Boston, 15 July 1997, and Ann Tanneyhill interview with author, 24 July 1995. Tanneyhill gave virtually the same information in each interview.

8. Gertrude Tanneyhill Cuthbert's recollections: Carmen Fields, "She asks lots of hard, serious questions," Sunday *Boston Globe*, 16 May 1976, pp. 270-273; Ann Tanneyhill's recollection of Mary Ann Taylor, Black Women Oral History Project, p. 3; W. E. B. Du Bois, *The Autobiography of W. E. B. Du Bois* (Canada: International Publishers Co., Inc. 2007), pp. 133-134.

9. Ann Tanneyhill, Black Women Oral History Project, p. 3. See also Elizabeth McHenry, *Forgotten Readers: Recovering the Lost History of African American Literary Societies* (Durham, NC: Duke University Press, 2002).

10. Ann Tanneyhill, Black Women Oral History Project, pp. 5-6; Interview with author, 1995.

11. Ann Tanneyhill, Black Women Oral History Project, p. 5; Vie Kaufman, "Ann Tanneyhill: Indomitable Spirit," *Equal Opportunity Journal*, February 1999, p. 39.

12. "Oldest Man Dies at 95," *Norwood Messenger*, 24 November 1933, p. 1. Norwood's *Boston Post* cane is kept on display in Norwood's town hall.

13. Kaufman, p. 39.

14. Fields, p. 271-272.

15. Dan Kochakian, "Say Hello to Highland Diggs," *Whiskey, Women and...*, No. 17 (Spring, 1988), p. 4.

16. Richard Vacca, *The Boston Jazz Chronicles: Faces, Places, and Nightlife, 1937-1962* (Concord, MA: Troy St. Publishing, 2012) p. 1, 184-185.

17. Kochakian, p. 9.

18. On music fence: Dudley Town Common, informational pamphlet, no pagination; John Tagiuri, metal sculptor and public artist, conversation with author, 25 August 2020.

19. "Veterans Day Ceremony at the State House," 11 November 2007, Boston.com.

20. Charles Joyce, "Report of the Morrill Memorial Library," *Annual Report of the Town of Norwood,* year ending December 31, 1962, p. 204.

21. Charles Joyce, "Report of the Morrill Memorial Library," *Annual Report of the Town of Norwood,* year ending December 31, 1966, p. 255.

22. Fields, p. 271; Gertrude Tanneyhill Cuthbert quoted in: Spotlight Team (Gerard O'Neill, Stephen A. Kurkjian, Alexander B. Hawes, Jr., and Joan Vennochi), "Blacks Receive Stiffer Sentences," *Boston Globe,* 4 April 1979, p. 50.

23. Kaufman, p. 40.

24. "Norwood Oasis in Tension Era," *Boston Record American,* 2 June 1968, p. 12.

25. "Remarks of Chairman Diggs to the Graduating Class June 7, 1970," *Annual Report of the Town of Norwood,* year ending December 31, 1970, p. 528.

26. Kaufman, p. 39; "Henry W. Diggs, 96, Was Devoted to Civic Work," *Martha's Vineyard Gazette,* 23 January 2003; *Annual Report of the Town of Norwood,* year ending December 31, 2003, p. 1.

27. "Norwood Oasis in Tension Era," *Boston Record American,* 2 June 1968, p. 12.

Acknowledgments

I wish to extend my gratitude to the staff of the Morrill Memorial Library, particularly Liz Reed, April Cushing, Lydia Sampson, and Charlotte Canelli; the Maxwell Library at Bridgewater State University; Dorothy De Simone, Dana Hall School; Amy Hague, Special Collections, Smith College. Thanks to Sarah Culver and Brian Halley of the University of Massachusetts Press; and Peter Benes, editor of The Dublin Seminar for New England Folklife Annual Proceedings for permission to reprint previously published material, and to Charles Donahue for permission to reprint the cover image.

I am indebted to John and Sue Anderson, Kyra Auerbach, Nancy Bailey, Heather Cole, Bob Donahue, Allison Hepler, Aira Koski Johnson, Bruce Jones, Seán Ó Coistealbha, and especially John Grove for their particular contributions to this project. My special thanks go to Janet Diggs Budrow, Kevan Budrow, Lucy Tanneyhill Cromwell, and Judith Diggs Potter.

Finally, I am most appreciative of my brother, Charles, who enjoys stories about Norwood as much as I do.

Index

[

About the Author

PATRICIA J. FANNING is a life-long Norwood resident. A professor of sociology emeritus at Bridgewater State University, she received her doctorate from Boston College. A former president of the Norwood Historical Society, she is the current president of the Old Parish Preservation Volunteers whose mission is to restore the Old Parish Cemetery in Norwood. Her publications include essays on connections between the arts, primarily photography and literature, and the wider American culture. She has written several books related to Norwood history including *Through an Uncommon Lens: The Life and Photography of F. Holland Day* (2008) and *Influenza and Inequality: One Town's Tragic Response to the Great Epidemic of 1918* (2010), both published by the University of Massachusetts Press.